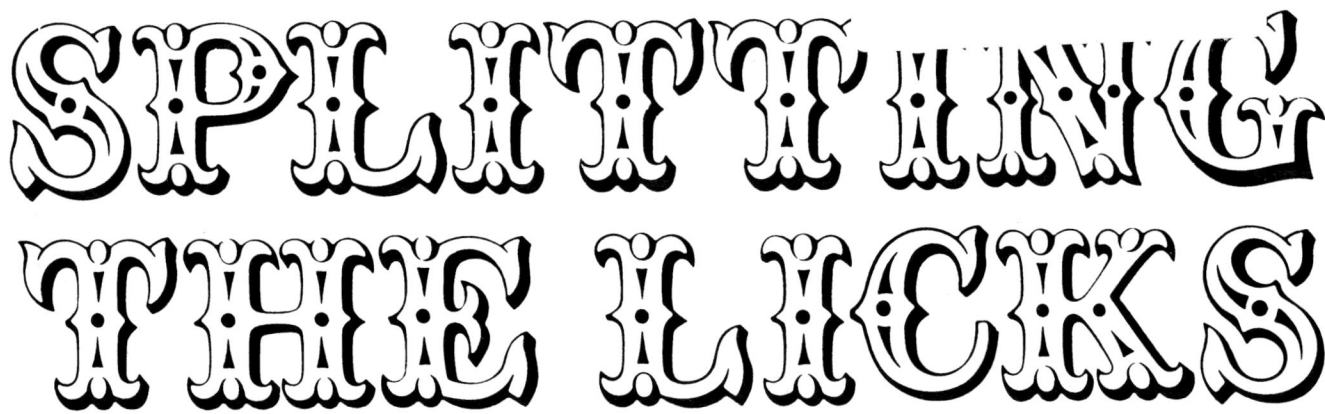

SPLITTING THE LICKS

Improvising and Arranging Songs on the 5-String Banjo

by Janet Davis

Cover photo is a picture of a handcrafted Liberty Banjo. Use of the photo is courtesy of The Liberty Banjo Company, 2472 Main Street, Bridgeport, Connecticut 06606.

Audio Contents

Audio 1

1. Introduction [:30]
2. Accent Patterns [:24]
3. Rhythm Patterns 1-4 [:59]
4. Roll Patterns [1:10]
5. Beginning Licks [:49]
6. Fill-In Licks—G Chord [:59]
7. G Chord Licks [1:13]
8. C Chord Licks [:48]
9. D Chord Licks [2:03]
10. A Chord Licks [:39]
11. F, B, & Em Chord Licks [:53]
12. Worried Man Blues [:46]
13. —Forward Roll [1:09]
14. —Other Rolls (1:23]
15. —Fill-In Rolls [1:24]
16. —Left-Hand Tech. [1:13]
17. —with Backup [:19]
18. Bury Me Beneath the Willow [:38]
19. —Forward Roll [:57]
20. —Other Rolls [:55]
21. —Fill-In Rolls [:59]
22. —Left-Hand Tech. [:52]
23. —with Backup [:32]
24. Red River Valley [:47]
25. —Forward Roll [:39]
26. —Other Rolls [:45]
27. —Fill-In Rolls [:42]
28. —Left-Hand Tech. [:52]
29. —with Backup [:23]
30. Roll in My Sweet Baby's Arms [:55]
31. —Forward Roll [:44]
32. —Other Rolls [:52]
33. —Fill-In Rolls [:48]
34. —Left-Hand Tech. [:49]
35. —with Backup [:18]
36. Goin' Down That Road Feelin' Bad [:34]
37. —Forward Roll [:39]
38. —Other Rolls [:40]
39. —Fill-In Rolls [:41]
40. —Left-Hand Tech. [:32]
41. —with Backup [:36]
42. Walking Cane [:41]
43. —Forward Roll [:37]
44. —Other Rolls [:39]
45. —Fill-In Licks [:37]
46. —Left-Hand Tech. [:37]
47. —with Backup [:41]
48. Wildwood Flower [:44]
49. —Forward Roll [:42]
50. —Other Rolls [:44]
51. —Fill-In Rolls [:44]
52. —Left-Hand Tech. [:38]
53. —with Backup [:23]
54. Cripple Creek [:49]
55. —Forward Roll [:42]
56. —Other Rolls [:38]
57. —Fill-In Rolls [:38]
58. —Left-Hand Tech. [:35]
59. —with Backup [:19]
60. Cumberland Gap [:29]
61. —Forward Roll [:25]
62. —Other Rolls [:19]
63. —Fill-In Licks [:20]
64. —Left-Hand Tech. [:23]
65. —with Backup [:11]
66. Jesse James [:13]
67. —Forward Roll [1:01]
68. —Other Rolls [1:05]
69. —Fill-In Rolls [1:06]
70. —Left-Hand Tech. [1:04]
71. —with Backup [:31]
72. Grandfather's Clock [1:26]
73. —Forward Roll [1:17]
74. —Other Rolls [1:22]
75. —Fill-In Licks [1:24]
76. —Left-Hand Tech. [1:19]
77. —with Backup [:46]

Audio 2

1. Circular Scale [:18]
2. G Major Scale [:20]
3. C Major Scale [:21]
4. D Major Scale [:23]
5. A, F, & E Minor Scale [:24]
6. G Chord Licks [1:33]
7. C Chord Licks [:48]
8. D Chord Licks [:45]
9. A Chord Licks [:11]
10. F Chord & E Minor Licks [:42]
11. Ending Licks— G-D-G [:43]
12. Ending Licks— D-G [:23]
13. Ending Licks— A-D-G, C-D-G [:15]
14. The Eighth of January [:39]
15. —with Backup [:24]
16. Banjo Joe [:43]
17. —with Backup [:21]
18. Bill Cheatham [1:02]
19. —with Backup [:36]
20. Devil's Dream [1:19]
21. —with Backup [:36]
22. Blackberry Blossom [:48]
23. —with Backup [:40]
24. Sailor's Hornpipe [:55]
25. —with Backup [:35]
26. Red Haired Boy [:38]
27. —with Backup [:34]
28. Turkey in the Straw [:50]
29. —with Backup [:17]
30. Fire on the Mountain [2:39]
31. —with Backup [:36]
32. Cripple Creek [:37]
33. —2nd Variation [:37]
34. —with Backup [:20]
35. John Hardy [:33]
36. —Melodic Variation [:30]
37. —with Backup [:41]
38. Old Joe Clark [1:34]
39. —with Backup [:34]
40. —Melodic Variation [1:11]
41. —with Backup [:41]
42. Exercise [:19]
43. Advanced G Chord Licks [1:13]
44. 2 Measure Licks in G [1:22]
45. Advanced C Chord Licks [1:29]
46. 2 Measure Licks in C [1:03]
47. Advanced D Chord Licks [:48]
48. 2 Measure Licks in D [1:20]
49. Ending Licks— G-D-G [:22]
50. Worried Man Blues [:25]
51. —with Backup [:20]
52. —2nd Variation [:27]
53. —with Backup [:16]
54. —3rd Variation [:26]
55. —with Backup [:16]
56. Roll in My Sweet Baby's Arms (2nd) [:34]
57. —with Backup [:20]
58. —3rd Variation [:36]
59. —with Backup [:16]
60. —4th Variation [:39]
61. —with Backup [:14]
62. Goin' Down That Road Feelin' Bad (2nd) [:32]
63. —with Backup [:16]
64. —3rd Variation [:30]
65. —with Backup [:16]
66. —4th Variation [:29]
67. —with Backup [:17]
68. Whoa Mule (2nd) [:25]
69. —with Backup [:19]
70. —3rd Variation [:27]
71. —with Backup [:14]
72. —4th Variation [:27]
73. —with Backup [:16]
74. Wabash Cannonball (2nd) [:28]
75. —with Backup [:19]
76. —Advanced Licks [:28]
77. —with Backup [:17]
78. Nine Pound Hammer (2nd) [:55]
79. —with Backup [:17]
80. —3rd Variation [:33]
81. —with Backup [:17]
82. Train 45 (2nd) [:53]
83. —with Backup [:19]
84. —3rd Variation [:41]
85. —with Backup [:14]
86. —4th Variation [:33]
87. —with Backup [:14]
88. —5th Variation [:35]
89. —with Backup [:15]
90. Salt River (2nd) [1:13]
91. —with Backup [:34]
92. —3rd Variation [1:19]
93. —with Backup [:33]
94. Hamilton County Breakdown (2nd) [1:15]
95. —with Backup [:32]
96. —3rd Variation [1:05]

Online Audio & Video

Audio
www.melbay.com/93998BCDEB

Video
dv.melbay.com/93998

You Tube
www.melbay.com/93998V

1 2 3 4 5 6 7 8 9 0

© 1985 BY MEL BAY PUBLICATIONS, INC., PACIFIC, MO 63069.
ALL RIGHTS RESERVED. INTERNATIONAL COPYRIGHT SECURED. B.M.I. MADE AND PRINTED IN U.S.A.
No part of this publication may be reproduced in whole or in part, or stored in a retrieval system, or transmitted in any form or by any means, electronic, mechanical, photocopy, recording, or otherwise, without written permission of the publisher.

Visit us on the Web at www.melbay.com — E-mail us at email@melbay.com

FOREWORD

This book takes you through step by step instructions on working out songs for the 5-string banjo from basic melodies in Bluegrass-style and in Melodic/Chromatic style. Each section also contains exercises and examples for improvising.

The first section and the second section deal with working out the basic arrangement of a song. The exercises involve replacing the x's around the melody with notes. The last section in the book deals with refining the arrangement of a song using advanced techniques. This section includes examples of songs showing how entire measures or licks can be replaced with licks from a sheet of suggested alternate, advanced licks.

All of the steps to arranging a song for the banjo discussed in this book, are based on the fact that banjo arrangements are actually combinations of specific patterns, (rolls, or licks), which are played according to the chords in the song. This method of arranging songs has worked well with my banjo students, and I hope it will work for you also.

Happy Pickin'

Janet Davis

P.S. 1983: SPLITTING THE LICKS has now been expanded to include over twice as much material as was contained in the first edition, which was published in 1977. This edition could easily serve as a supplement to the earlier edition, for those who have that edition. The following pages include many new licks and many additional songs which demonstrate the process of building an arrangement of a song to be played on the banjo. Also, the instructional material has been expanded to include answers to questions from people who studied the first edition of the book.

INTRODUCTION

To play a song on the 5-string banjo, you actually play combinations of finger patterns, (also referred to as rolls or licks). To improvise* or arrange a song on the banjo, you must work the melody into these finger patterns, according to the chords of the song.

Before attempting to arrange a song on your own, you should be able to play several arrangements (from tablature) of songs in the style you will use, in order to familiarize yourself with the rhythm, the finger patterns, and the overall feeling of playing in this style.

This book will deal with two very popular styles of picking the banjo with three fingers:

1.) Bluegrass-Style—where the melody is surrounded by background notes.
2.) Melodic-Style (Chromatic)—where each note picked is essentially a melody note.

These styles can be combined within one song, or one song can be played entirely in one of these styles.

One noticeable difference between each style of playing is the rhythm . . . where the accent (melody) or stress falls.

Comparison of Accent of the Two Styles

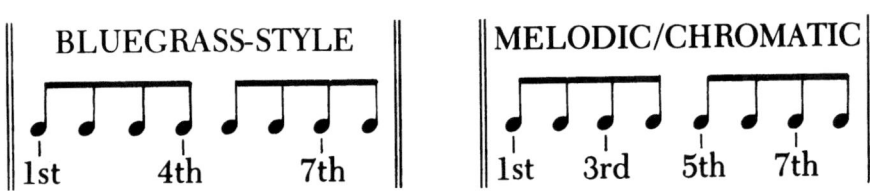

Note: stress the notes indicated with arrows. Generally your melody notes are these notes.

In learning these styles, it is best to learn them one at a time, so that you will become familiar with the finger patterns particular to that style.

*To improvise generally implies arranging on the spur of the moment. One musical dictionary defines "improvise" as — to arrange, however. For the purposes of this book, the terms "improvise" and "arrange" will refer to the same things.

TABLE OF CONTENTS

INTRODUCTION 3
EXPLANATION OF TABLATURE
  & RHYTHM 5
RHYTHM EXERCISES 6
BLUEGRASS-STYLE—Discussion Of 7
  Standard Roll Patterns 8
  Fill-in Licks 9
  Arranging Songs—Steps To Follow 13
  Songs—Exercises on Improvising:
    WORRIED MAN BLUES 13
    BURY ME BENEATH THE WILLOW ... 19
    RED RIVER VALLEY 22
    ROLL IN MY SWEET BABY'S ARMS ... 25
    GOIN' DOWN THAT ROAD
      FEELIN' BAD 28
    WALKING CANE 30
    WILDWOOD FLOWER 32
    CRIPPLE CREEK 35
    CUMBERLAND GAP 37
    JESSE JAMES 39
    GRANDFATHER'S CLOCK 43
MELODIC STYLE—Discussion Of 49
  Scale Patterns 49
  Fill-In Licks 52
  Arranging Songs—Steps To Follow 55
  Songs—Exercises on Improvising:
    THE EIGHTH OF JANUARY 57
    BANJO JOE 58
    BILL CHEATHAM 59
    DEVIL'S DREAM 60
    BLACKBERRY BLOSSOM 61
    SAILOR'S HORNPIPE 62
    RED HAIRED BOY 64
    TURKEY IN THE STRAW 65
    FIRE ON THE MOUNTAIN 66

    CRIPPLE CREEK 67
COMPARISON OF SCRUGGS-STYLE &
  MELODIC-STYLE 68
  Songs—One Arrangement in Each Style:
    JOHN HARDY 68
    OLD JOE CLARK 70
  (See also "Cripple Creek", p. 35 & 67.)
COMBINING STYLES OF PLAYING 72
  Advanced Fill-In Licks 73
  Arranging Songs—Steps To Follow 77
  Songs Using Advanced Licks:
    WORRIED MAN BLUES 77
    ROLL IN MY SWEET BABY'S ARMS ... 80
    GOIN' DOWN THAT ROAD
      FEELIN' BAD 82
    WHOA MULE 84
    WABASH CANNONBALL 86
    NINE POUND HAMMER 88
    TRAIN 45 90
    SALT RIVER 92
    HAMILTON COUNTY
      BREAKDOWN 94
    UNDER THE DOUBLE EAGLE 96
BUILDING ENDINGS FOR SONGS 98
  Tag Endings 99
  Two Measure Endings 101
CHORDS—Discussion Of 102
Chord Charts:
  Moveable Chord Chart for Major
    Chords 103
  Major Chords 104
  Minor Chords 105
  Locating Chord Positions Without
    A Chart 106

EXPLANATION OF TABLATURE AND RHYTHM

I. <u>TABLATURE</u> -- The tablature format used in this book is fairly standard:

The <u>five</u> lines represent the <u>five strings</u>; the top line is the first string, and the bottom line is the 5th string, (the short string).

The <u>number</u> tells you which <u>fret</u> to push down with your left hand. (O means open--don't push the string down with the left hand when picking it with the right hand).

T, I, M = are <u>fingering indications</u> for the <u>right hand</u>. M means pick the string with the middle finger; I means index finger; T means thumb.

t, i, m, r, p = <u>Left</u> hand <u>fingering:</u> t=thumb; i=index; m=middle; r=ring; p=pinky.

H, P, Sl, Ch = are left hand techniques used for sounding the strings with the <u>left hand</u>; (the right hand picks the note preceding them).
<u>H</u> means to <u>hammer</u> the fret indicated, by pushing down the string with the left finger, hard enough to sound the tone.
<u>P</u> means to <u>pull off</u> of the string from the fret <u>before</u> the one to be sounded by the pull off, therefore sounding the tone indicated above the P.
<u>SL</u> means to sound the tone by <u>sliding</u> to the fret number above the Sl with the left finger(s) from the number <u>before</u> it.
<u>Ch</u> means to <u>bend</u> the string with the left finger, (do not pick the string with the right hand, just bend it). <u>(Ch=choke)</u>

× = <u>pause,</u> do not play, for that count. (An × is a rest.)

> OR - means to stress or <u>accent</u> this tone...play it louder.

<u>NOTE:</u> For more complete explanations of the above indications, refer to a beginning banjo book.

II. <u>RHYTHM</u> -- The rhythm used in this book is based upon standard notation. If you already understand rhythmic notation, all of the music in this book can be counted in $\frac{4}{4}$ time, with each eighth note (♪) receiving $\frac{1}{2}$ count. Each X equals an eighth rest, and also receives $\frac{1}{2}$ count. (Each measure contains eight $\frac{1}{2}$ counts.)

The following explanation is for those who do not already know how to play the rhythm of the notes. (For the sake of simplicity, it is explained in $\frac{8}{8}$ time, with each eighth note equaling 1 count.)

Each measure consists of 8 counts.
The measures are divided by bar lines.

The <u>STEMS</u> under the notes (or numbers) tell you how long to let each note ring:

♪ = 1 count. Each eighth note receives one count. Eighth notes are written alone, ♪ , in pairs, ♩♩ , or in fours, ♩♩♩♩ .

0 × = 2 counts. Hold the tone played for the duration of two tones.

0 = $\frac{1}{2}$ count. Play two sixteenth notes in the same amount of time you play one eighth note: 0 0 = 0 ♪ .

X = 1 count. (An eighth) rest indicates silence for the indicated duration. (Pause for one count.)

‖: :‖ Repeat sign. It means to repeat (play again) what has just been played. (Return to the previous ‖: if there is one. Otherwise, return to the beginning and repeat the section.)

RHYTHM

When working out a song on the banjo, correct RHYTHM is very important. Without the correct timing, no one will know what song you are playing. Counting is often thought to be difficult, but it is really very simple. In the tablature in this book, <u>each measure consists of eight equal counts.</u> The measures are divided by bar lines.

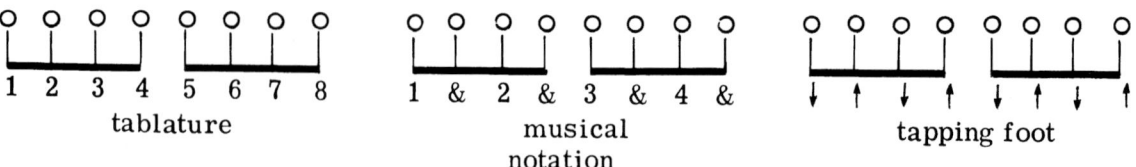

Any way you say it*, there are eight equal counts. If an X is above the stem instead of a number, <u>pause</u>, (don't play), for that count. In other words, silence is played for that count. By the way, when playing, do not pause for the bar lines... they merely separate the notes into groups of equal counts for simplicity.

If you have difficulty reading rhythm and playing it, the following exercises may help. Remember to keep your rhythm EVEN.

EXERCISES: (watch the stems on the notes!)

* For people who read music: this tablature can be played in 4/4 time. To make counting easier to understand, the above explanation is in 8/8 time.

BLUEGRASS-STYLE

This style of picking was popularized by a banjo player named Earl Scruggs in the early 1940's. It consists of playing combinations of specific finger patterns or "rolls" or "licks" with the Thumb, Index, and Middle fingers of the right hand, and it makes frequent use of left-hand techniques for sounding notes within these "rolls". The melody is usually picked by one finger of the right hand, while the other two fingers pick background notes surrounding the melody. (Generally the Thumb picks the melody and the Index & Middle fingers pick the background notes, or the Index picks the melody while the Thumb and Middle finger pick the background notes.) The 5th string, also picked with the Thumb, acts as a drone; it is usually played on the third and sixth notes in a "roll". (There are eight notes in one roll.)

Before attempting to improvise on your own, you should be <u>thoroughly</u> familiar with the Standard Rolls, especially the forward, reverse, and the alternating thumb rolls. You will use these rolls to play the melody. You should also be "at home" with several "fill-in-rolls" for at least G, C, and D, chords. The more of these you learn, the faster you will be able to work out a smooth arrangement for a song.

NOTE: <u>STANDARD BLUEGRASS-STYLE "ROLLS"</u> are used to play the melody.

<u>FILL-IN-"ROLLS"</u> are used to "fill in" the pauses between melody lines, and also for changing from one chord to another and for beginning and ending songs.

NOTE: You should play all eight notes in a "roll" consecutively, <u>without a pause.</u> Stress the fingers accented (>); they play the melody.

NOTE: After learning the fill-in "rolls", try substituting one roll for another in a song you already know. i.e. where you have been playing roll 1. in a song, substitute roll 2. (of the same chord). These are very important to arranging your own songs, (and also to backing on the banjo.)

STANDARD BLUEGRASS-STYLE
ROLL PATTERNS

The Finger Indications, which your right fingers follow, are arranged in combinations of patterns, called ROLLS. These patterns are what make up the Bluegrass-style of playing the banjo.

Play each roll over and over several times in a row. Then try to combine several of the rolls without a break in your rhythm.

Keep in mind, when improvising, the idea that the melody note (generally) falls where the Finger Indication is accented (>).

Each standard roll can be played while holding ANY chord position with the left hand. (The rolls are right hand fingering patterns.)

FORWARD ROLL:

    standard   *alternate   pattern

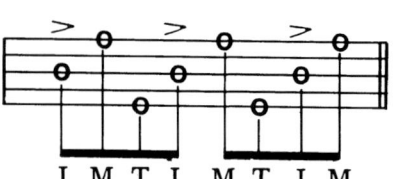 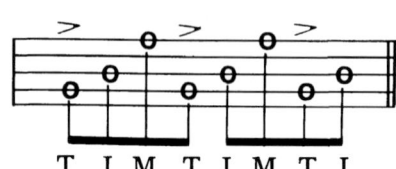 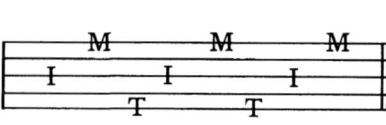

BACKWARD ROLL:

    standard   alternate   pattern

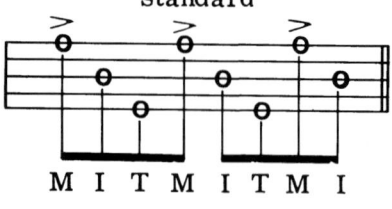 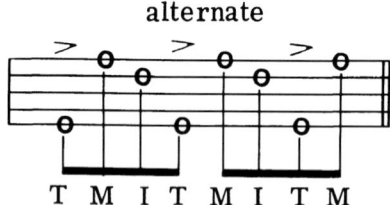 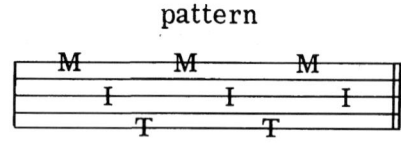

FORWARD-REVERSE ROLL:

    standard   alternate   pattern

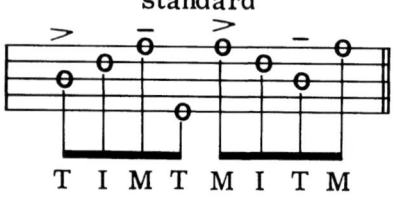 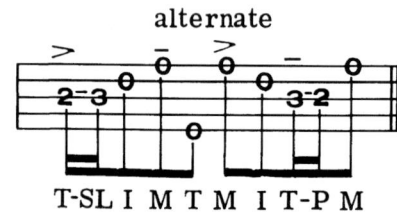 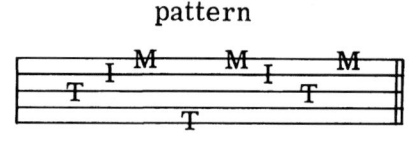

MIXED ROLL (ALTERNATING THUMB):

    standard   alternate   pattern

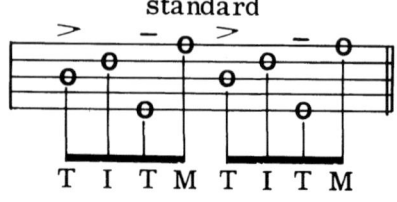 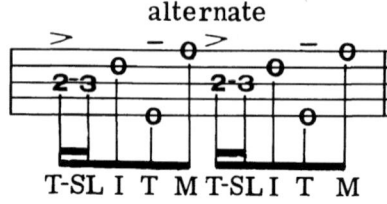 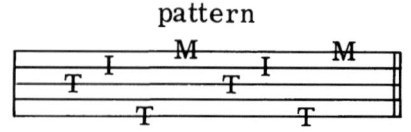

*NOTE: The pattern demonstrates the direction your fingers "roll".
Any finger can begin the roll pattern, and the roll can begin on any string. (See alternate roll). The name of the roll is determined by the order in which the fingers follow one another.

NOTE: Each roll contains 8 equal counts. Do NOT pause at the end of a roll when playing two or more rolls...there should be NO break in the rhythm.

BLUEGRASS-STYLE "FILL-IN-ROLLS"
FOR BEGINNINGS, ENDINGS, AND PAUSES

These rolls are commonly heard in Bluegrass-style arrangements.
Each of the "rolls" below is used only for the chord specified.
The first "roll" might be called, for example, a "G Beginning Lick".
("Lick" is another term frequently used for "Fill-In Roll").

BEGINNING "LICKS": (pick-up notes)

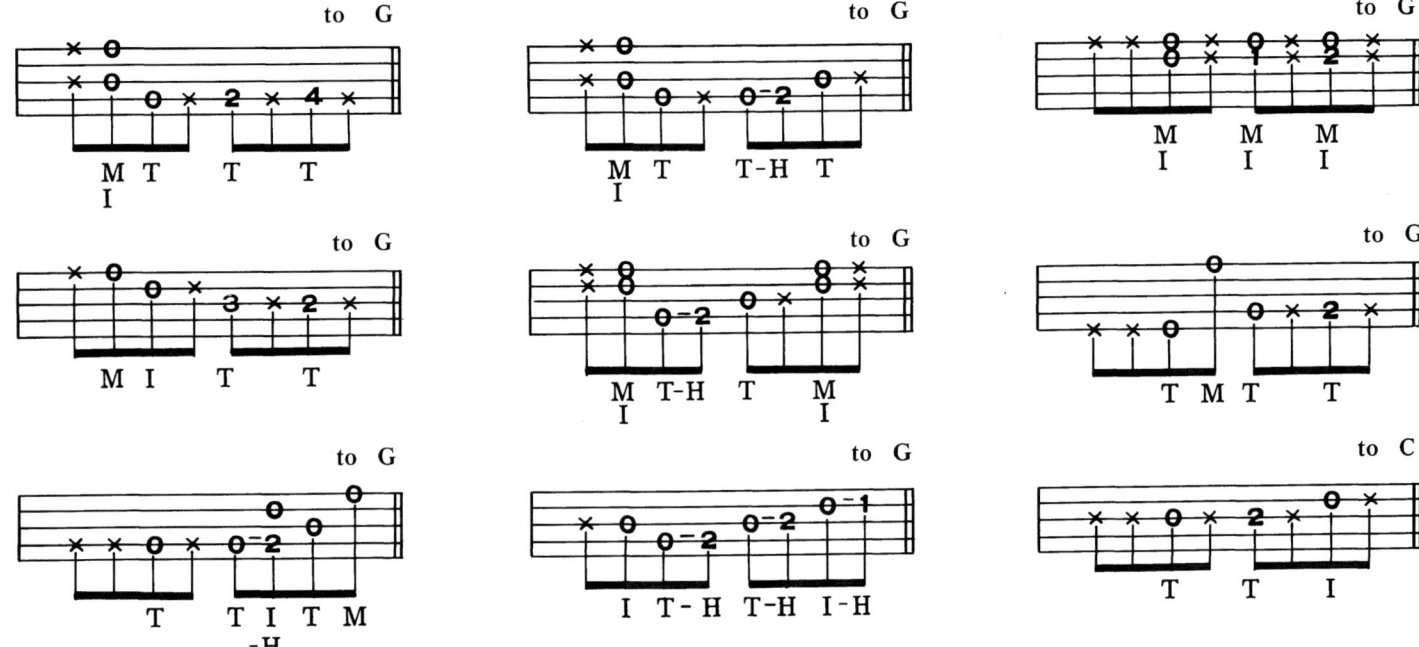

FILL-IN LICKS FOR PAUSES:

G CHORD LICKS:

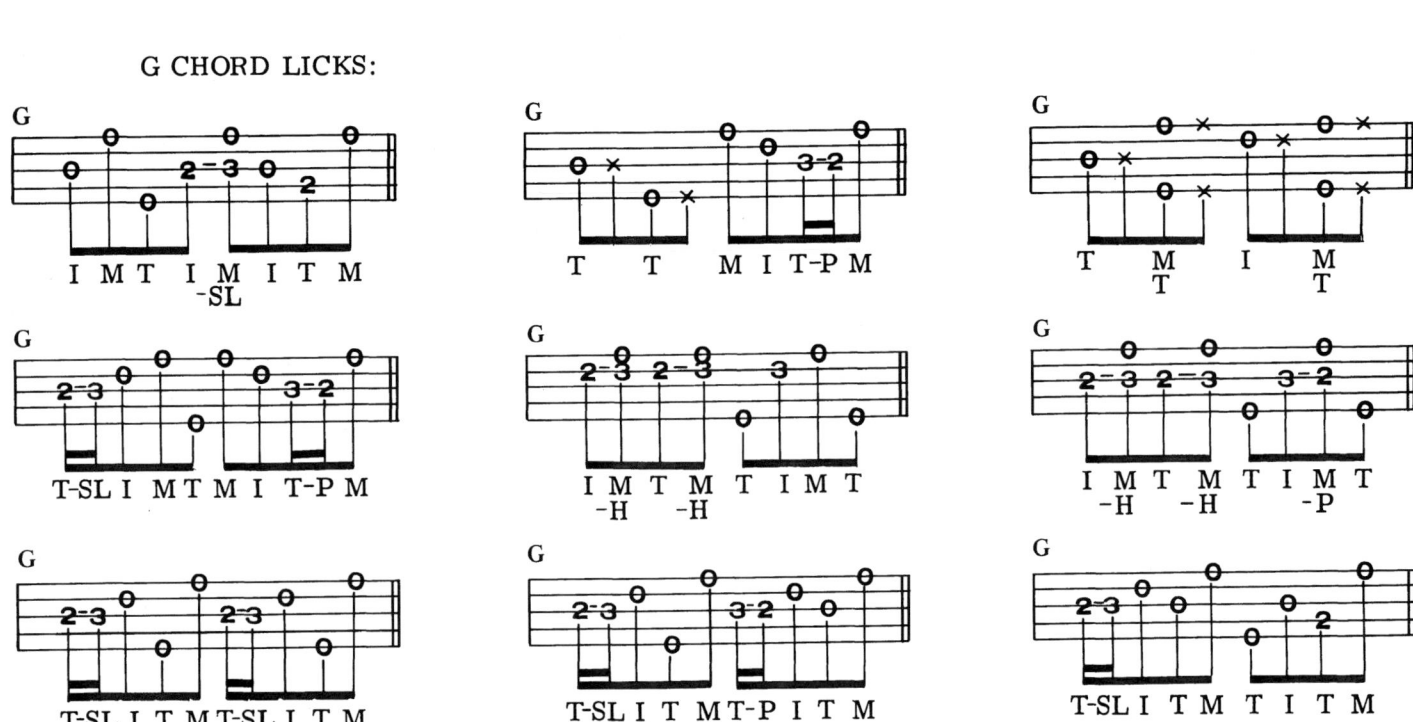

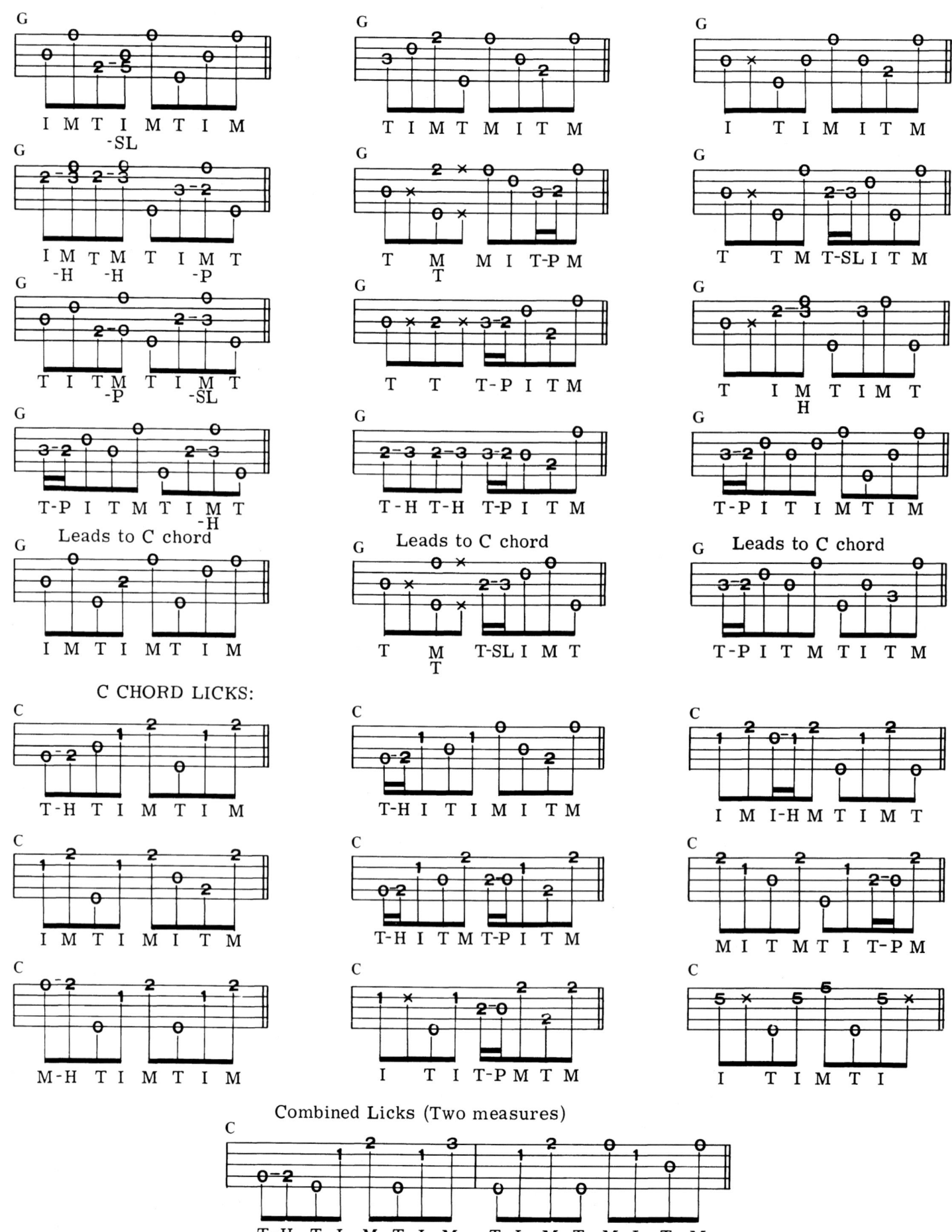

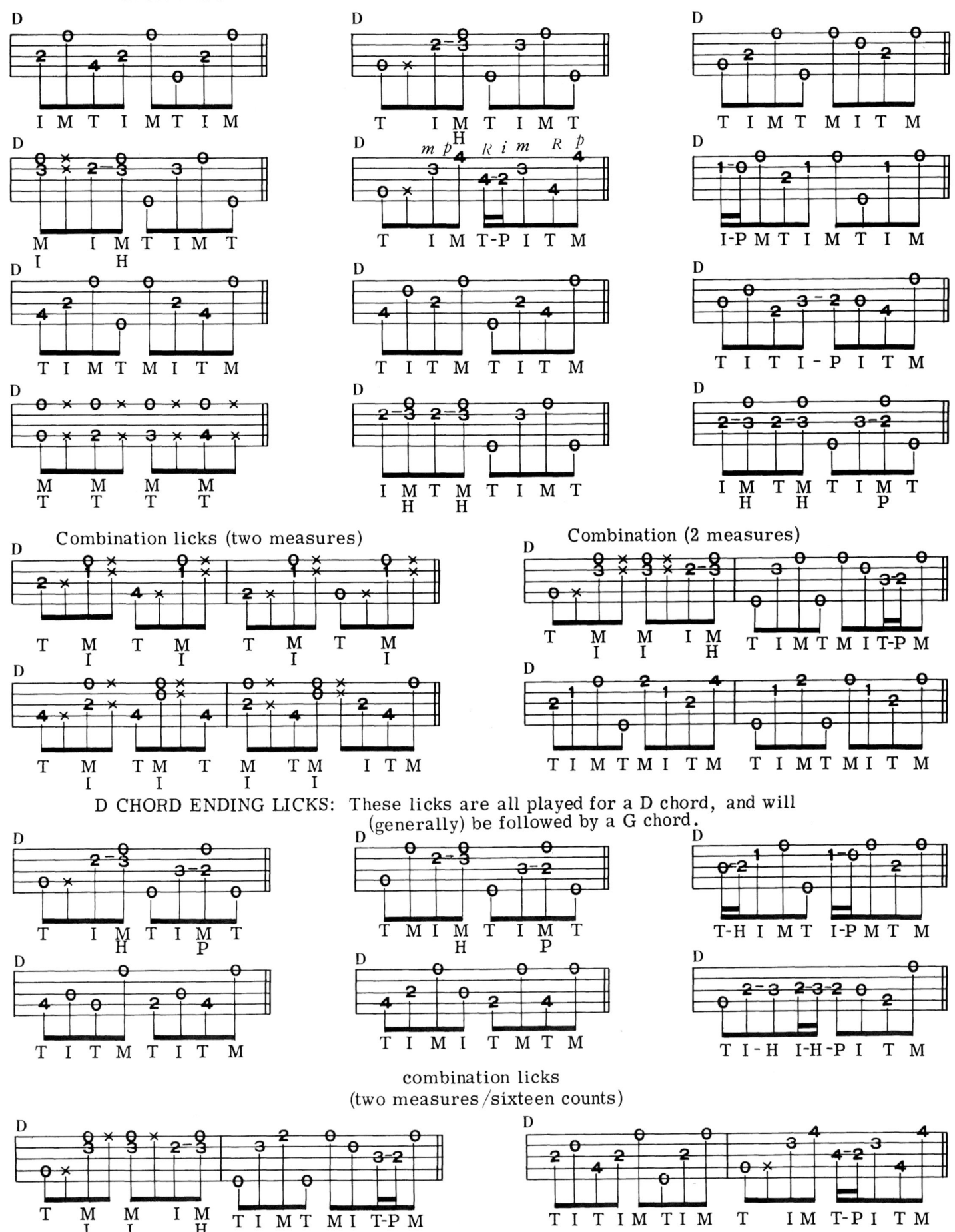

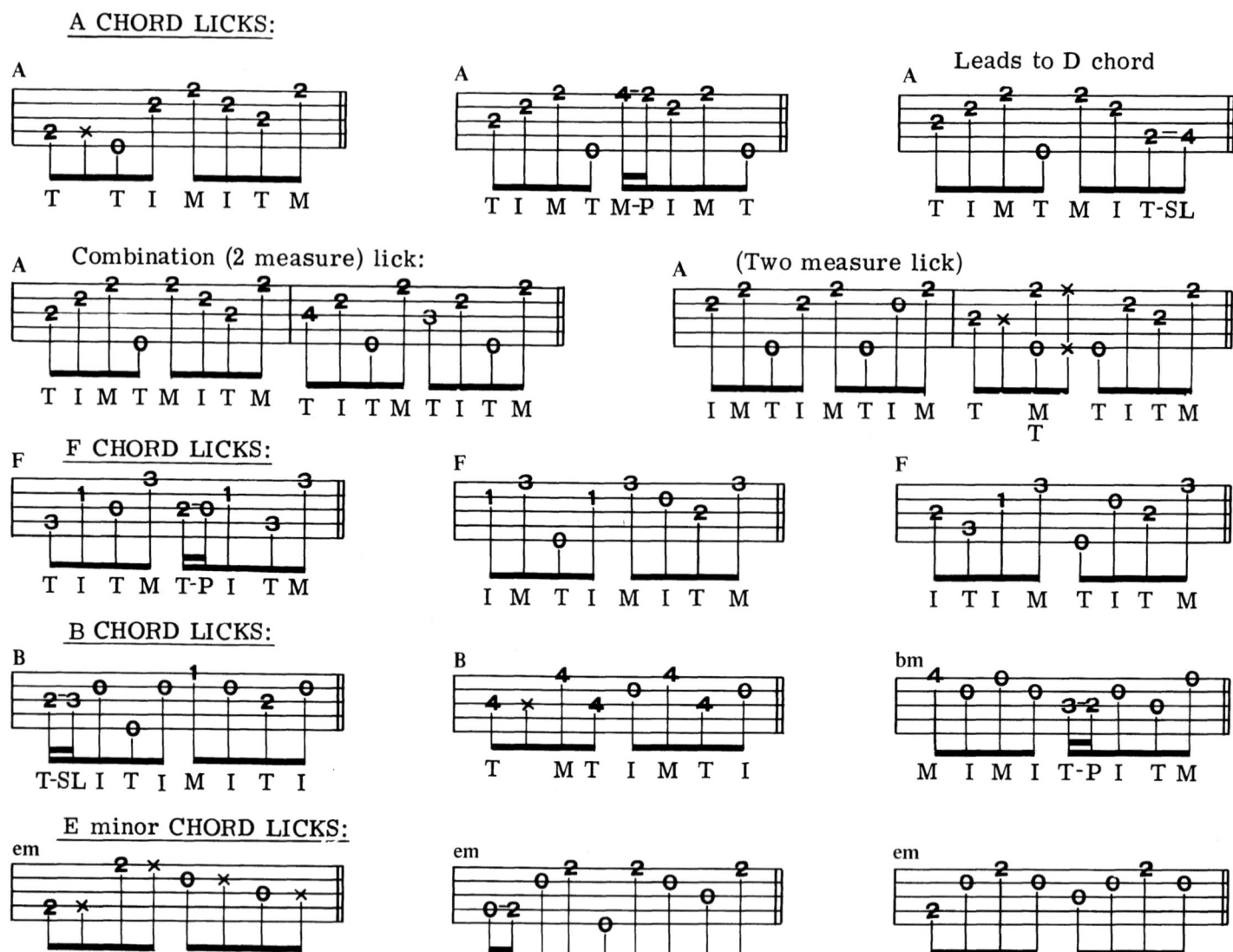

NOTE: Notice that the fill-in licks make frequent use of left-hand techniques such as hammering, pulling off, and sliding. (If these techniques were omitted from the licks, most of the above examples would simply be standard roll patterns.)

NOTE: ROLLS are specific right hand finger patterns which can be played while holding ANY chord position with the left hand.

LICKS are specific finger patterns which are played only for specific chords. (Fill-In Rolls & Fill-In Licks apply to the same things in this book.)

NOTE: Two of the fill-in licks will often be played together as one continuous lick... especially in the pauses between the melody lines, (when a vocalist would take a breath), and frequently for the D chord at the end of the song, just before the final G chord.

ARRANGING SONGS FOR THE BANJO
BLUEGRASS-STYLE

Before attempting to work out your own arrangements of songs on the banjo, you should be able to play several songs from tablature in Bluegrass-style, you should be VERY familiar with the chord positions of the major chords, (G, C, D, & A in particular), and you should be at ease with the standard Bluegrass-style rolls and fill-in-rolls.

PROCEDURE FOR ARRANGING A SONG: (follow step by step)

1.) Learn the CHORDS of the song you want to play.

2.) Pick out the MELODY on your banjo with your right Thumb or Index finger.

3.) Form the chords with the left hand, while picking the melody with the right hand.

    Note: Hold the C chord in Worried Man Blues. (The G and D chords work primarily from open positions.)

EXAMPLE: "WORRIED MAN BLUES"
(MELODY & CHORDS ONLY)

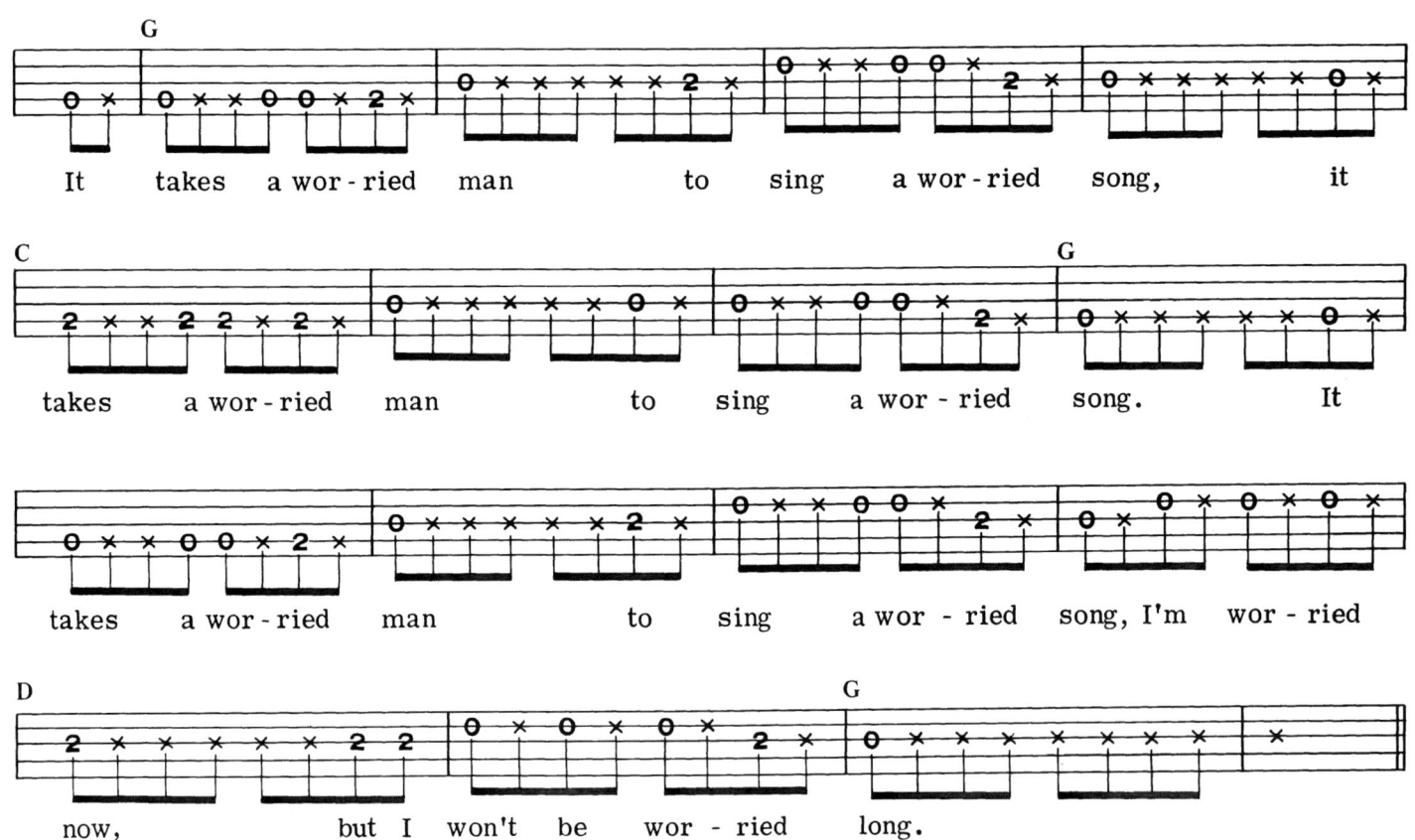

NOTE: There are 8 counts in each measure of tablature (divided by bar lines.)

NOTE: X means pause...pause for each X.

NOTE: The melody notes are placed in each measure to fit the Forward Roll pattern. (See 4. on the following page.) (Also, see last Note on p.18.)

4.) Now is the time to FIT THE MELODY INTO THE STANDARD ROLLS. When first working out a song, you should choose one roll and try to use only that roll, repeating it over and over again, playing the melody notes where they belong.

You can use any of the standard rolls as a primary roll, but I have found that the "Forward Roll", (I M T I M T I M; or T I M T I M T I) best incorporates the "bluegrass rhythm" with the melody of the song. In other words, I strongly suggest using the Forward Roll as your primary roll pattern when working out a song. However, if you find that it isn't working for you on a song, try using a different standard roll.

NOTE: There will be a few places in every song where your primary roll doesn't sound good, or is difficult to play. Use another standard roll for these places. This problem will be dealt with in more detail in a later step.

NOTE: If the melody note is on the 1st string, find the same note or tone on the 2nd string, in order to use the I M T I M T I M pattern.

NOTE: Remember to hold the C chord with the left hand when the song calls for that chord. (The G and D chords primarily use open strings, fretting notes only when necessary.)

The following example adds notes to the X's in the previous example, by playing the Forward Roll for each measure.

EXAMPLE: "WORRIED MAN BLUES"
(USING FORWARD ROLL PATTERN)

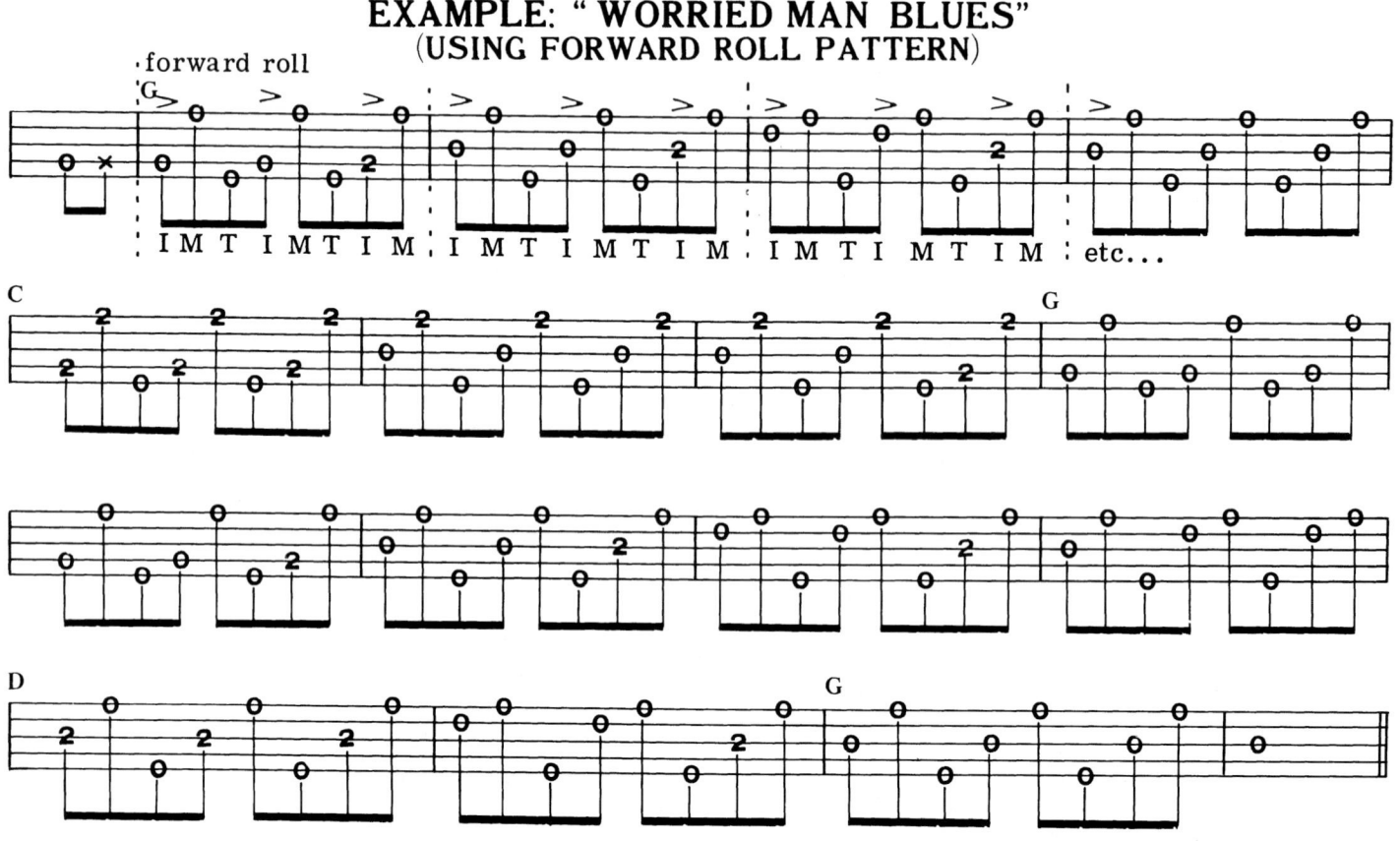

NOTE: The roll patterns are divided by bar lines. There are 8 counts to a roll.
(Don't pause at the bar lines. Pause only for each X.)
When playing the Forward Roll, the right Index finger picks the melody: IMTIMTIM
(> = melody note)

5.) SUBSTITUTE other Standard Rolls in the places where the primary roll is difficult to play with the melody, or where the primary roll doesn't sound good to you. Ad lib if you run into difficulty. Remember, this is your song. Anything will work as long as each measure has 8 counts, and as long as you don't pick with the same right hand finger, two notes in a row.

NOTE: The following example begins with the alternate Forward Roll pattern, which begins with the thumb. Keep in mind when playing these rolls, that each roll pattern can begin with any finger; the order in which the fingers pick the strings determines the name of the roll.

NOTE: HOLD THE C Chord with the left hand when it occurs: ; also, hold the D7 chord position for the D chord on the last line. Move the left fingers as needed for notes which do not naturally fall on the frets of the chord position. Remember, songs work from chords! The melody note is usually a chord tone, or can be found close to the chord position with the left hand; the other notes picked in the roll pattern will supply chord tones for the <u>correct</u> chord as background notes.

EXAMPLE: "WORRIED MAN BLUES"
(SUBSTITUTING OTHER STANDARD ROLLS)

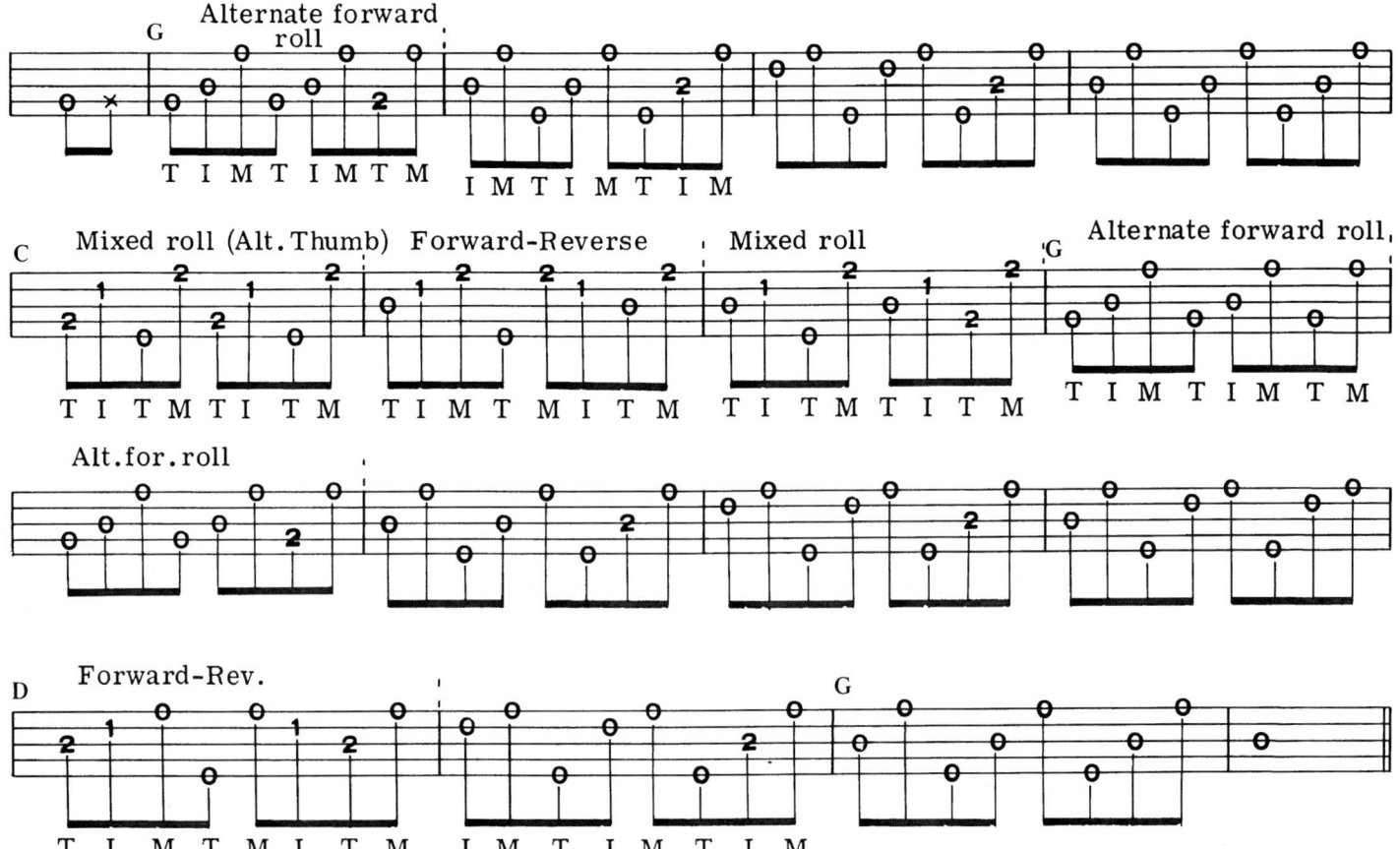

6.) **ADD THE FILL-IN ROLLS.** You should have a fairly smooth arrangement at this point. The Fill-In Rolls are used to give your arrangement character, and also to fill in the gaps or pauses at the ends of phrases, (i.e. where a singer might take a breath). Fill-In Rolls really give a song the "Bluegrass Sound"!

NOTE:
1.) Fill-In Rolls can be substituted for any measure of a song. (Too many fill-in rolls may garble the song, however, and you may lose the melody.)
2.) Substitute Fill-In Rolls according to chords. i.e. when playing a C chord, you must use C chord Fill-In Rolls.
3.) When replacing a Standard Roll, you MUST substitute the correct number of notes, or beats. You can even make up your own rolls, as long as each roll has 8 counts.

SUGGESTIONS FOR USING FILL-IN ROLLS:

1.) BEGINNING: Choose a beginning to your arrangement from the page of Fill-In Rolls labeled "Beginnings". These are usually pick up notes which lead you into the song.
2.) PAUSES: a.) Use fill-in rolls for chords at the end of the melody lines, or phrases, i.e. where the vocalist takes a breath;
b.) Where you have substituted standard rolls for the primary roll in your arrangement, use fill-in rolls for the same chord, instead.
3.) ENDINGS: Fill-in Rolls are frequently used for the final chords of a verse or chorus to a song, (i.e. for the final D chord & G chord in songs which are played in the key of G.) These rolls add a driving force to the close of the verse. (To end your arrangement, refer to the examples of fill-in rolls labeled "Fill-In Rolls-Endings".)

EXAMPLE: "WORRIED MAN BLUES"
(USING FILL-IN ROLLS)

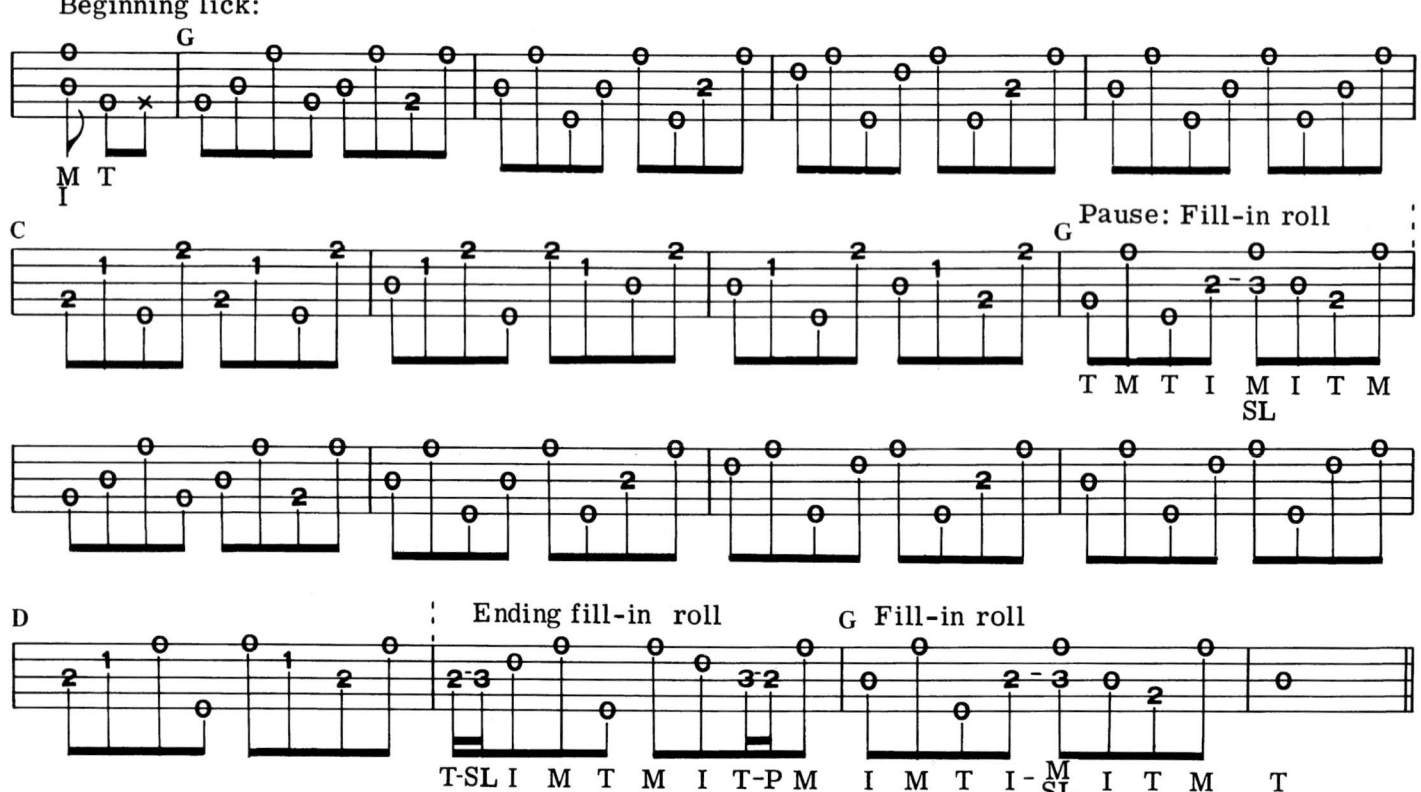

NOTE: WHEN USING Fill-In Rolls, you may lose the melody somewhat, if not entirely. This is fine. The melody will surround these rolls in the standard rolls, and for this reason, the song will sound like it should.

NOTE: Notice that many of the Fill-In Rolls include left-hand techniques such as hammers, slides, and pull-offs. This is the primary reason that these rolls can only be used for specific chords. If the left hand techniques were omitted from the Fill-In Rolls, most of these rolls would be reduced to standard roll patterns.

7.) ADDING LEFT HAND TECHNIQUES: HAMMERS, SLIDES, PULL-OFFS, ETC. Left hand techniques can be added to an arrangement for the sake of embellishment. This is not a necessary step to improvising, but it often gives the song a little more polish.

NOTE: To decide WHICH technique to use: (These are merely general guidelines.) (The last note of each example is the melody note.)

HAMMER OR SLIDE to a higher pitched note: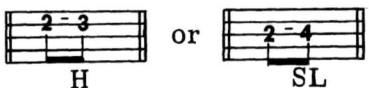

PULL OFF or PUSH OFF in order to sound a lower tone:

EXAMPLE: "WORRIED MAN BLUES"
(USING STANDARD ROLLS, FILL-IN ROLLS, AND LEFT HAND TECHNIQUES)

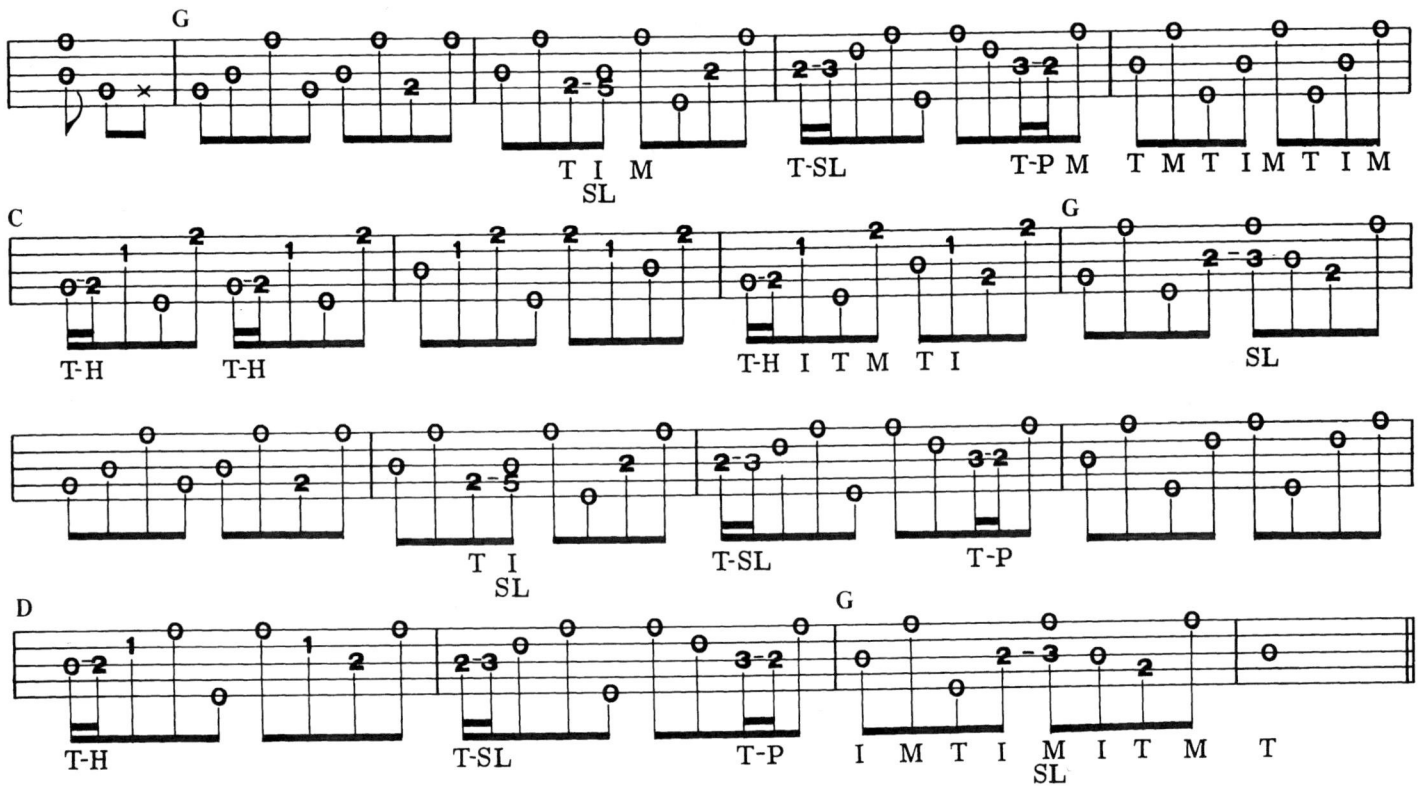

SUMMARY: These are the basic steps to working out your own arrangement to a song in Bluegrass-style. You will get better at it with practice. When you run into a problem--ad-lib--be creative. Keep in mind that nothing is absolute. These are simply guidelines and suggestions to get you started.

The following songs are exercises in improvising. The variations exemplify each step to arranging. The first variation of each song is the melody only. Before looking at the other variations, work on replacing the X's with notes by using the Forward Roll in each measure. Follow the steps to improvising and see what you get. Then check yourself with the rest of the variations offered...you may even like yours better.

(For more practice on working out songs, you may want to get the book, 3 FINGER PICKIN' BANJO SONGBOOK, by Mike Bailey, Mel Bay Publications. It contains the melodies of many bluegrass songs in tablature, along with the chords. The melodies are divided into measures, but arranging the songs for the banjo, giving each measure eight counts, is left up to you. (The songs which say 4 beats per measure should have 8 notes per measure. The songs which say 3 beats per measure should have 6 notes per measure. One beat=two eighth notes in music.) [To play the songs in $\frac{3}{4}$ time, simply omit two notes (the last two) of the roll pattern used for each measure, and play only six notes.] A complete arrangement is _also_ provided for each tune in this book, on the page opposite the melody tab. for the song.)

NOTE: When working out a song using a primary roll pattern, some of the melody notes may have to be omitted, in order to accomodate the roll pattern. This often occurs when two melody notes happen right together, as in "It takes a worried man..". The important melody notes will automatically be included in the roll, due to their rhythmic position in the song. Don't worry about trying to fit in every single note that might be sung.

BURY ME BENEATH THE WILLOW
– EXERCISE IN IMPROVISING –
– WORKING OUT A SONG –

The principal steps to working out a song on the banjo are:

    I. PLAY THE MELODY.

    II. ADD THE FORWARD ROLL, (Play notes for the x's in the melody).

    III. SUBSTITUTE OTHER STANDARD ROLLS, (in "rough spots").

    IV. ADD FILL-IN ROLLS, (i.e. for pauses, and at close of arrangement).

    V. ADD LEFT HAND TECHNIQUES, (to polish the arrangement).

"Bury Me Beneath the Willow" takes you through these, one step at a time. Try to work out each step first, then check your playing with the following examples.

    I. MELODY and Chords ONLY:

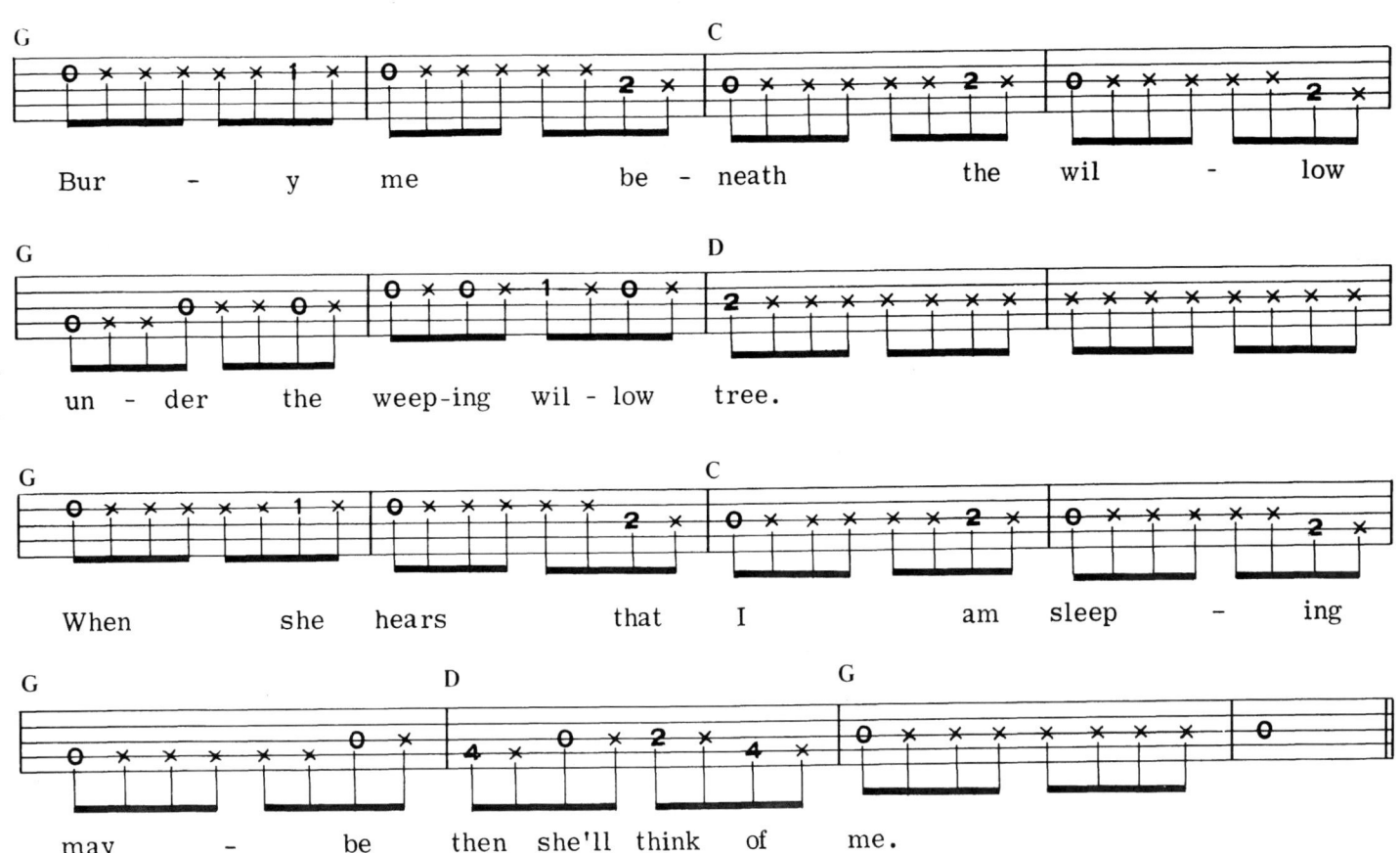

Play through the melody, pausing for each X. Then try, on your own, to replace the X's with notes by playing the Forward Roll, (IMTIMTIM), for each measure. The I will pick the melody notes. Check yourself in Step II.

II. ADD THE FORWARD ROLL (IMTIMTIM) for each measure:

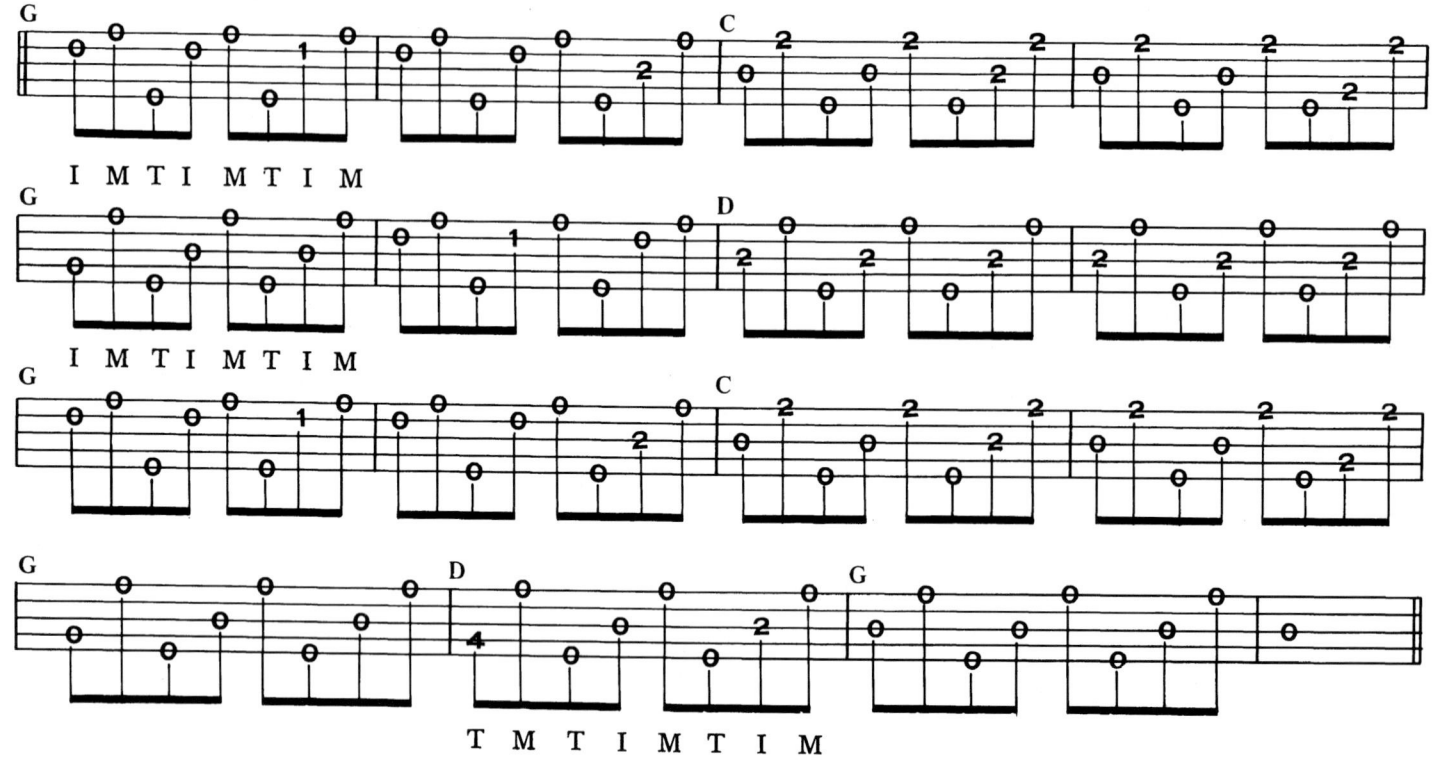

NOTE: Some of the measures in step II above may be awkward to play when using the forward roll. Substitute other standard rolls for these measures, and compare with step III. Other measures may sound better to your ear, using other rolls. (The C chord often sounds fuller with the Forward-Reverse Roll or the Mixed Roll pattern.)

III. SUBSTITUTE OTHER STANDARD ROLLS:

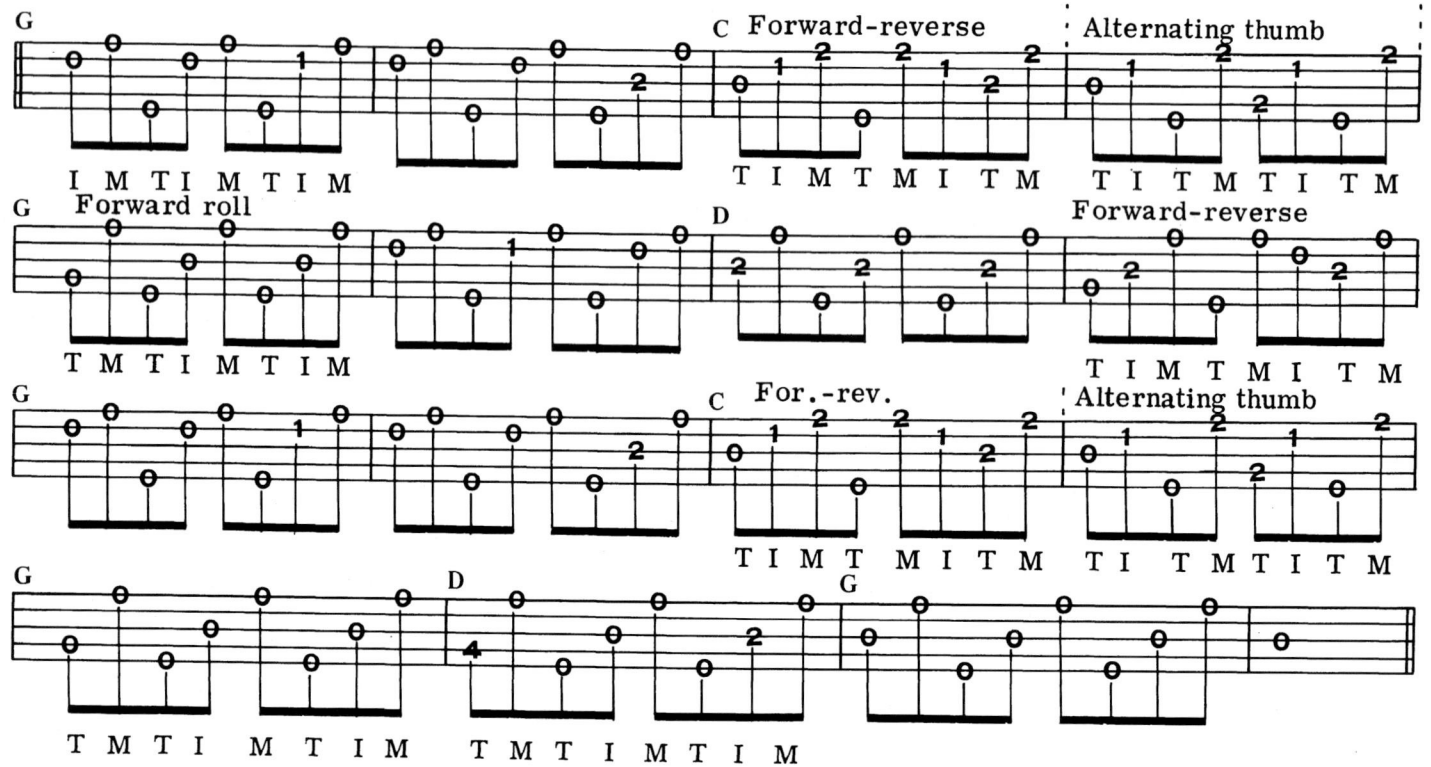

IV. ADD FILL-IN ROLLS:

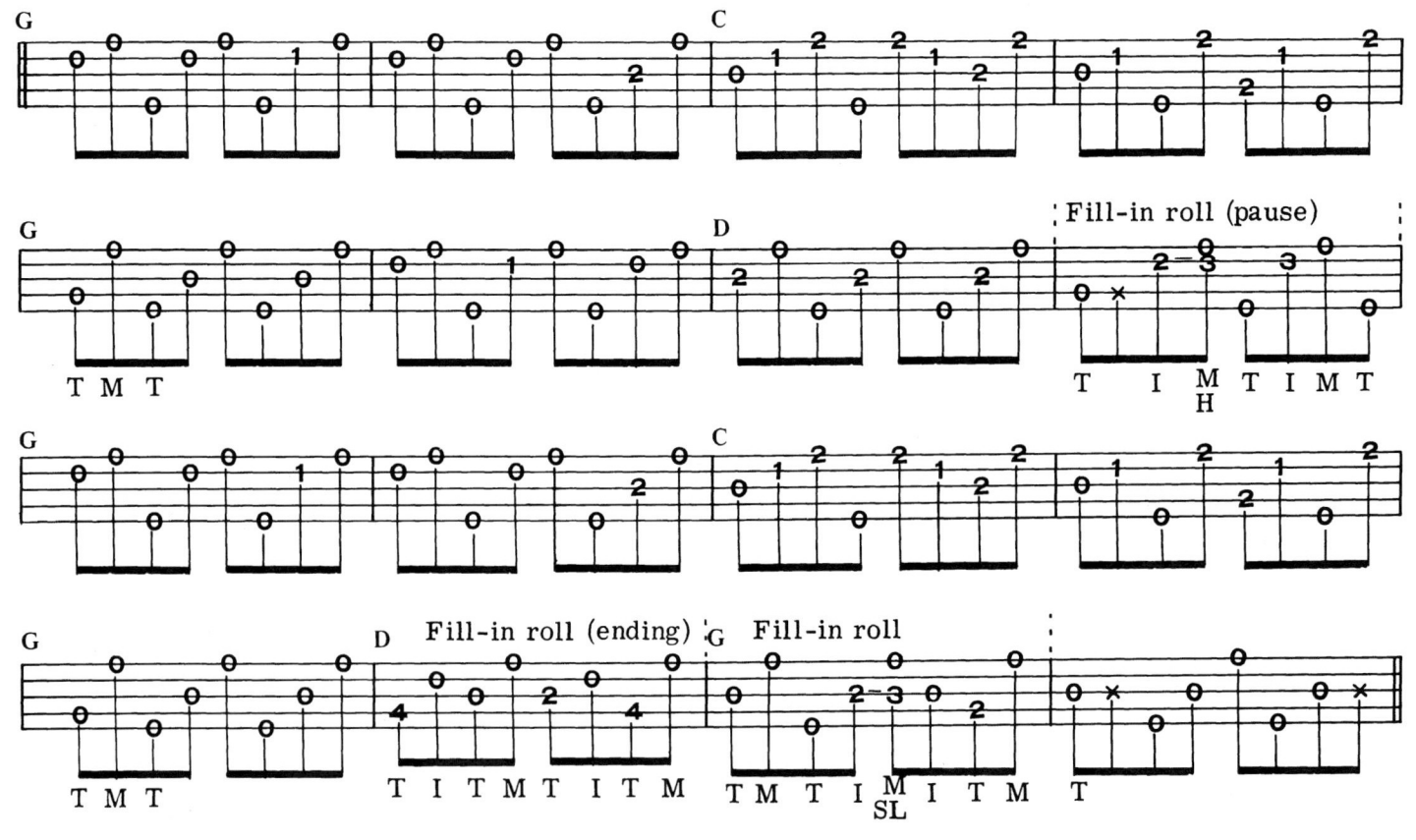

V. ADD LEFT HAND TECHNIQUES:

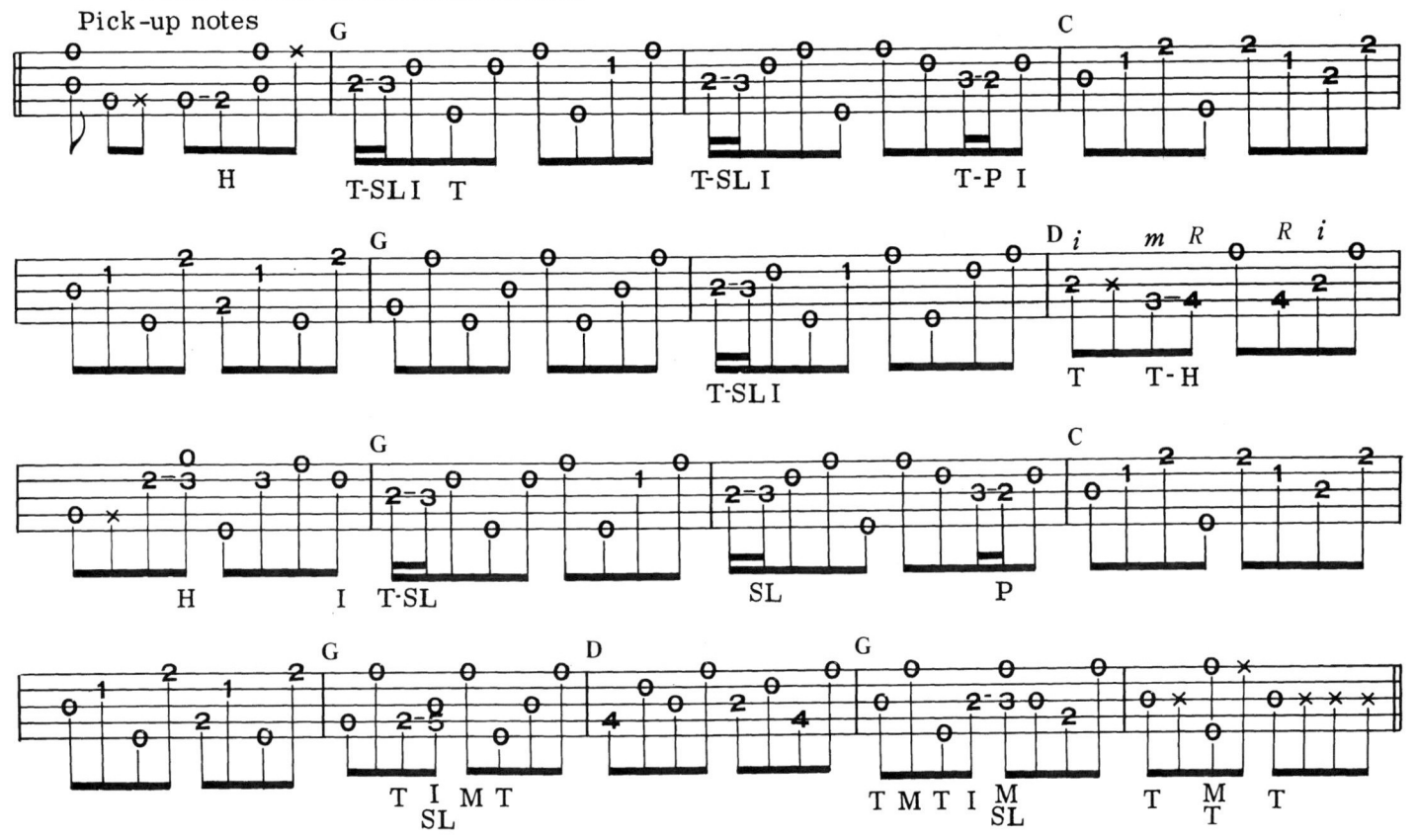

RED RIVER VALLEY

I. <u>MELODY</u> and <u>CHORDS</u> <u>ONLY</u>:

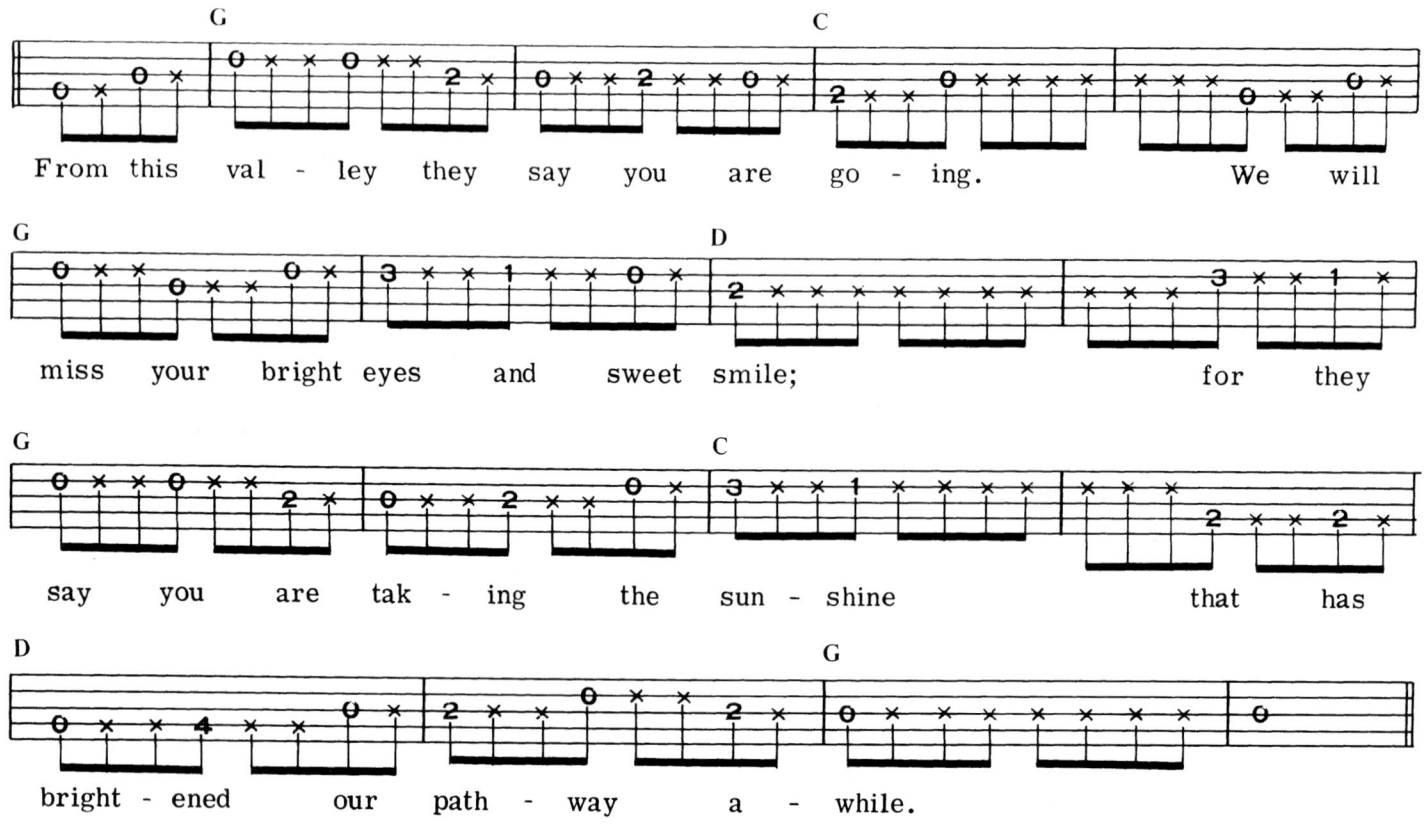

II. ADD THE FORWARD ROLL: (IMTIMTIM)

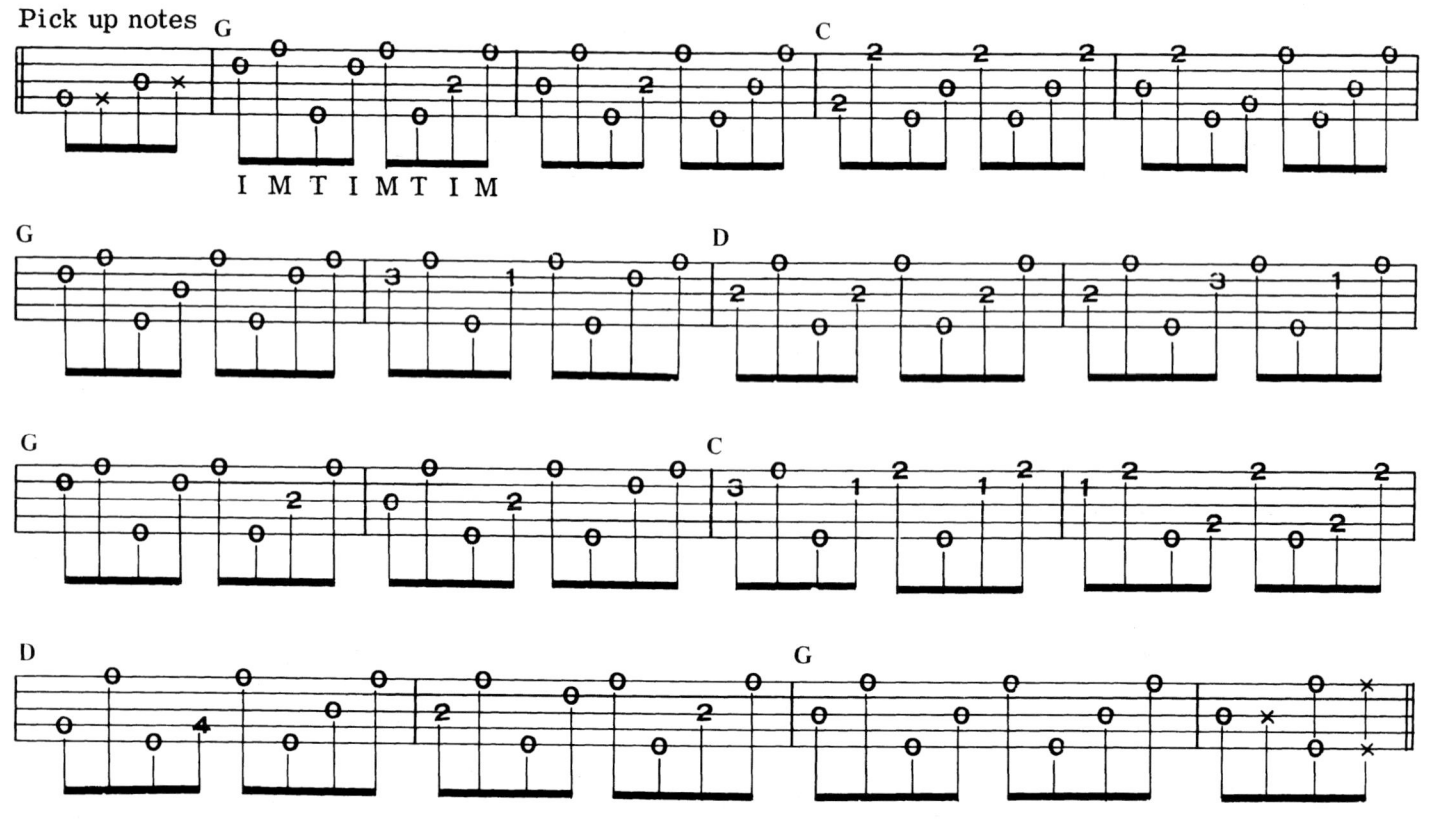

22

III. SUBSTITUTE OTHER STANDARD ROLLS:

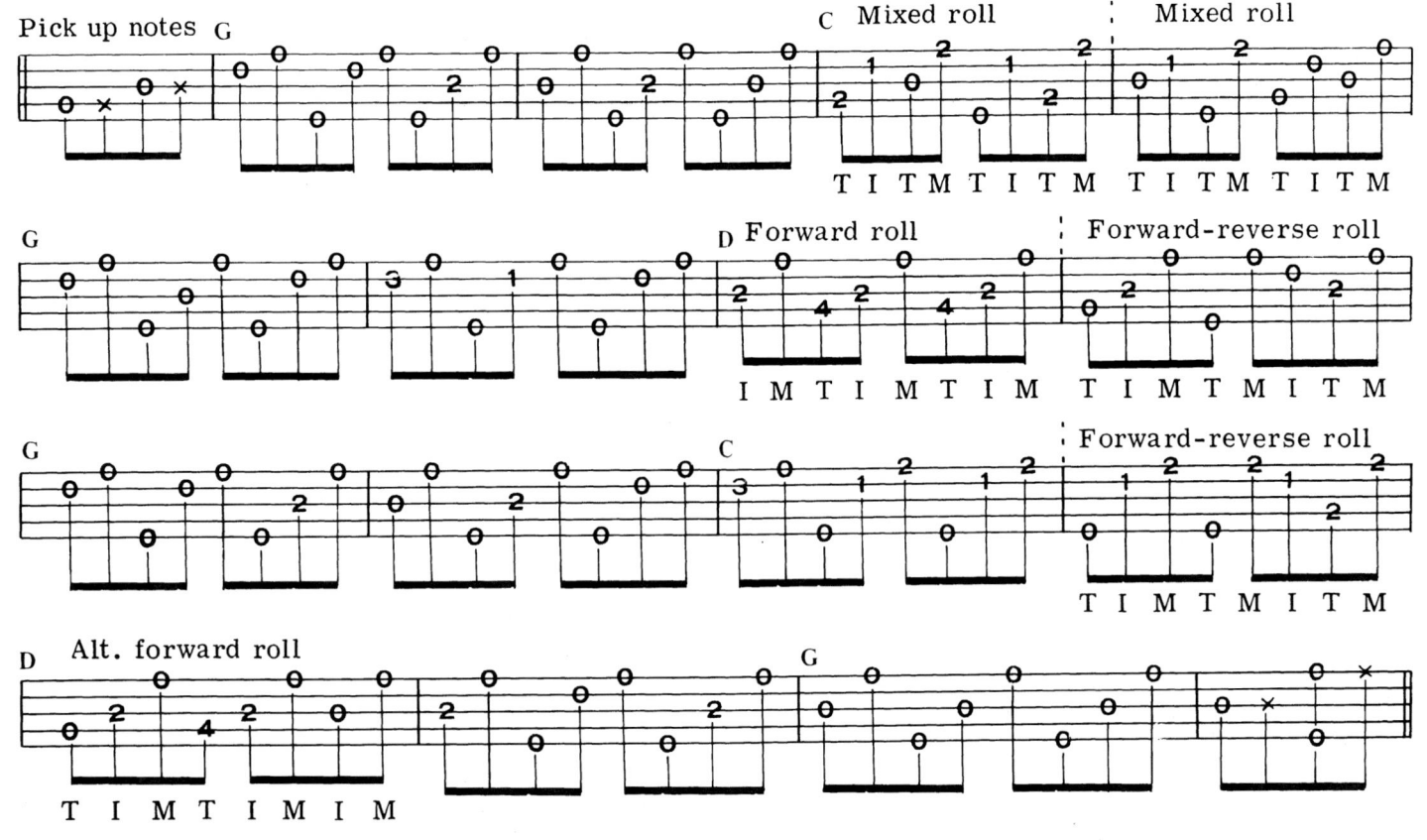

IV. ADD FILL IN ROLLS:

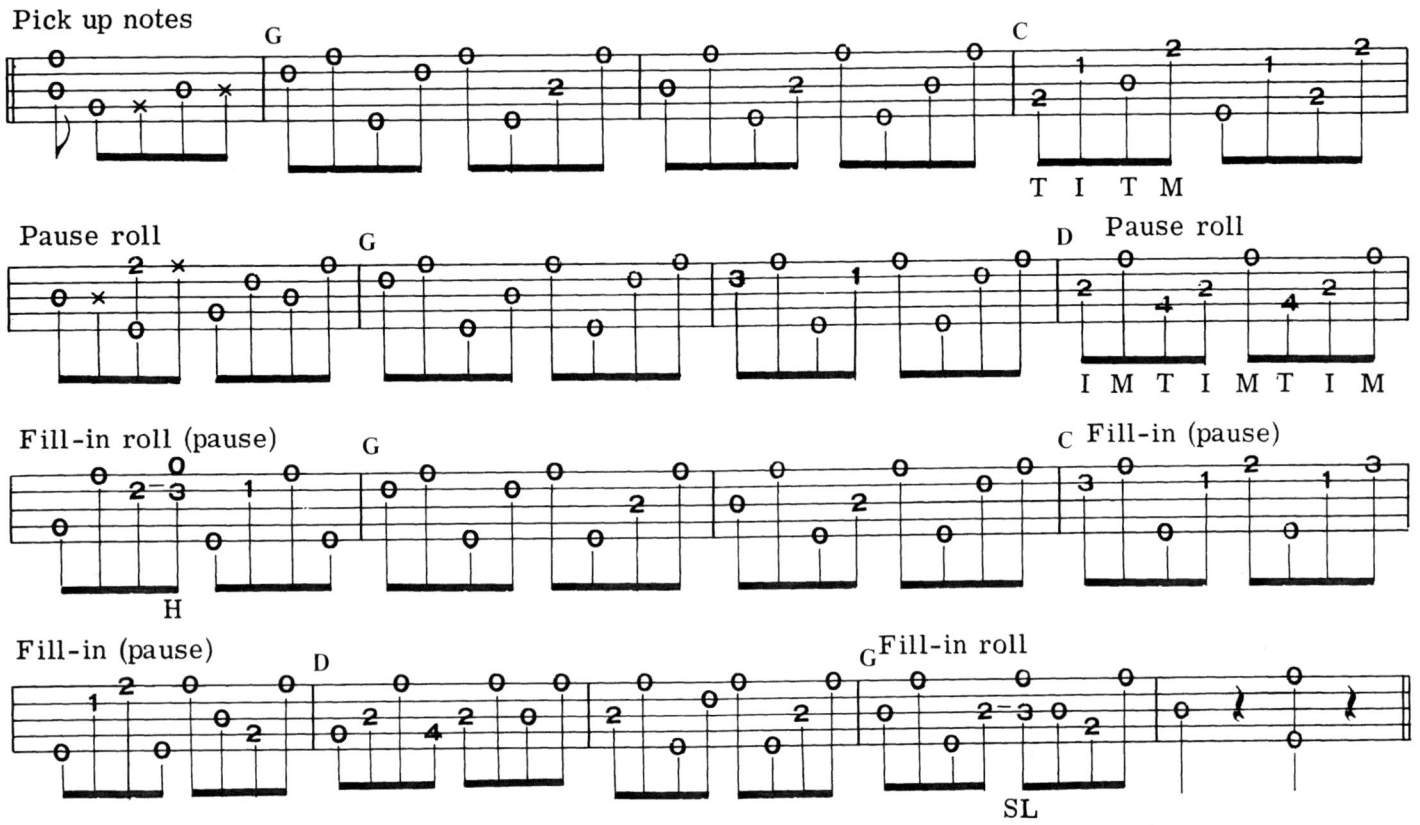

V. ADD LEFT-HAND TECHNIQUES: (i.e. Sl, H, P etc.)

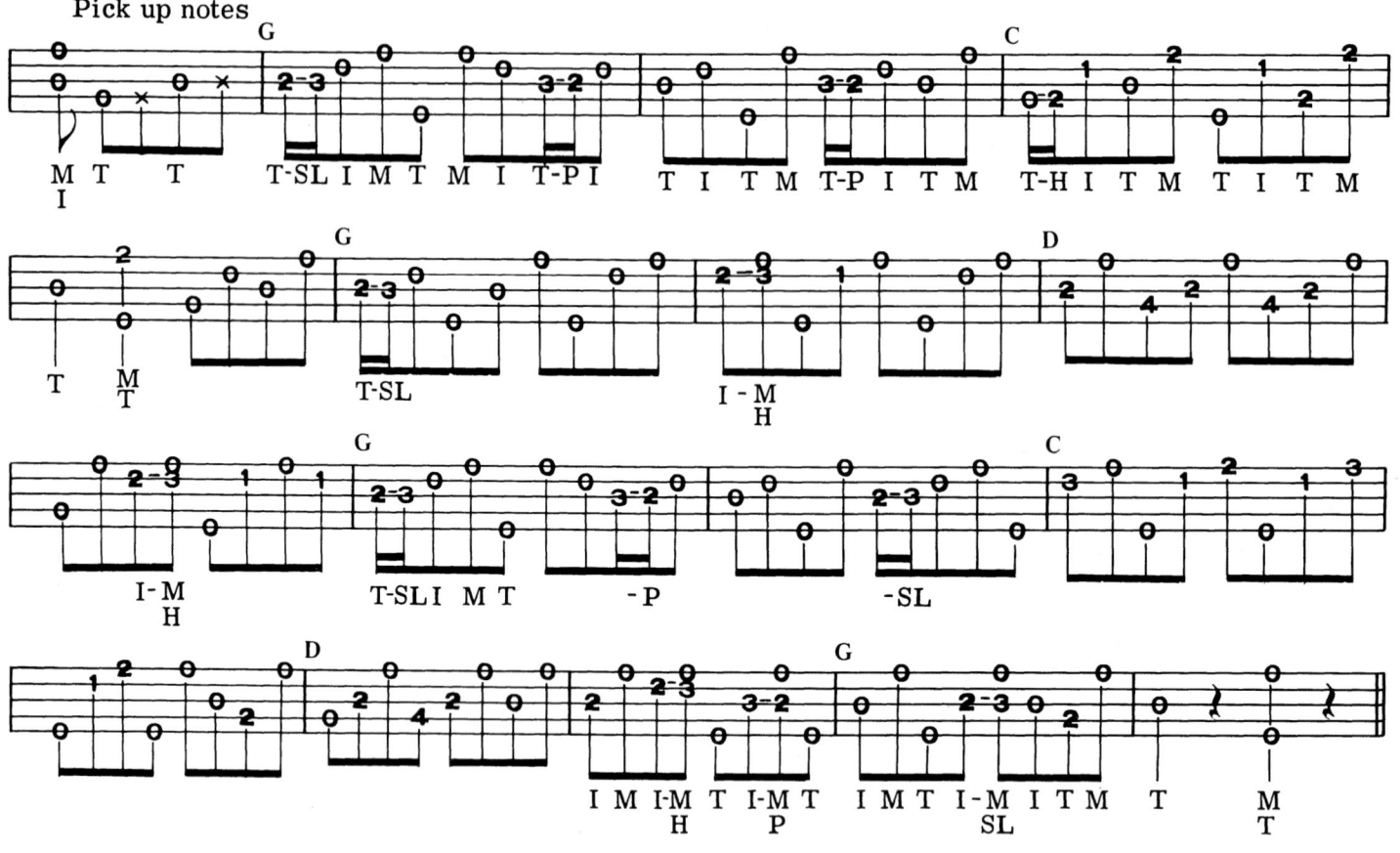

ROLL IN MY SWEET BABY'S ARMS

I. <u>MELODY</u> and <u>CHORDS ONLY</u>:

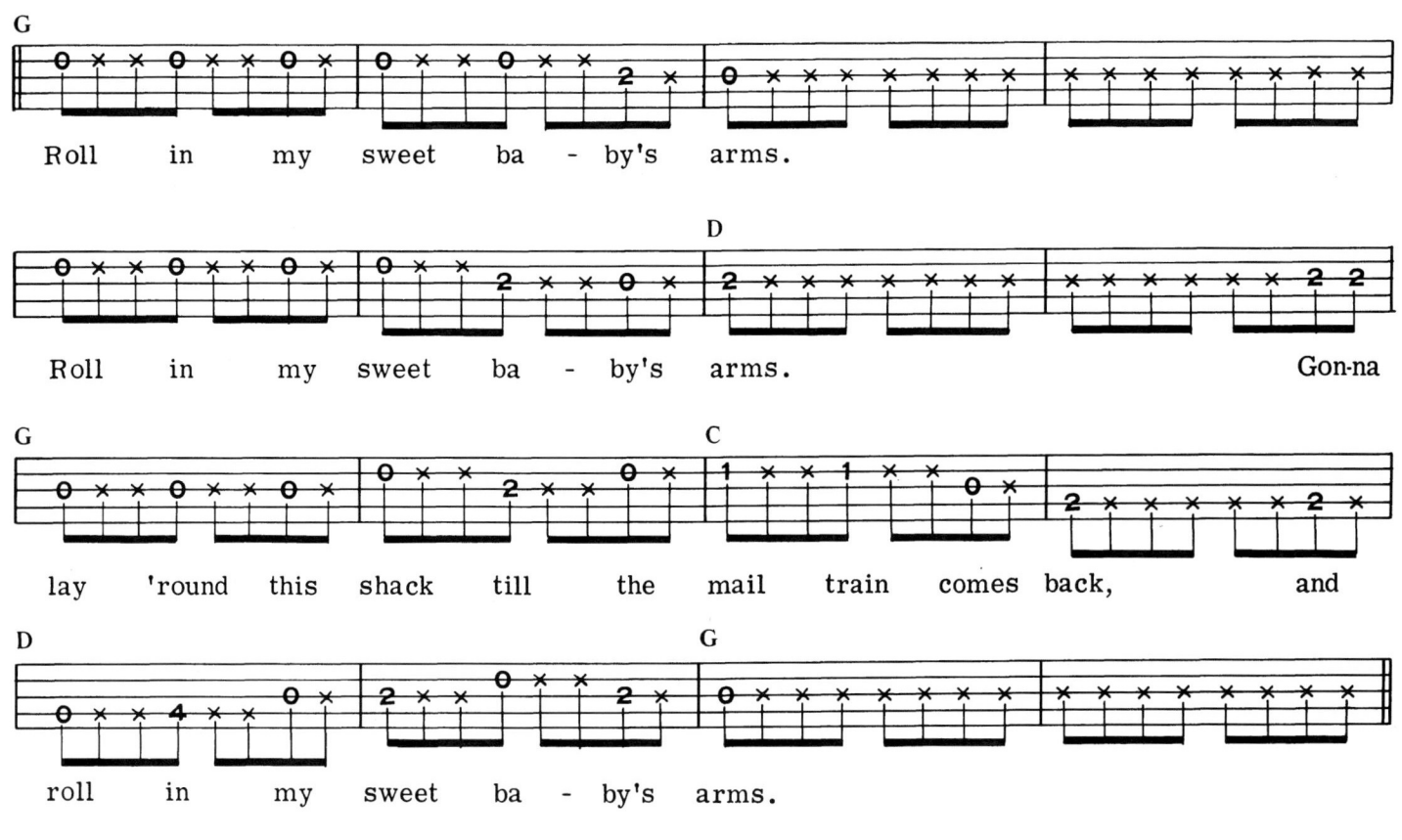

II. ADDING THE FORWARD ROLL: (The right index finger picks the melody.)

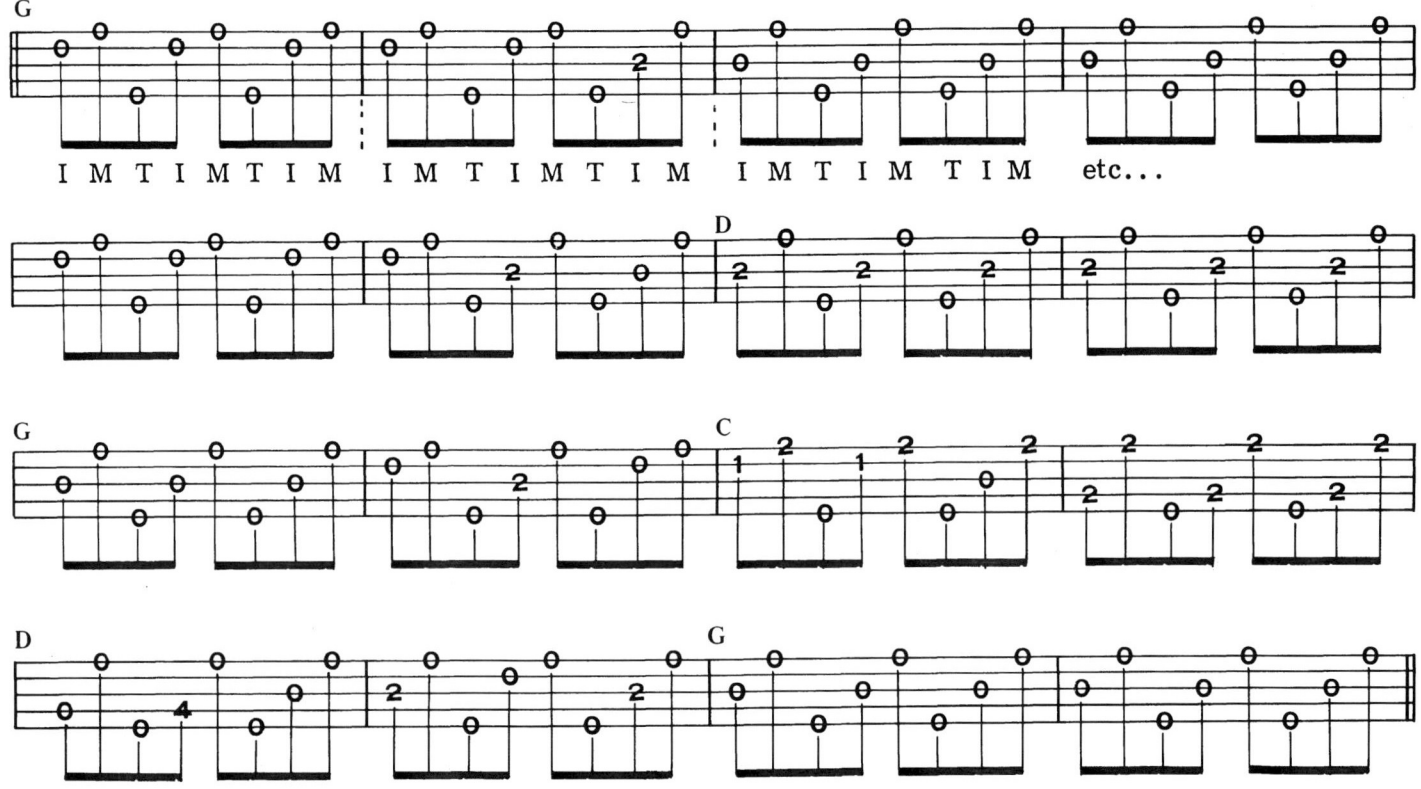

25

III. <u>SUBSTITUTING</u> <u>OTHER</u> <u>STANDARD</u> <u>ROLL</u> <u>PATTERNS</u>: (The Mixed Roll and the Forward-Reverse Roll enable the melody notes to be picked by the thumb of the right hand, instead of the index finger.)

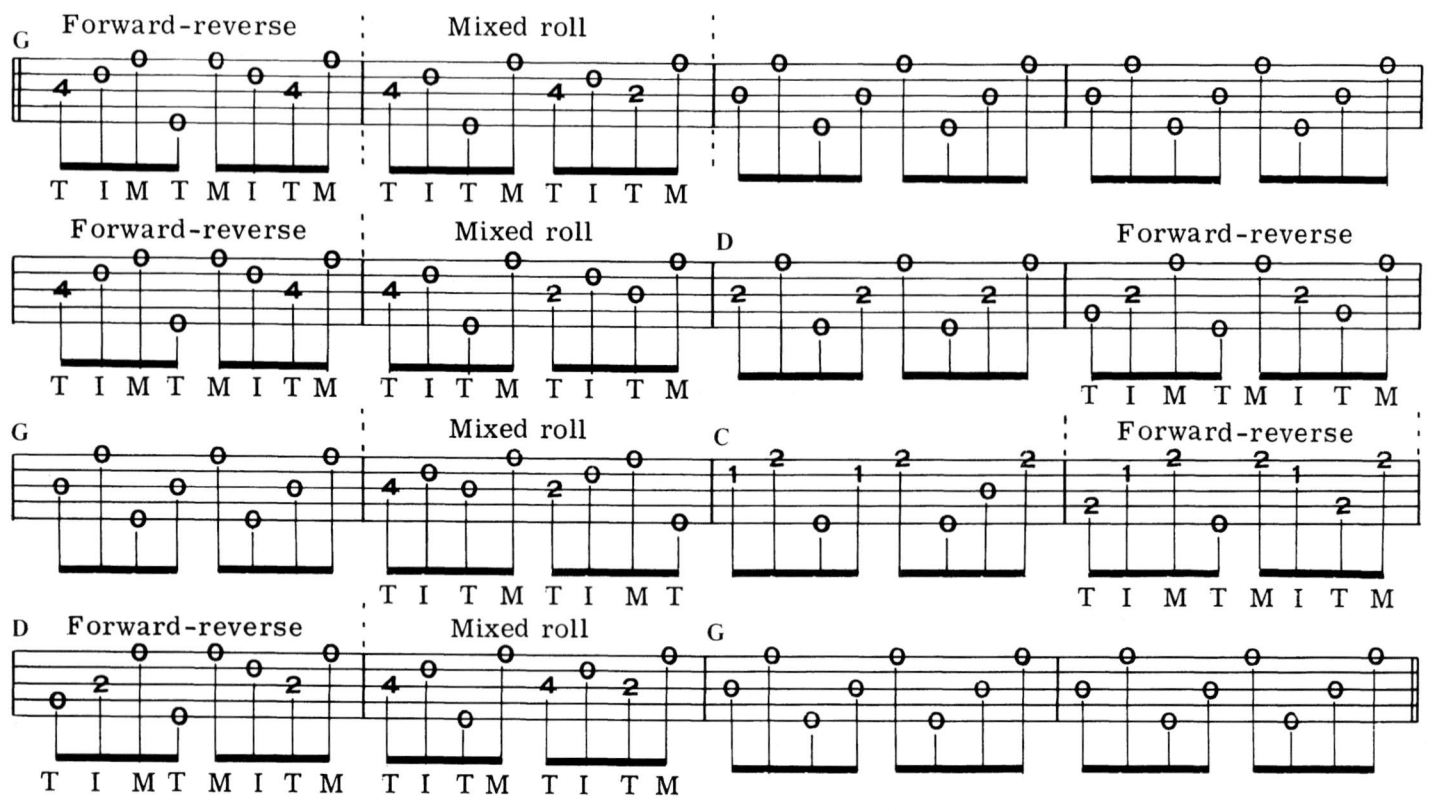

IV. <u>ADDING</u> <u>FILL-IN</u> <u>LICKS</u>:

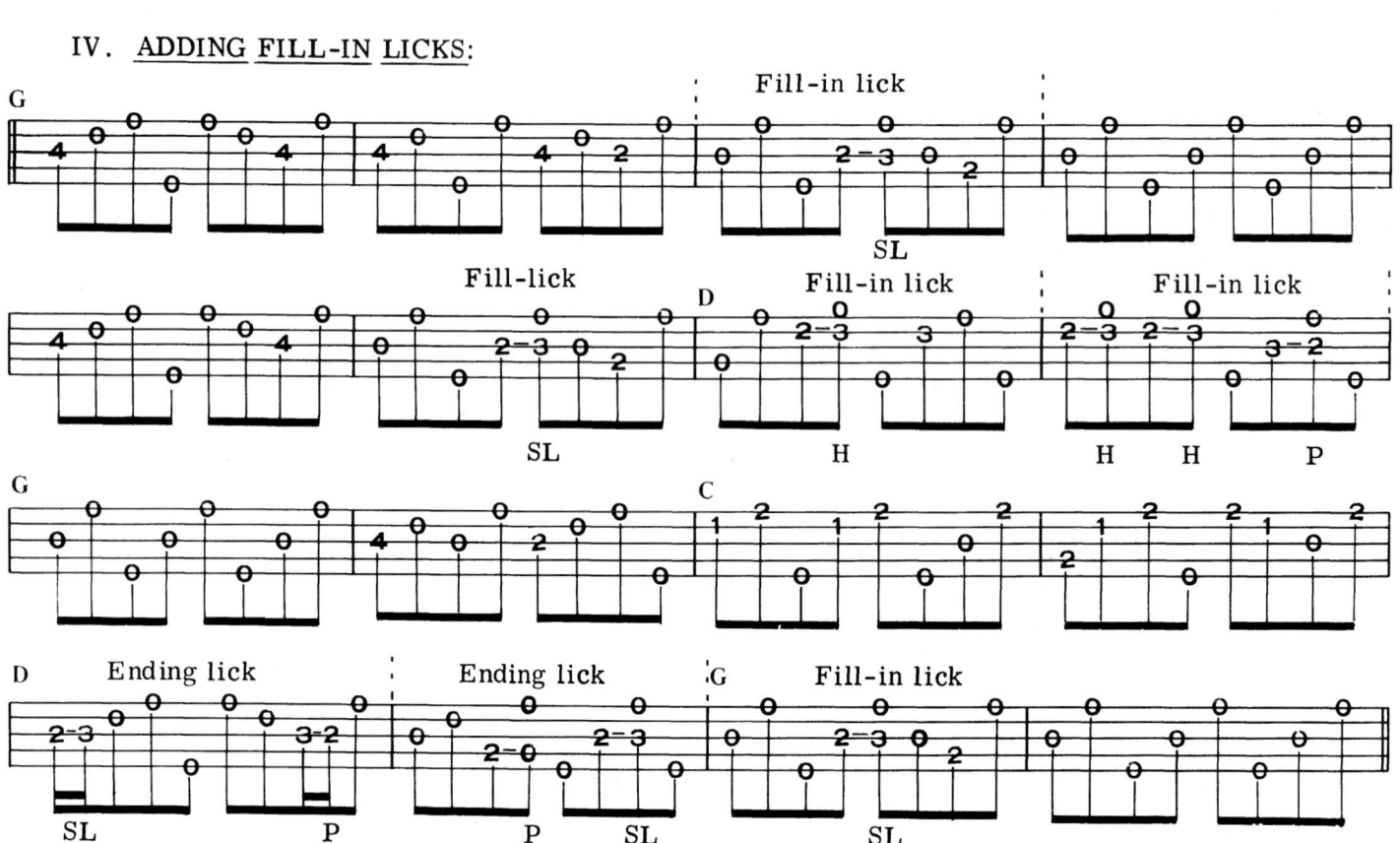

V. ADDING LEFT-HAND TECHNIQUES: Slightly accent (play louder) the first note of each measure to bring out the melody, or tune to the song. (This tone will often be a melody note, in any song.)

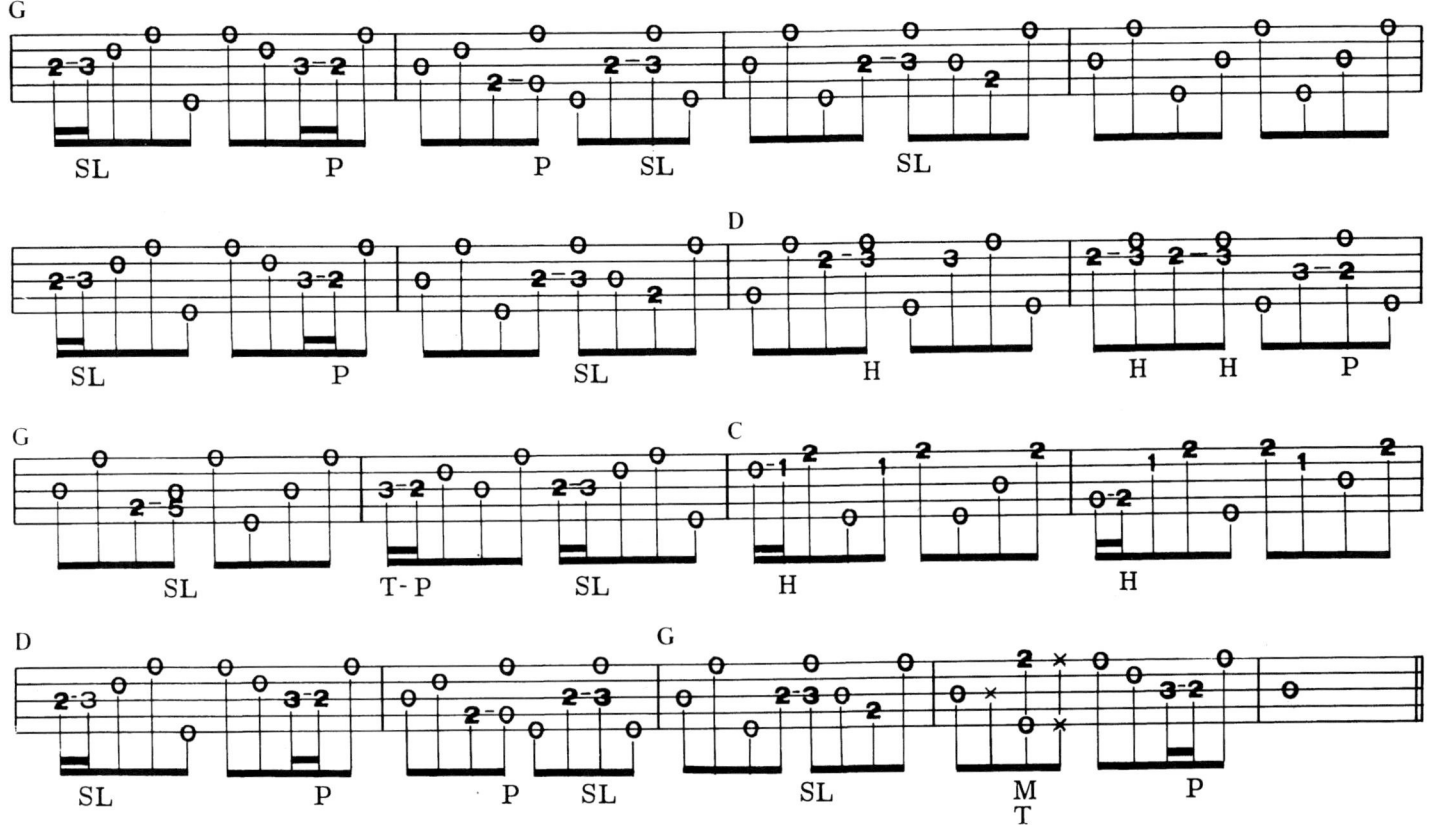

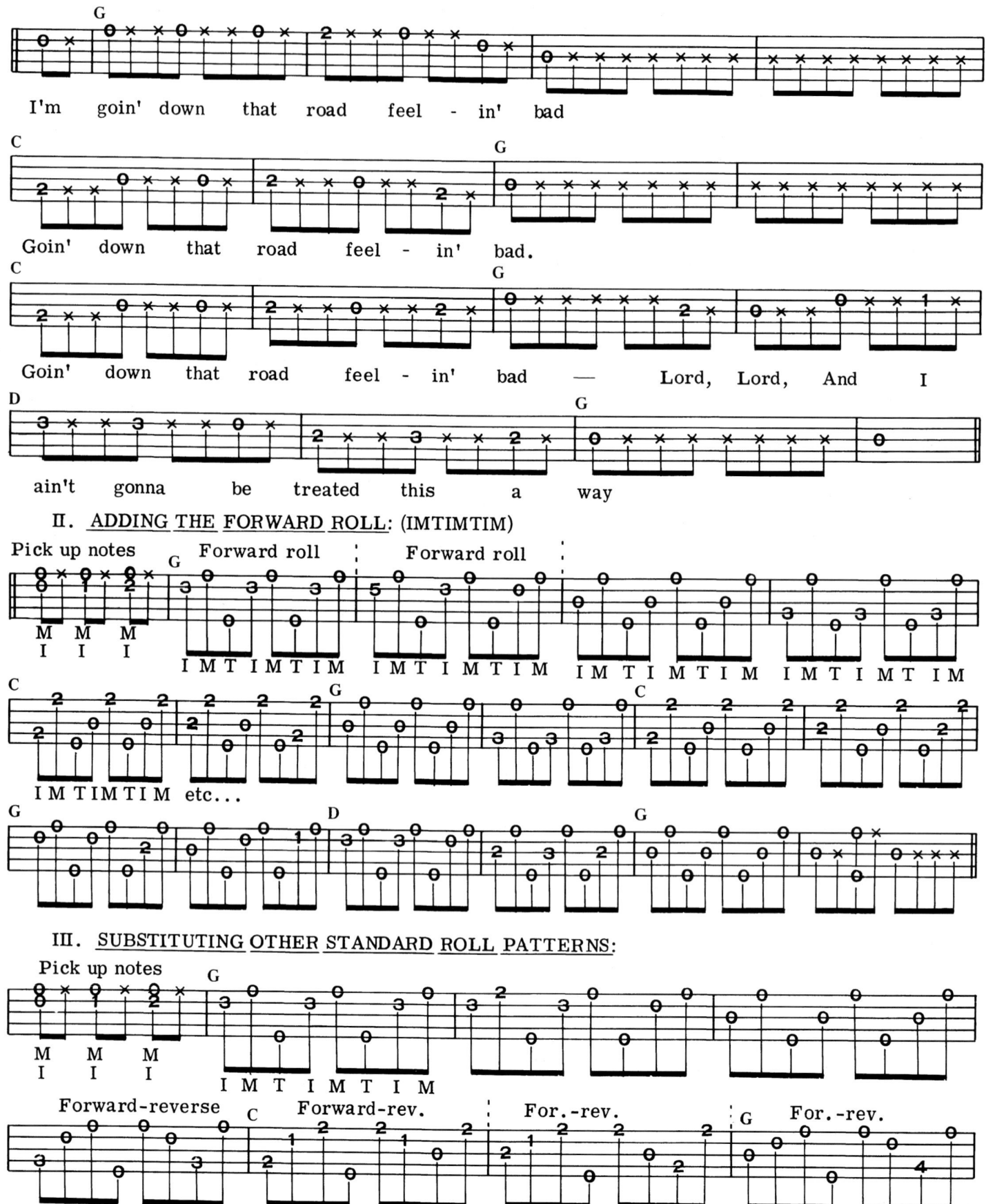

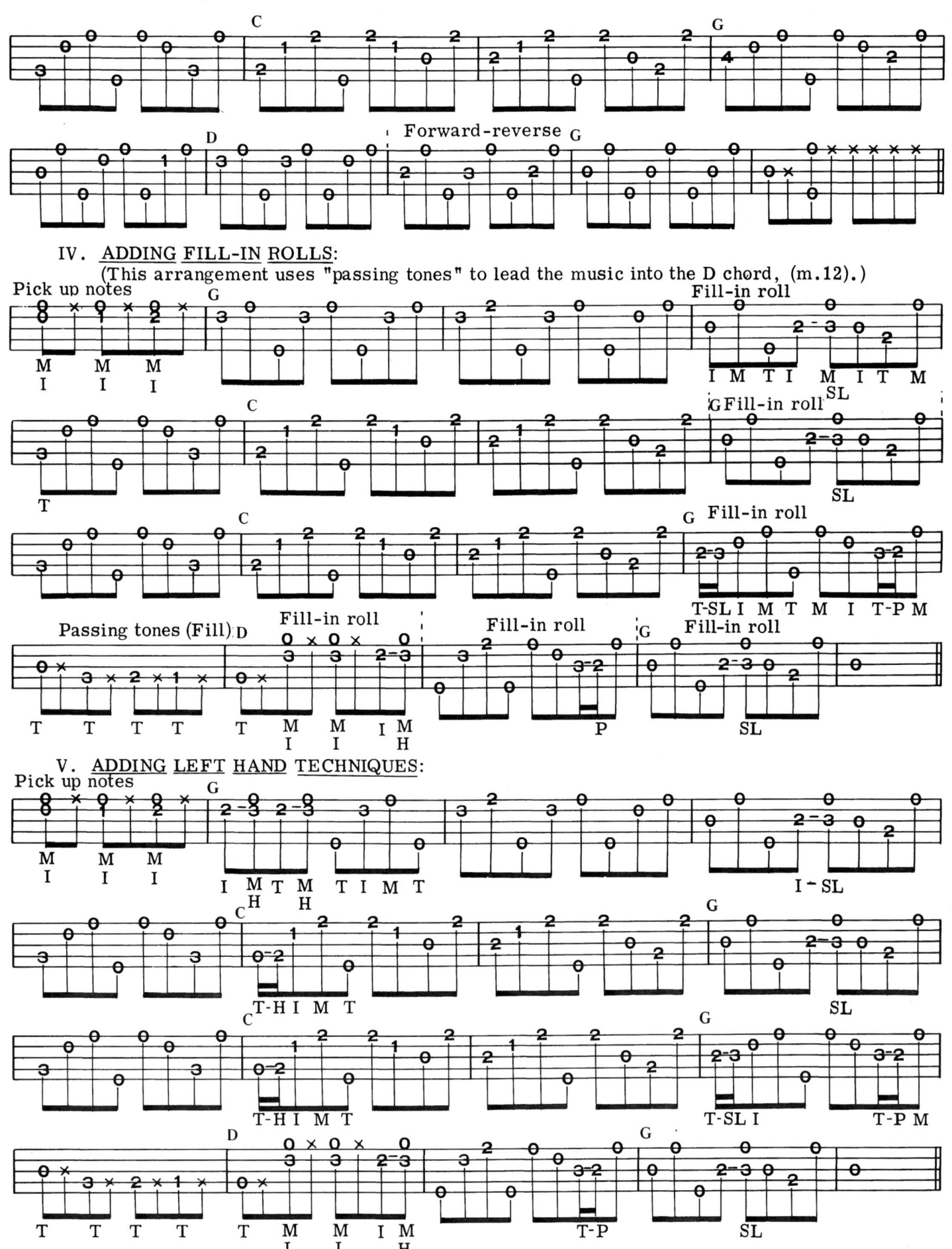

WALKING CANE

I. <u>MELODY</u> and <u>CHORDS</u> ONLY:

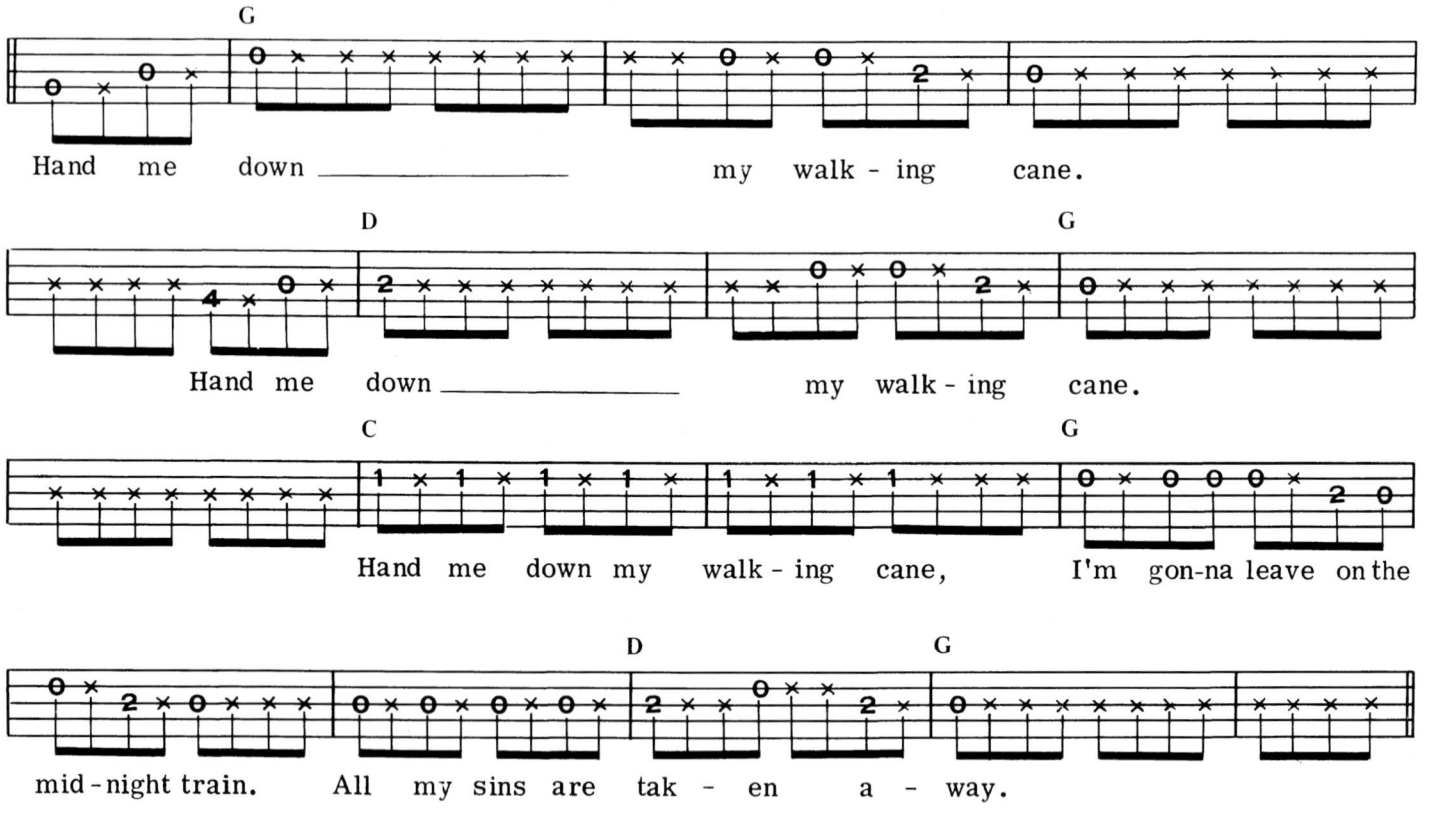

II. <u>USING</u> <u>THE</u> <u>FORWARD</u> <u>ROLL</u> <u>PATTERN</u>:

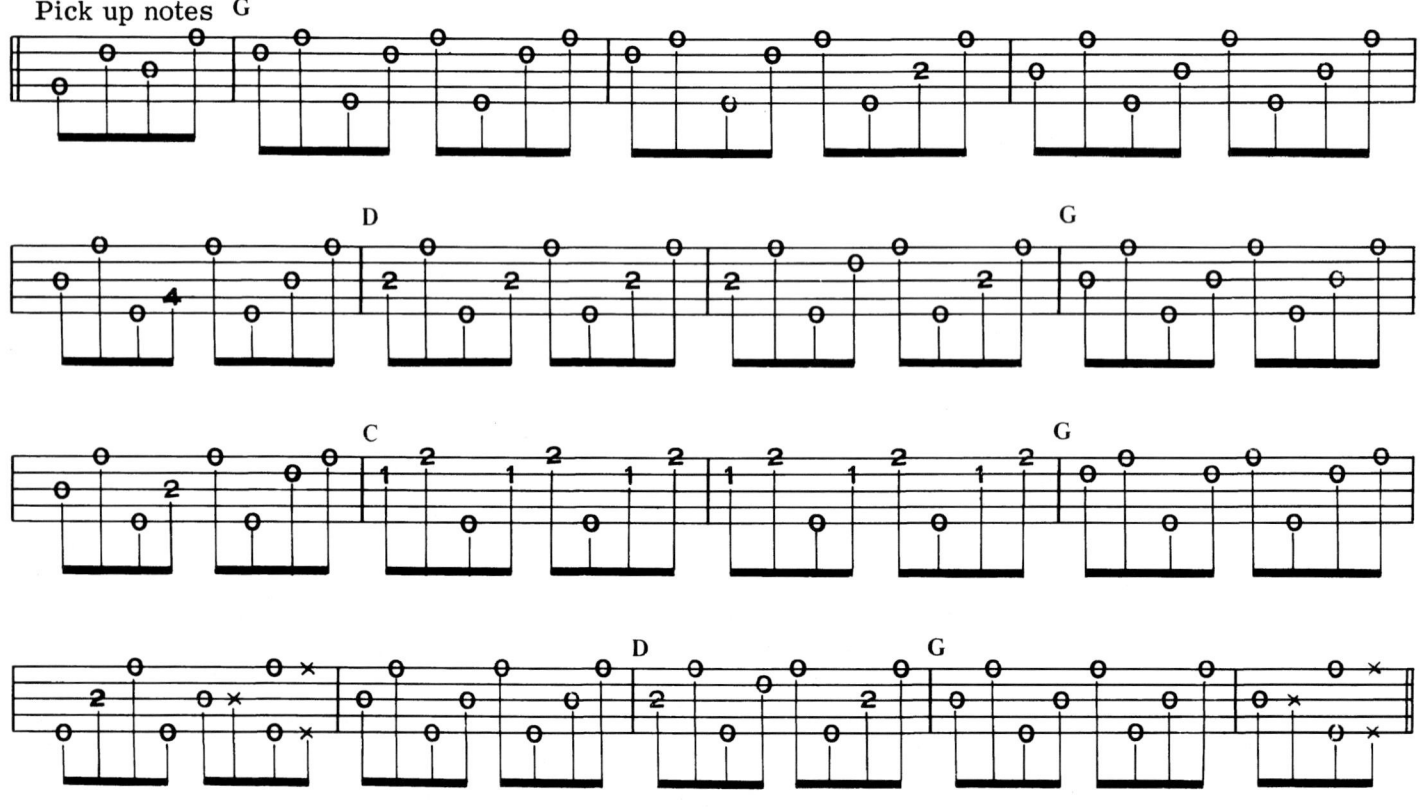

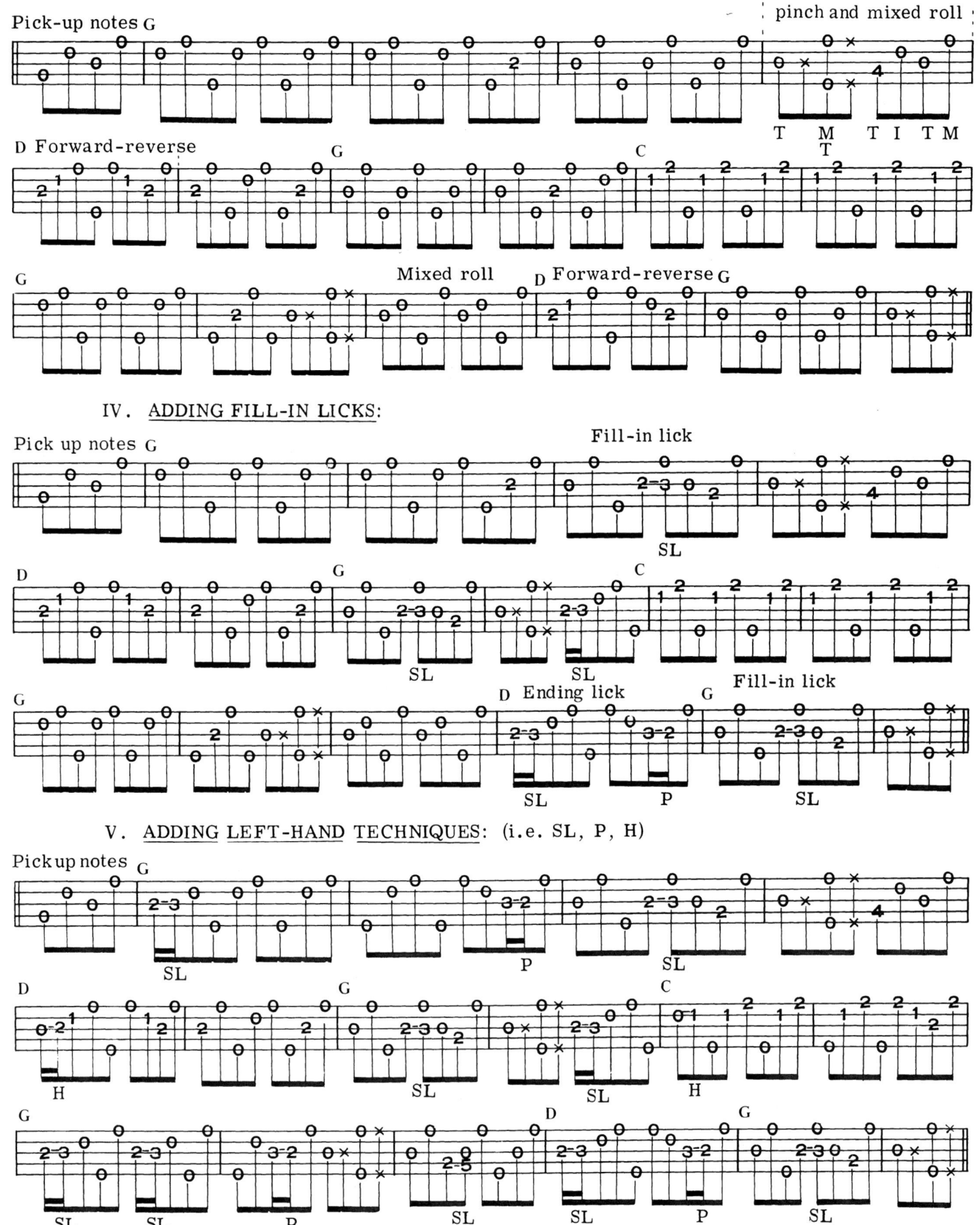

WILDWOOD FLOWER

This tune is divided into two parts, which are labeled Part A & Part B. The melody for part B begins with notes which are located in the up-the-neck area of the fingerboard of the banjo.

I. <u>MELODY</u> and <u>CHORDS</u> ONLY:

Part A:

[Tablature with lyrics:]
I'll en-twine and I'll min-gle my ra-ven black  hair. With the ro-ses so red and the 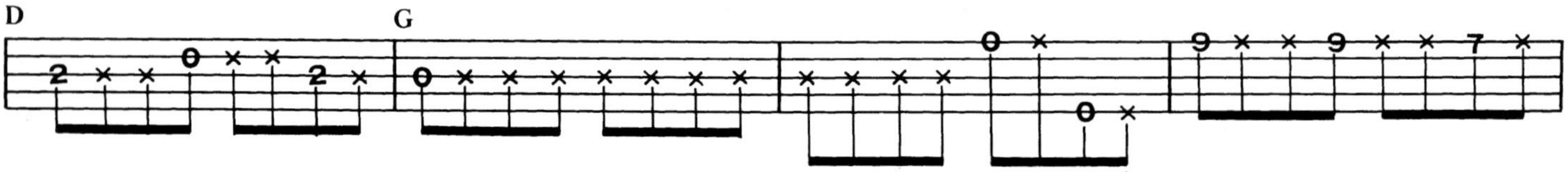 lil-lies so fair. And the myr-tle so 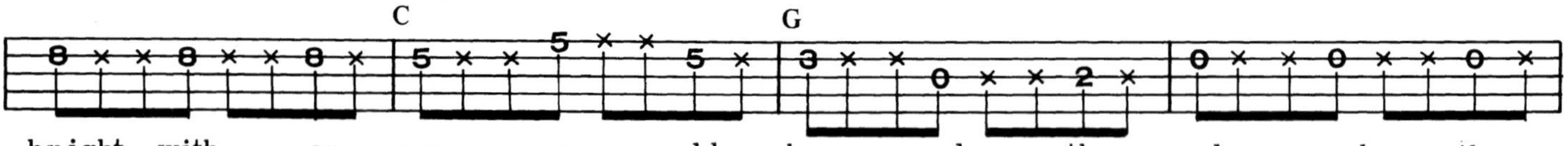 bright with an em-er-ald hue and the pale and the  lea-der and eyes look so blue.

II. <u>ADDING</u> <u>THE</u> <u>FORWARD</u> <u>ROLL</u> <u>PATTERN</u>: (IMTIMTIM)

(The first measure of Part B uses an alternate form of the Forward Roll, for the middle finger of the right hand begins the roll. Remember, any finger can begin the roll pattern; the <u>order</u> in which the right fingers pick the strings determines the name of the roll.)

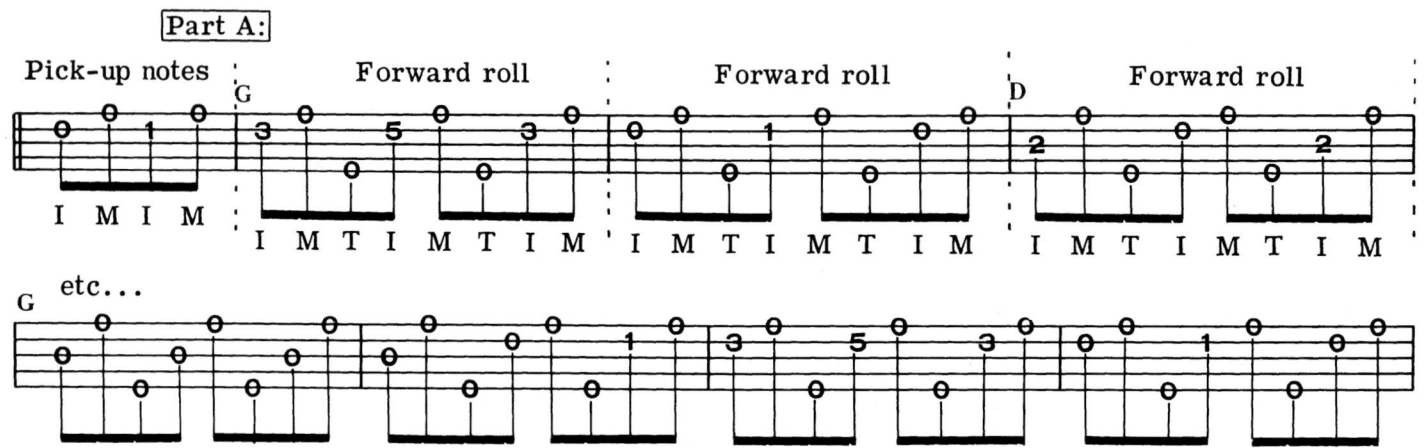

32

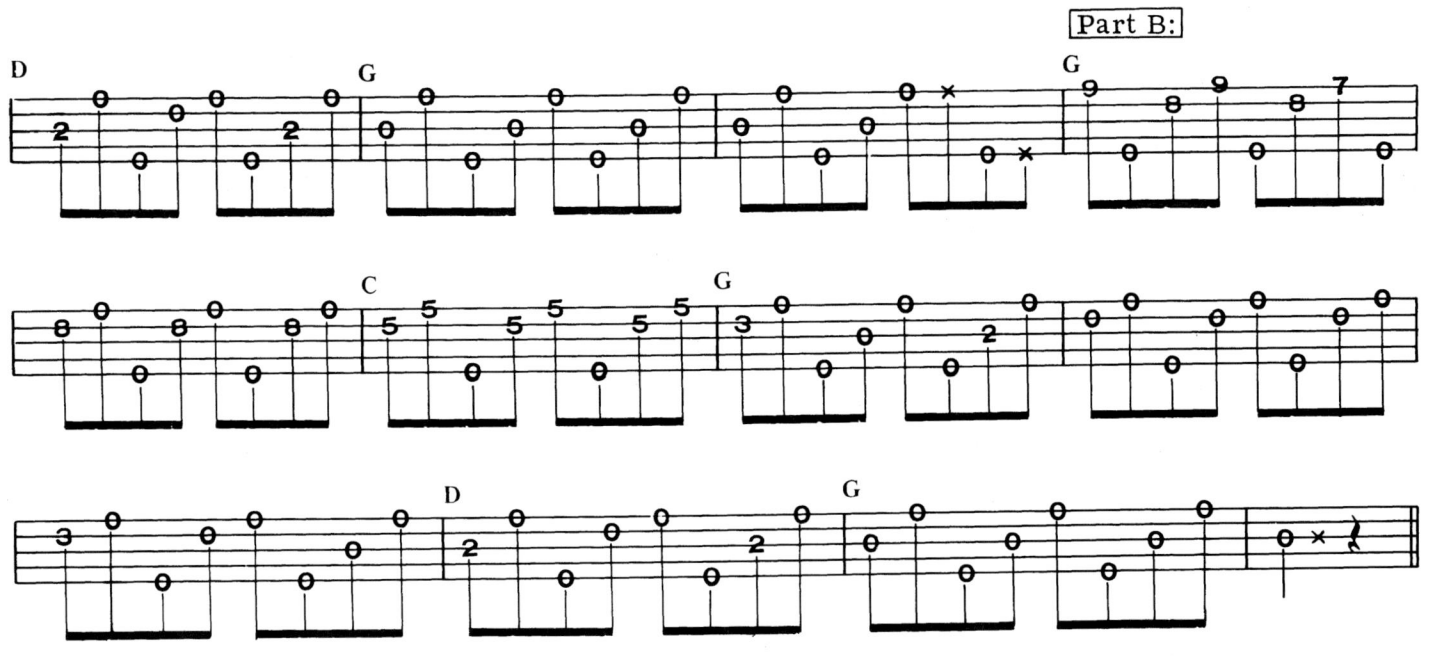

III. SUBTITUTING OTHER STANDARD ROLL PATTERNS:

NOTE: A melody note can be emphasized by pausing after the note. (Substitute an "x" (rest) for the note which should follow the melody note. i.e. See measures 2 and 3 of Part B.)

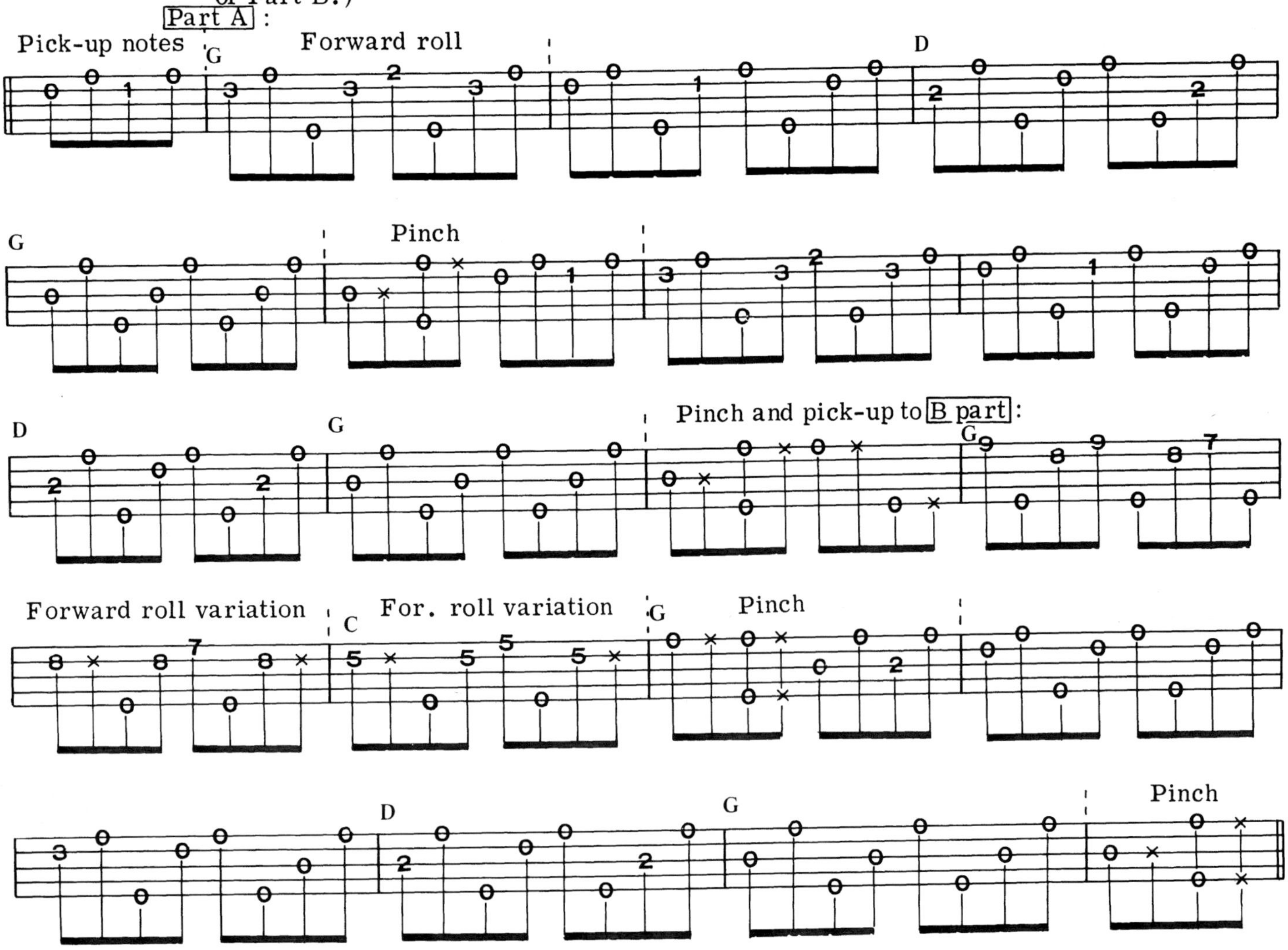

IV. ADDING FILL-IN ROLLS:

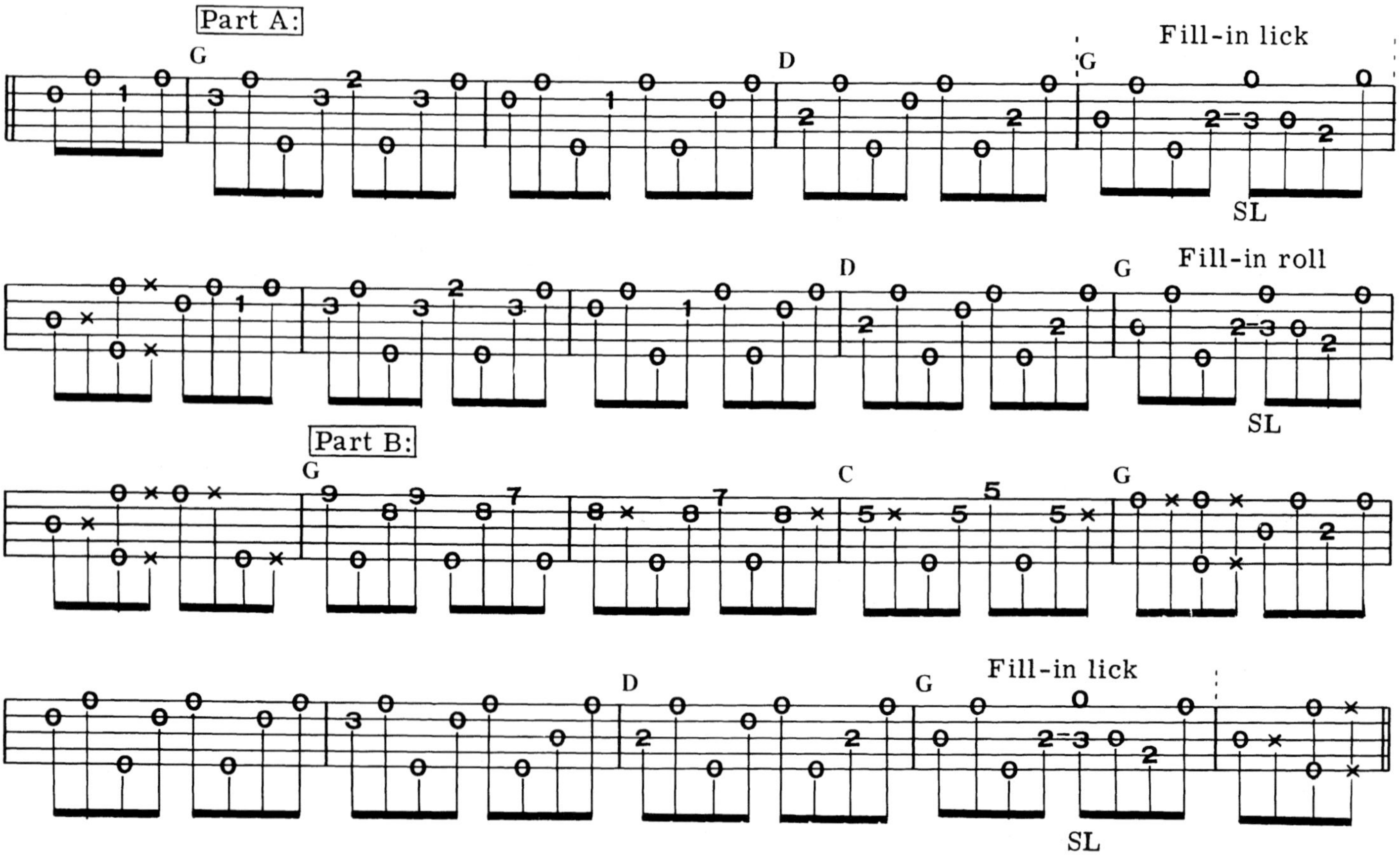

V. ADDING LEFT HAND TECHNIQUES:

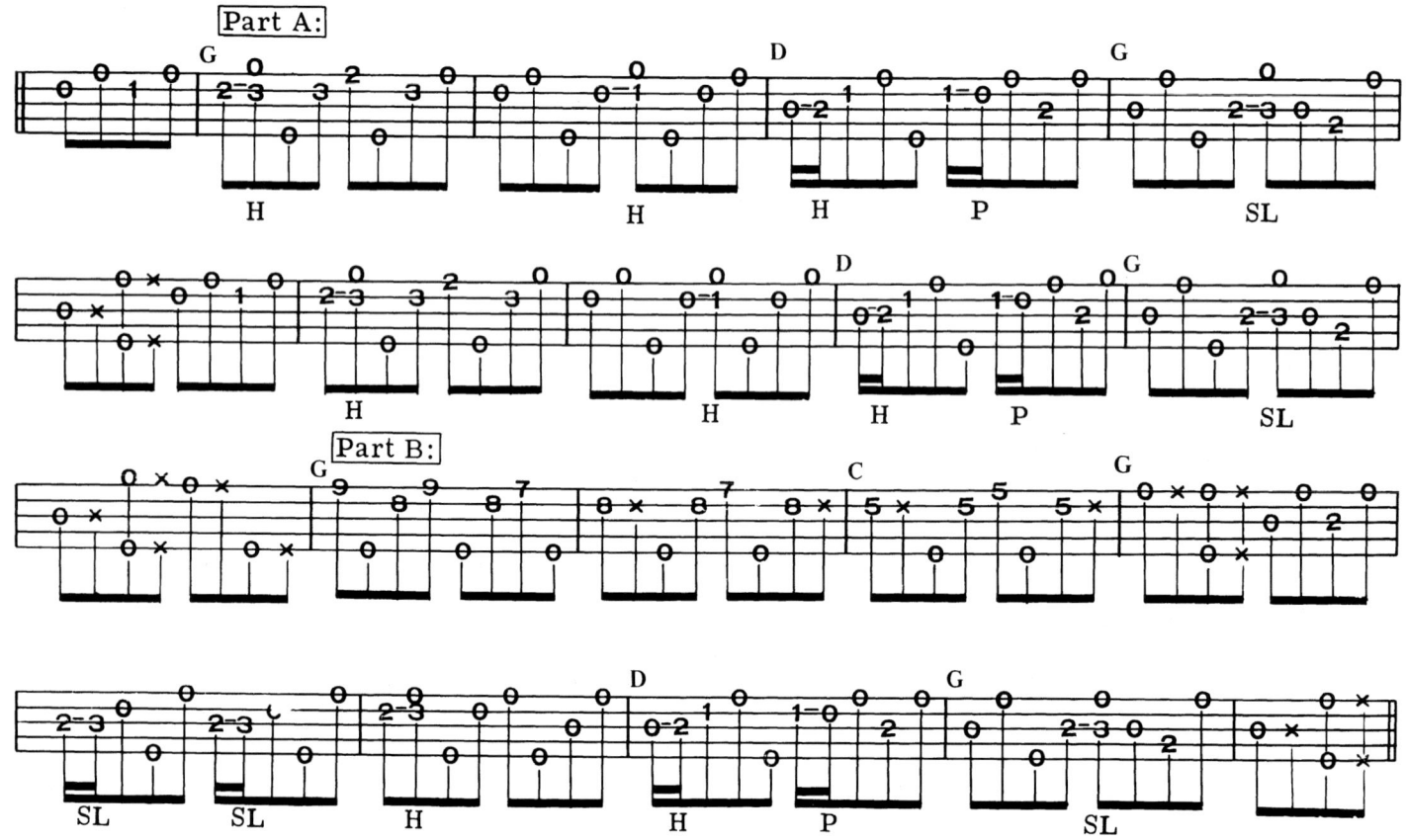

CRIPPLE CREEK

Notice when playing through the melody for this tune, that two chords are used in the 2nd measure of the verse, and also in the 4th measure. When this situation occurs in a song, simply divide the roll pattern in half, playing four notes for the first chord of the measure, and four notes for the second chord. (The "Mixed Roll" is particularly effective when this occurs. i.e. see III. below.)

NOTE: play the verse twice, then play the chorus twice in I.-IV. (||:   :|| means repeat)

I. <u>MELODY</u> and <u>CHORDS</u> <u>ONLY</u>:

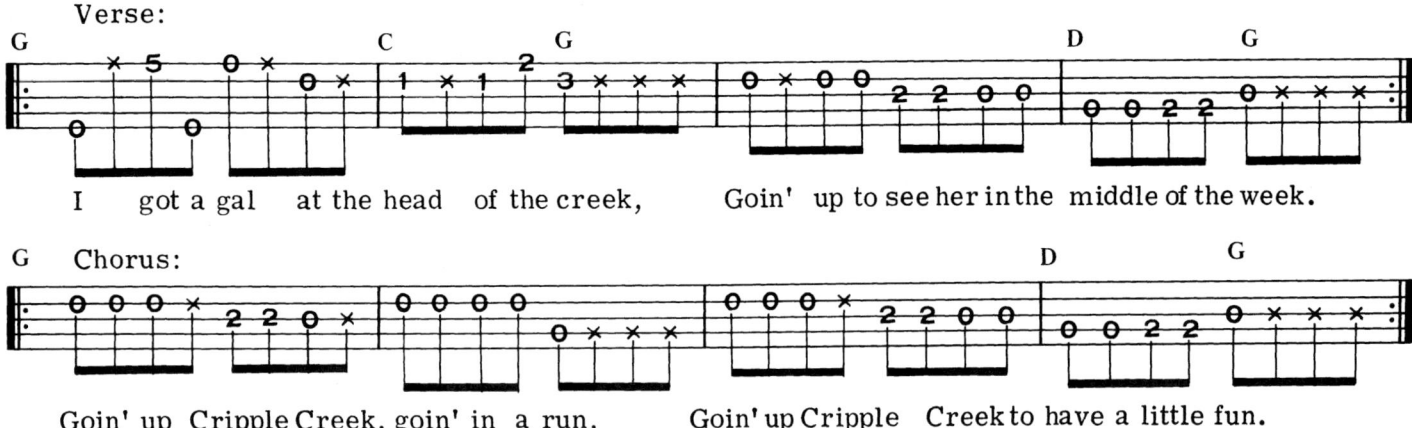

II. ADDING THE FORWARD ROLL PATTERN:

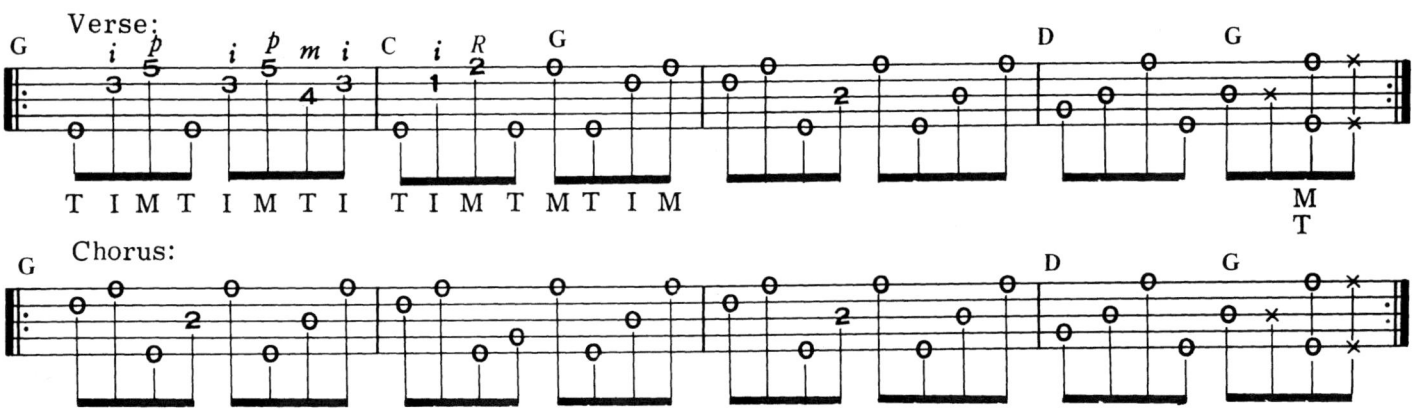

III. <u>ADDING OTHER STANDARD ROLL PATTERNS</u>:

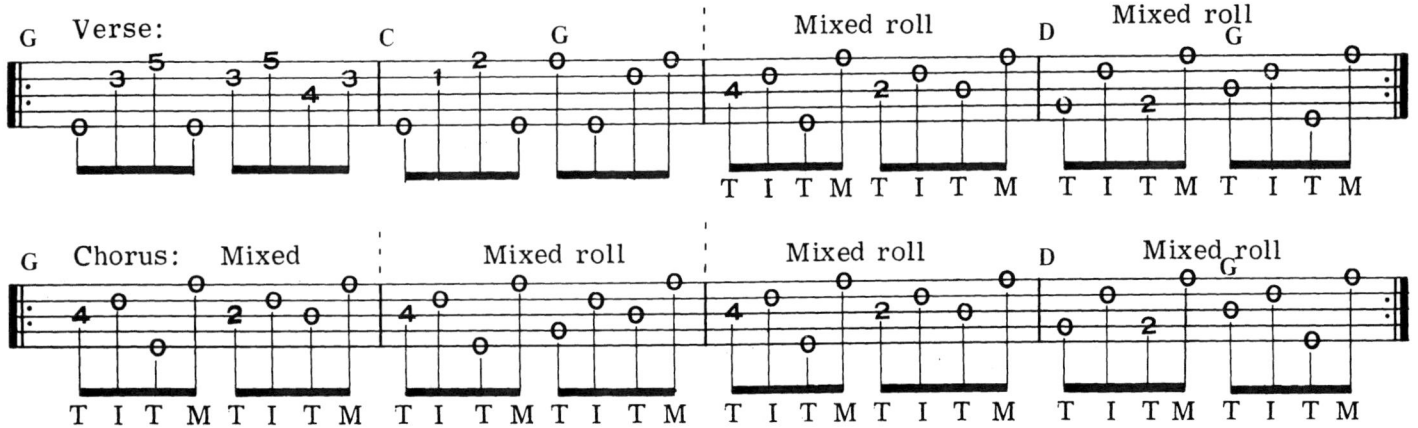

35

IV. <u>ADDING</u> <u>FILL-IN</u> <u>ROLLS</u>:

Verse:

Chorus:

V. <u>ADDING</u> <u>LEFT-HAND</u> <u>TECHNIQUES</u>: When playing through this arrangement, do not repeat the verse before playing the chorus; the repeats are written out.

NOTE: ♫♩ = (fast slide)   (♫ = ♪)
       SL

Pick up   Verse:
notes

G Chorus:

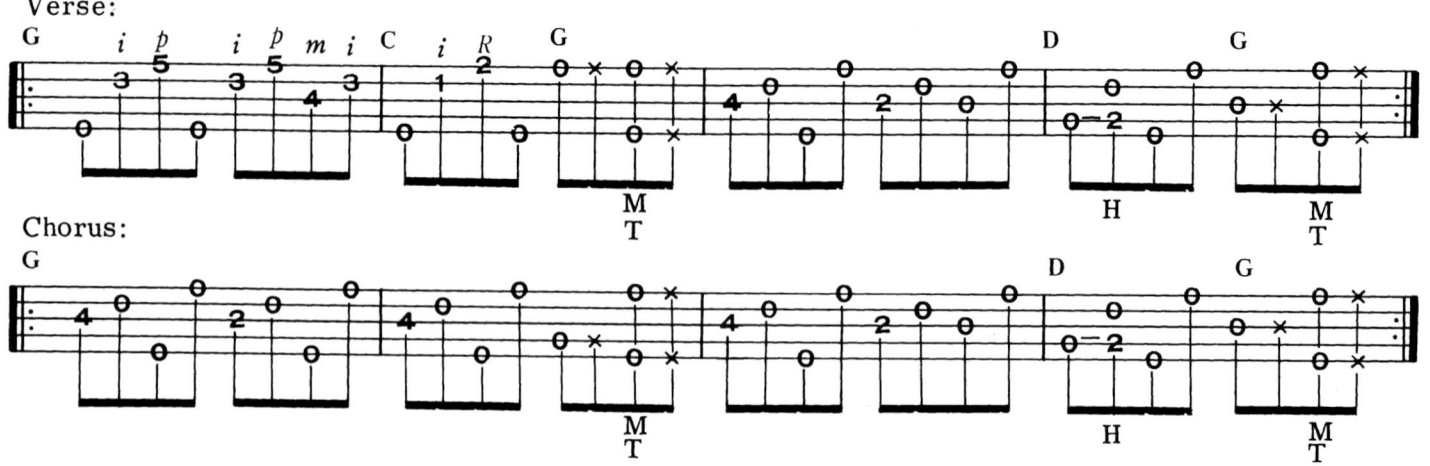

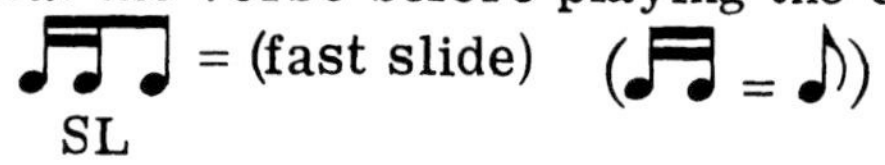

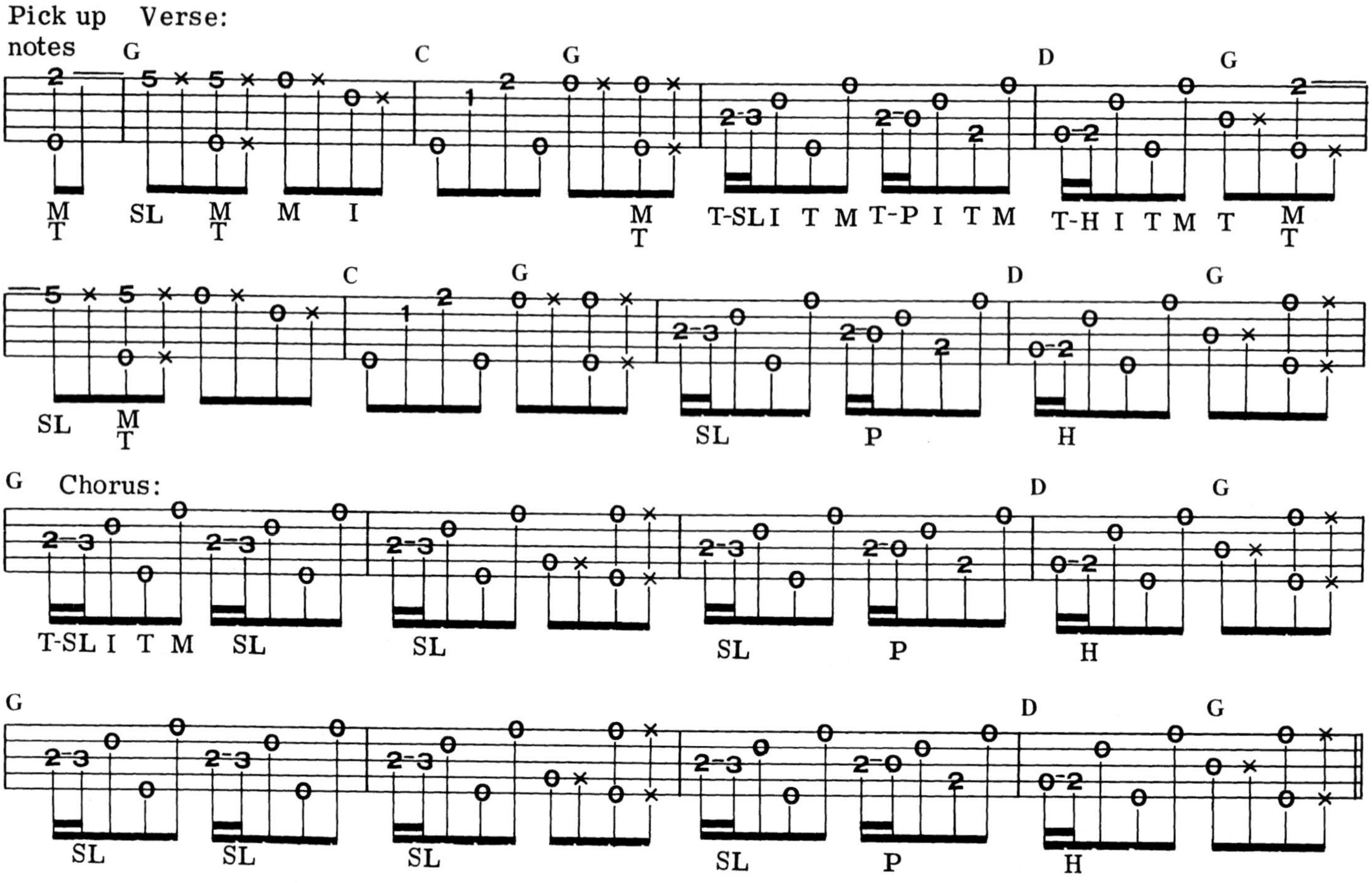

CUMBERLAND GAP

I. <u>MELODY</u> and <u>CHORDS</u> <u>ONLY</u>:

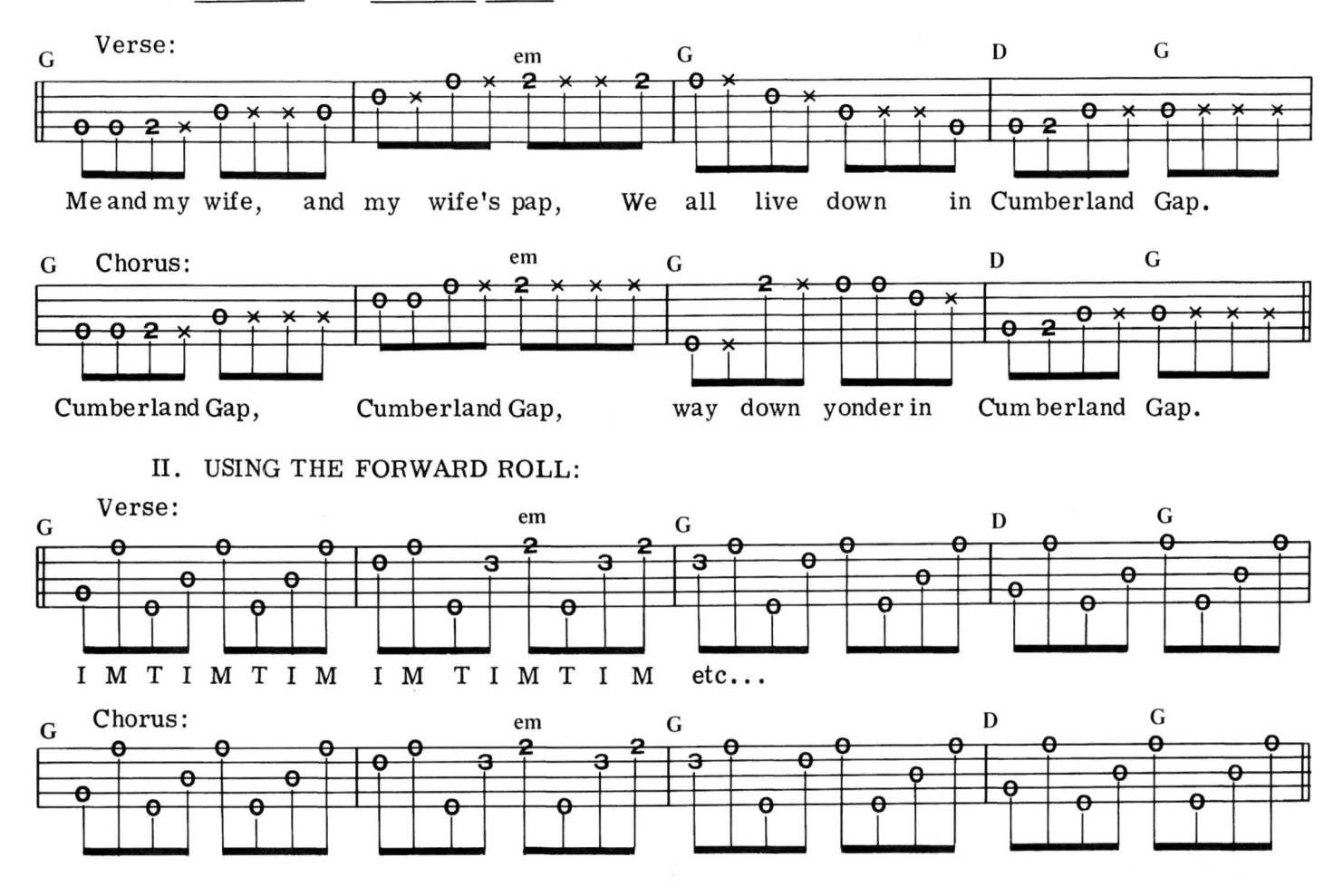

Verse: Me and my wife, and my wife's pap, We all live down in Cumberland Gap.

Chorus: Cumberland Gap, Cumberland Gap, way down yonder in Cumberland Gap.

II. USING THE FORWARD ROLL:

Verse: I M T I M T I M   I M T I M T I M   etc...

Chorus:

NOTE: In III through V below, the Forward-Reverse Roll Pattern is used to musically "link" the verse and the chorus. (It drives the verse into the chorus, giving the song a feeling of continuation.)

III. <u>SUBSTITUTING</u> <u>OTHER</u> <u>STANDARD</u> <u>ROLLS</u>:

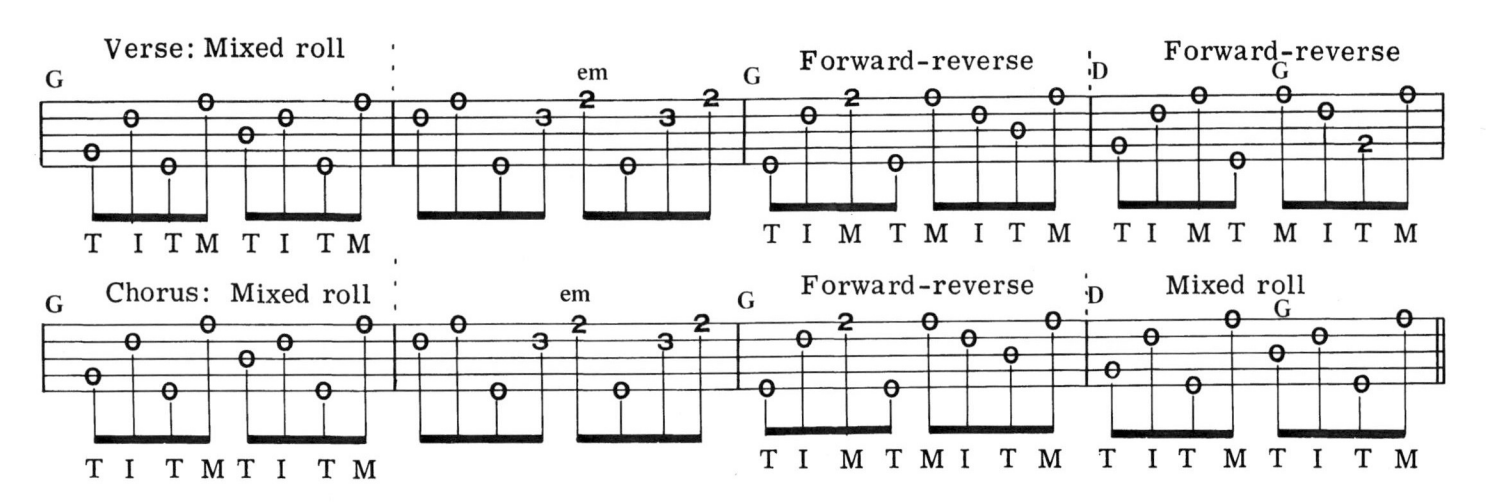

Verse: Mixed roll — Forward-reverse — Forward-reverse
T I T M T I T M   T I M T M I T M   T I M T M I T M

Chorus: Mixed roll — Forward-reverse — Mixed roll
T I T M T I T M   T I M T M I T M   T I T M T I T M

IV. **ADDING FILL-IN LICKS:** (The "pinch" is frequently used for pausing.)

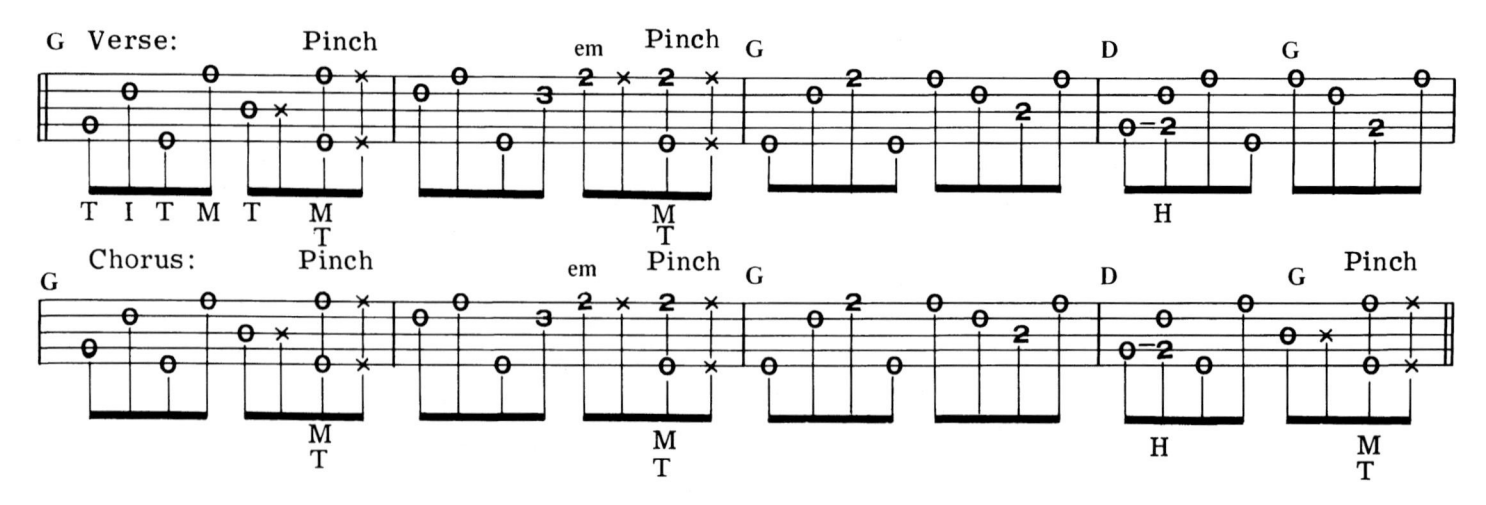

[Tablature: G Verse with Pinch, em Pinch, G, D, G chord progressions]

[Tablature: G Chorus with Pinch, em Pinch, G, D, G Pinch chord progressions]

V. **ADDING LEFT-HAND TECHNIQUES:**

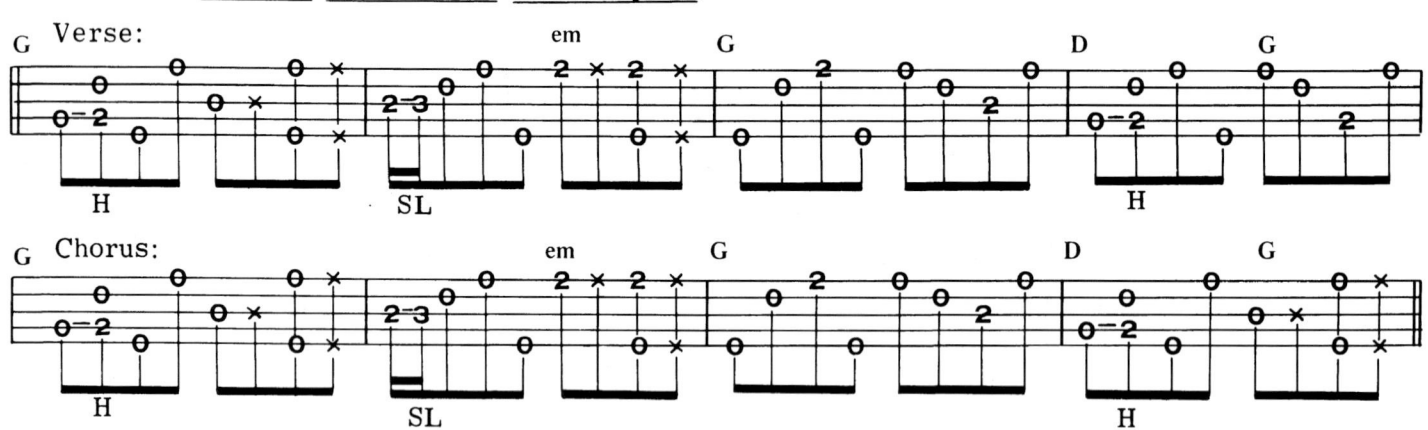

[Tablature: G Verse with H, SL, em, G, D, G, H markings]

[Tablature: G Chorus with H, SL, em, G, D, G, H markings]

* Notice in the final arrangement of this tune, that the Forward Roll Pattern has been retained for only two of the measures. Although the Forward Roll can usually be used as the primary roll pattern throughout a song, it is not always the best pattern. When a song has an average of four or more melody notes per measure, the Mixed Roll and/or the Forward - Reverse Roll often work better than the Forward Roll. (See also "Cripple Creek").

JESSE JAMES

This tune is divided into two parts, the verse, and the refrain, (which follows each verse). Remember to hold the C chord with the left hand when playing this tune, where it is required.

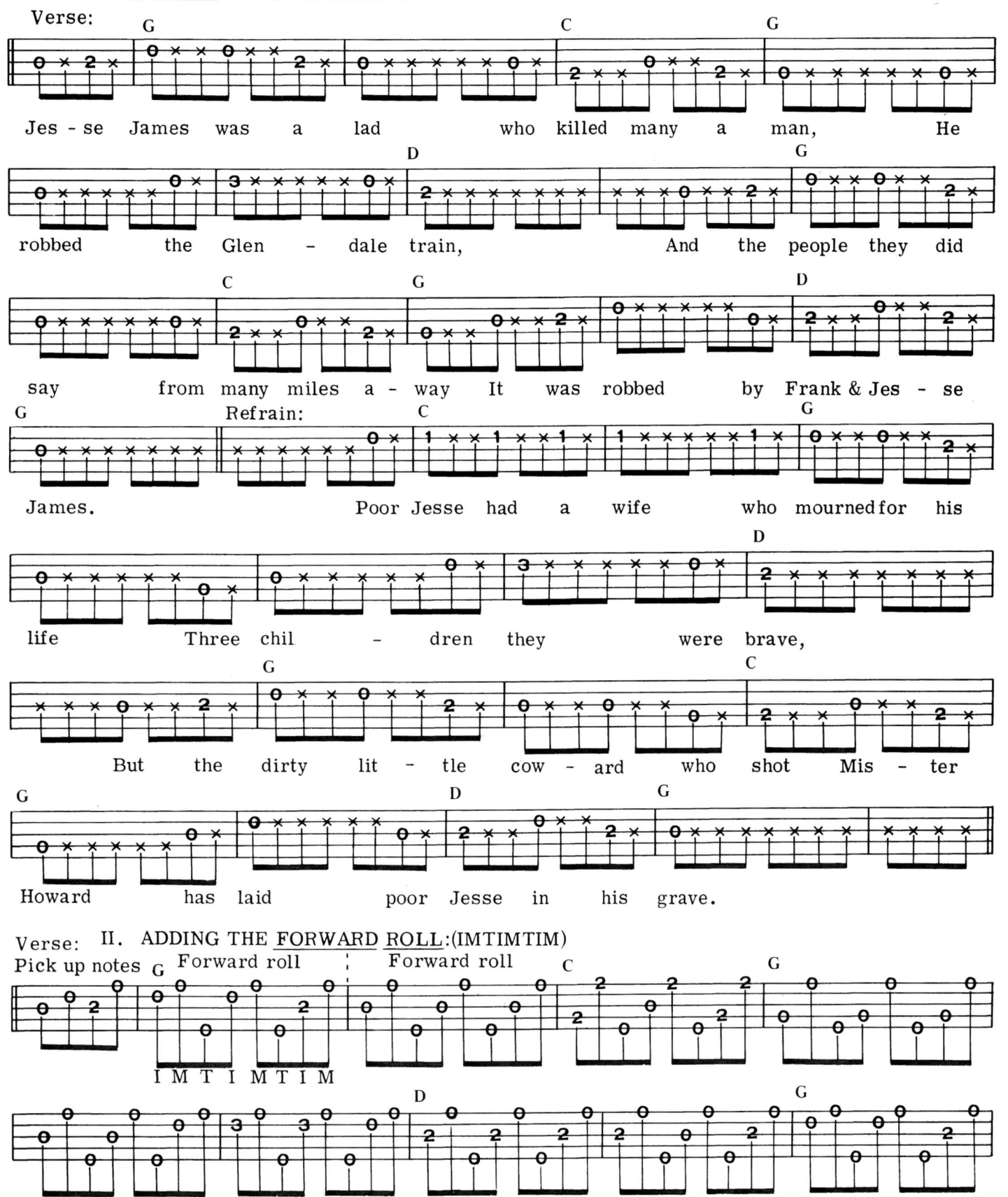

I. MELODY AND CHORDS ONLY:

Verse:

Jes-se James was a lad who killed many a man, He robbed the Glen-dale train, And the people they did say from many miles a-way It was robbed by Frank & Jes-se James.

Refrain:

Poor Jesse had a wife who mourned for his life Three chil-dren they were brave, But the dirty lit-tle cow-ard who shot Mis-ter Howard has laid poor Jesse in his grave.

II. ADDING THE FORWARD ROLL: (IMTIMTIM)

Verse: Pick up notes Forward roll   Forward roll

I M T I M T I M

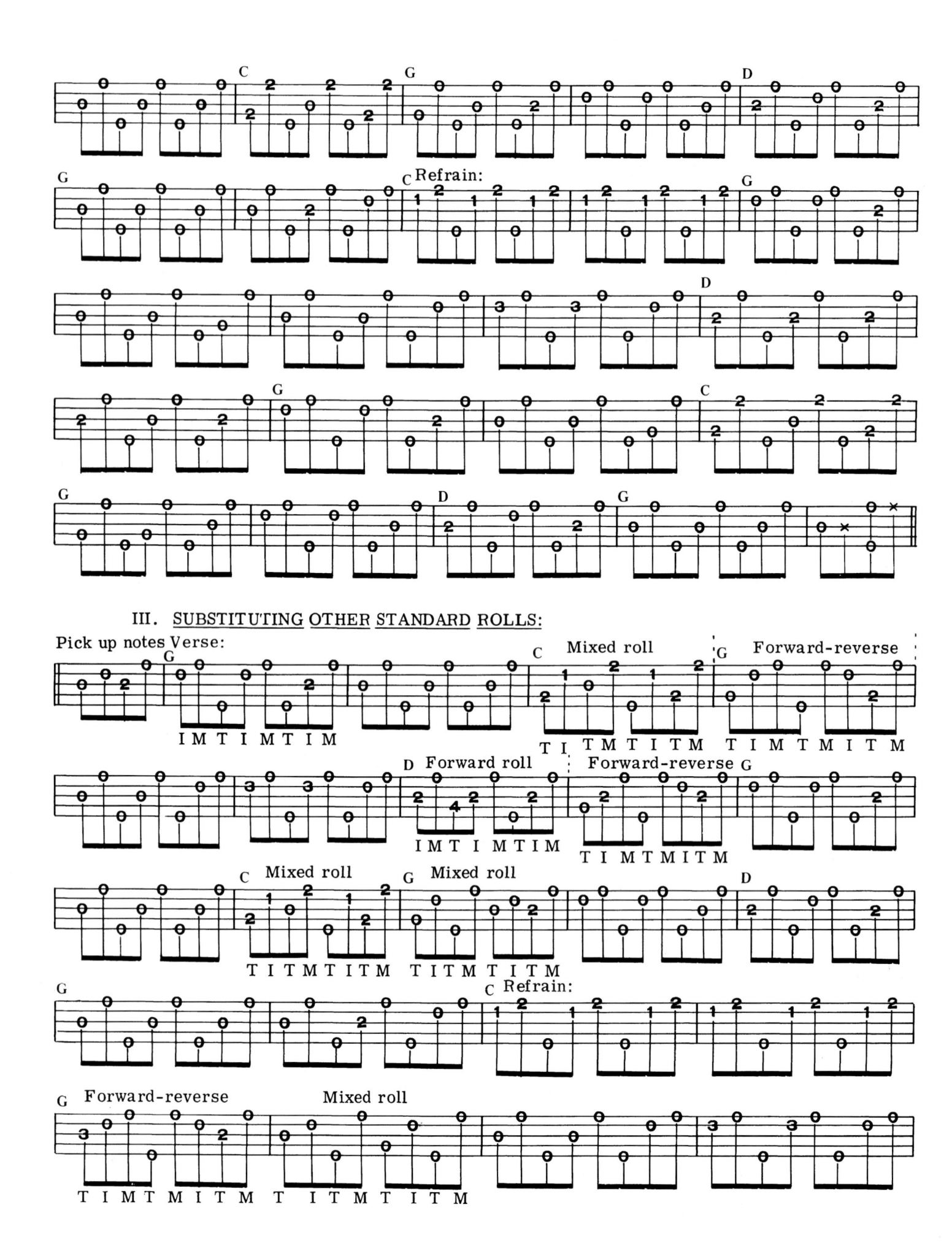

III. SUBSTITUTING OTHER STANDARD ROLLS:

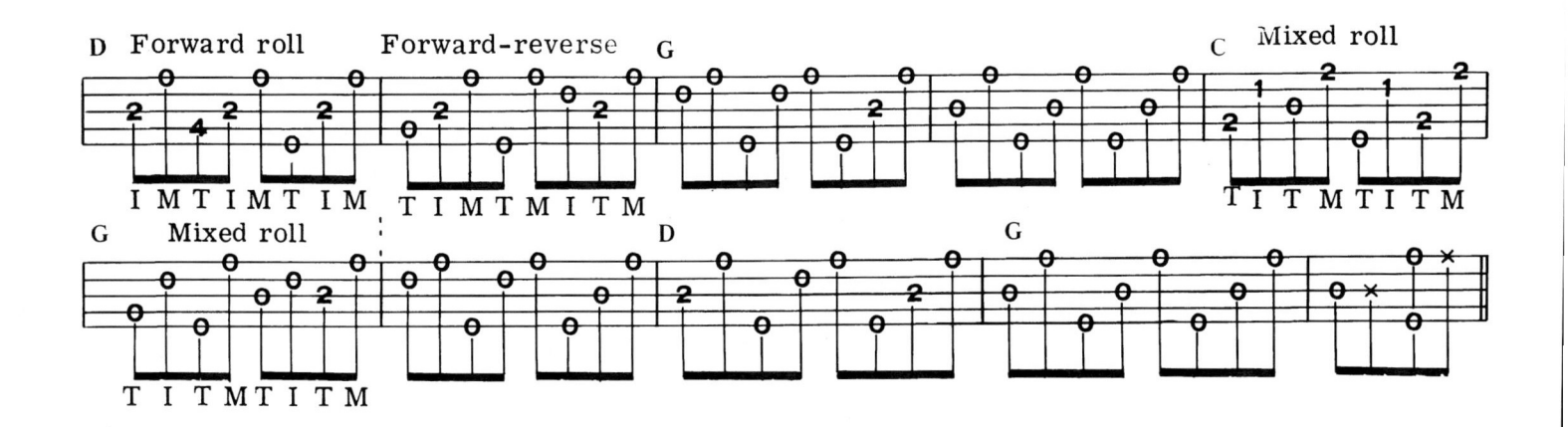

IV. ADDING FILL-IN ROLLS:

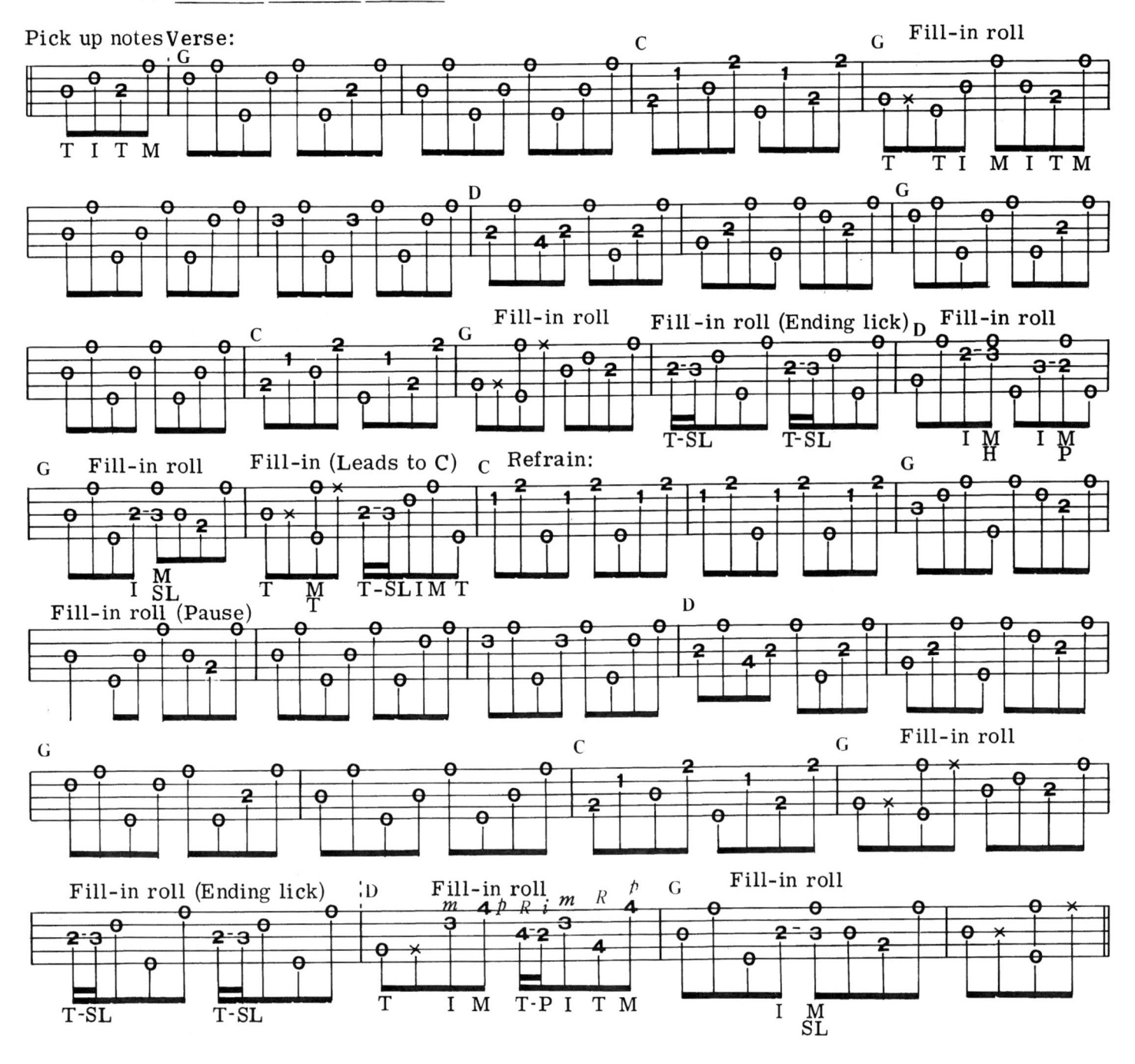

V. ADDING LEFT-HAND TECHNIQUES:

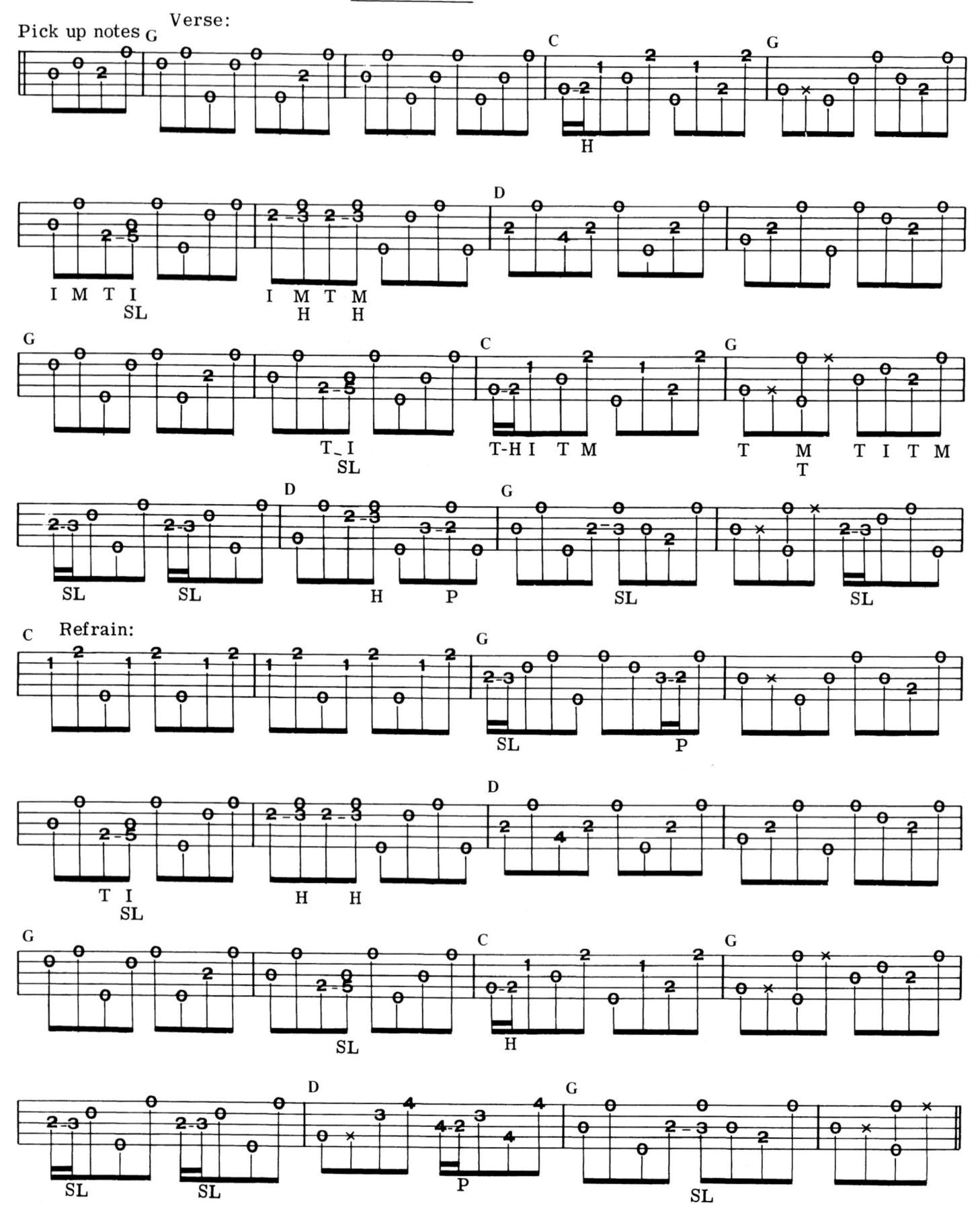

GRANDFATHER'S CLOCK

I. **MELODY** and **CHORDS** ONLY:
Find the melody notes on the 2nd, 3rd, and 4th strings in order to use the Forward Roll Pattern: IMTIMTIM.

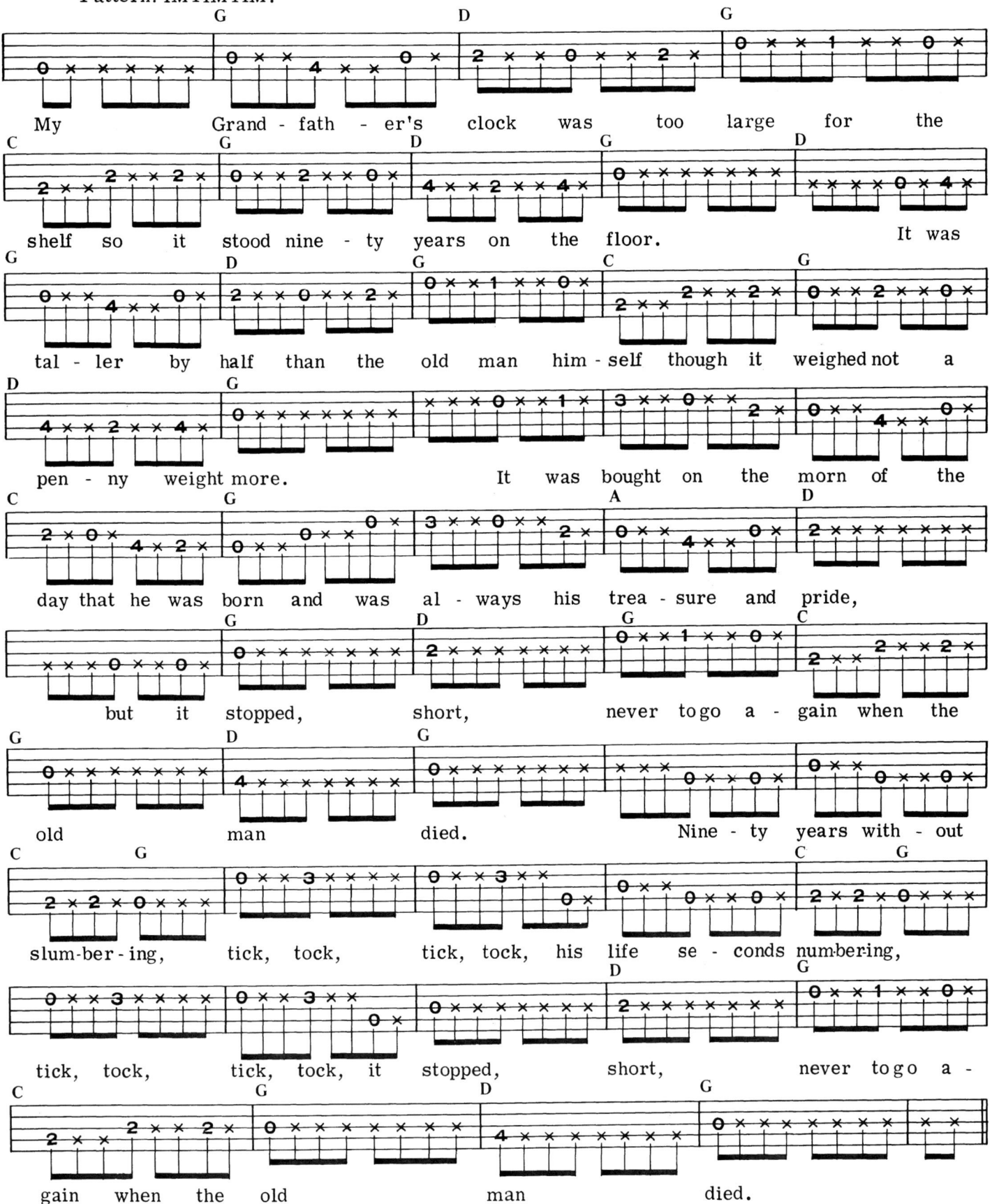

II. ADDING THE FORWARD ROLL: (I M T I M T I M)

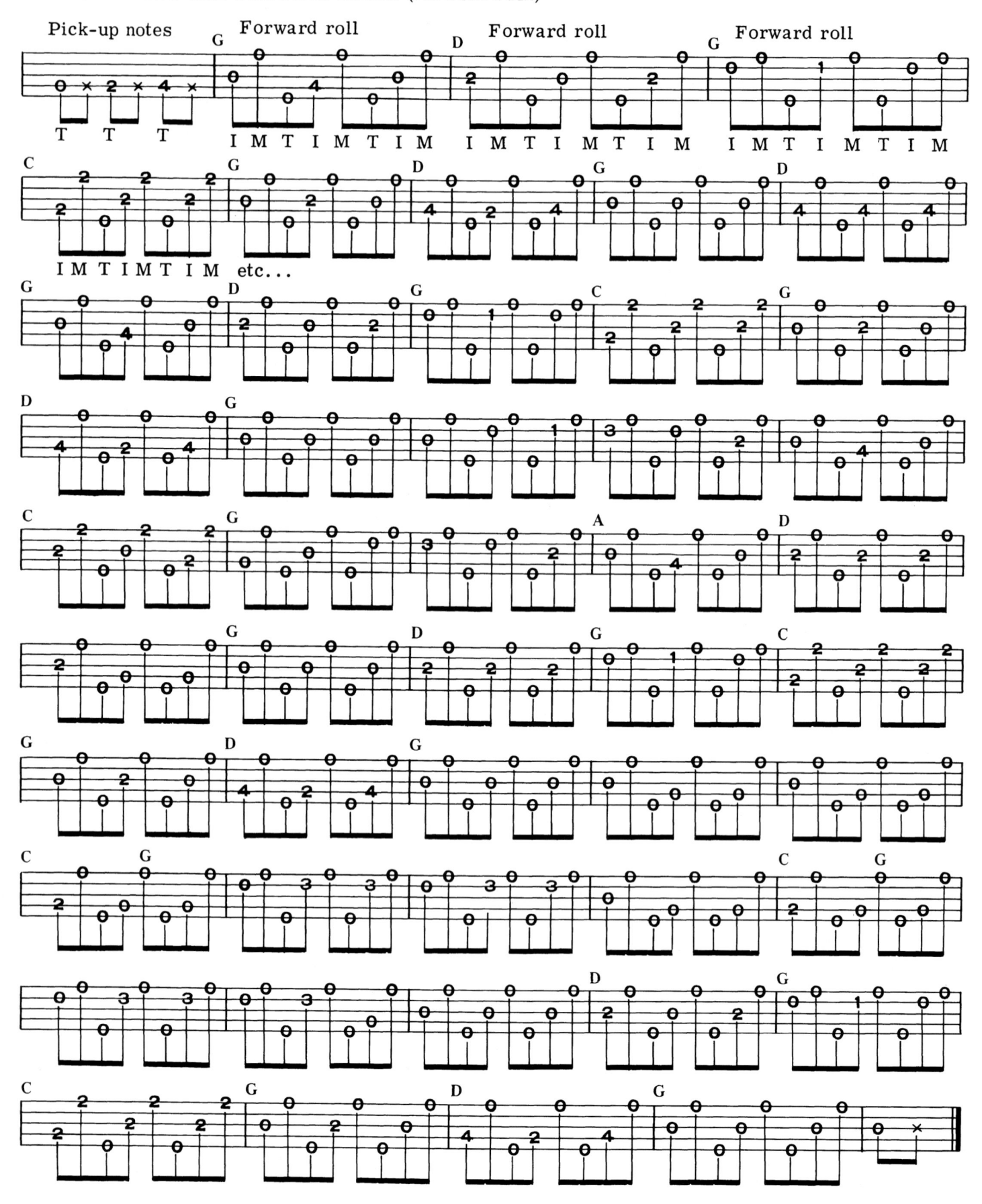

III. SUBSTITUTING OTHER STANDARD ROLL PATTERNS:

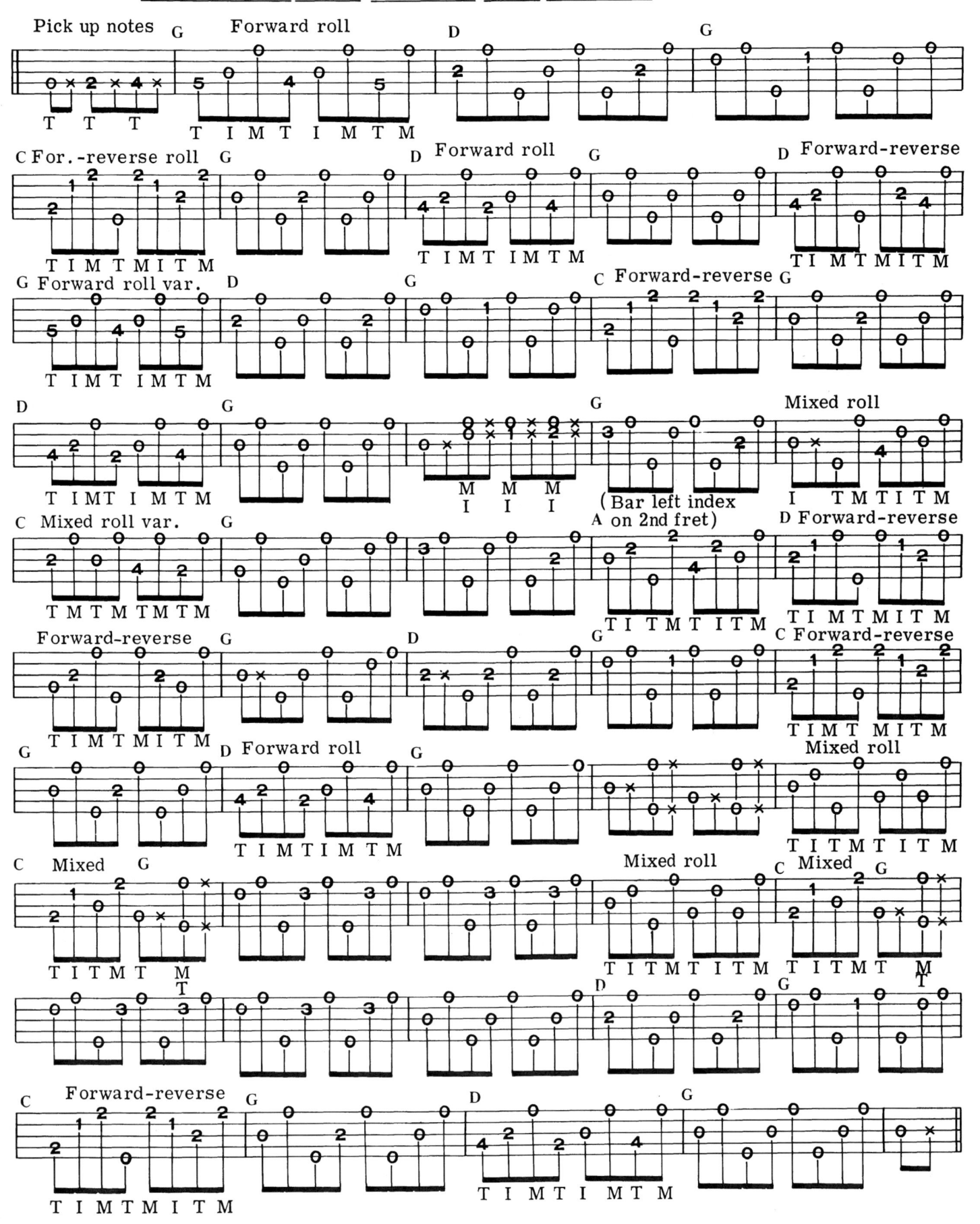

IV. ADDING FILL-IN LICKS:

NOTE: This arrangement also uses a technique referred to as "Harmonics".**
To play "harmonics" (chimes) lay the left middle finger <u>lightly</u> across the strings over the 12th fret <u>bar</u>. Do not depress the strings. Although this is actually a left hand technique, it is being included at this stage because this song is rarely played on the banjo without the harmonics.
(**. . . . . . .)

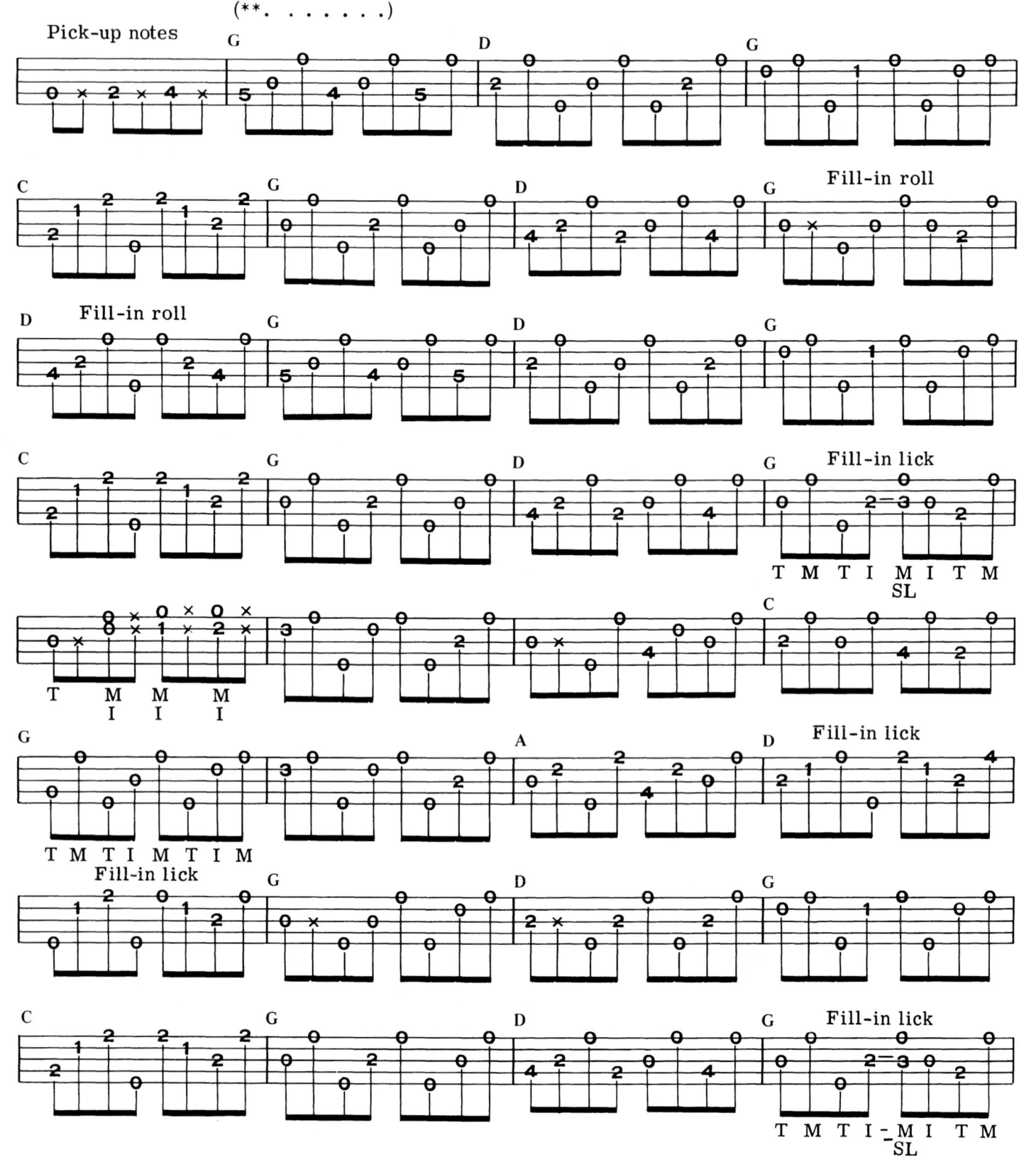

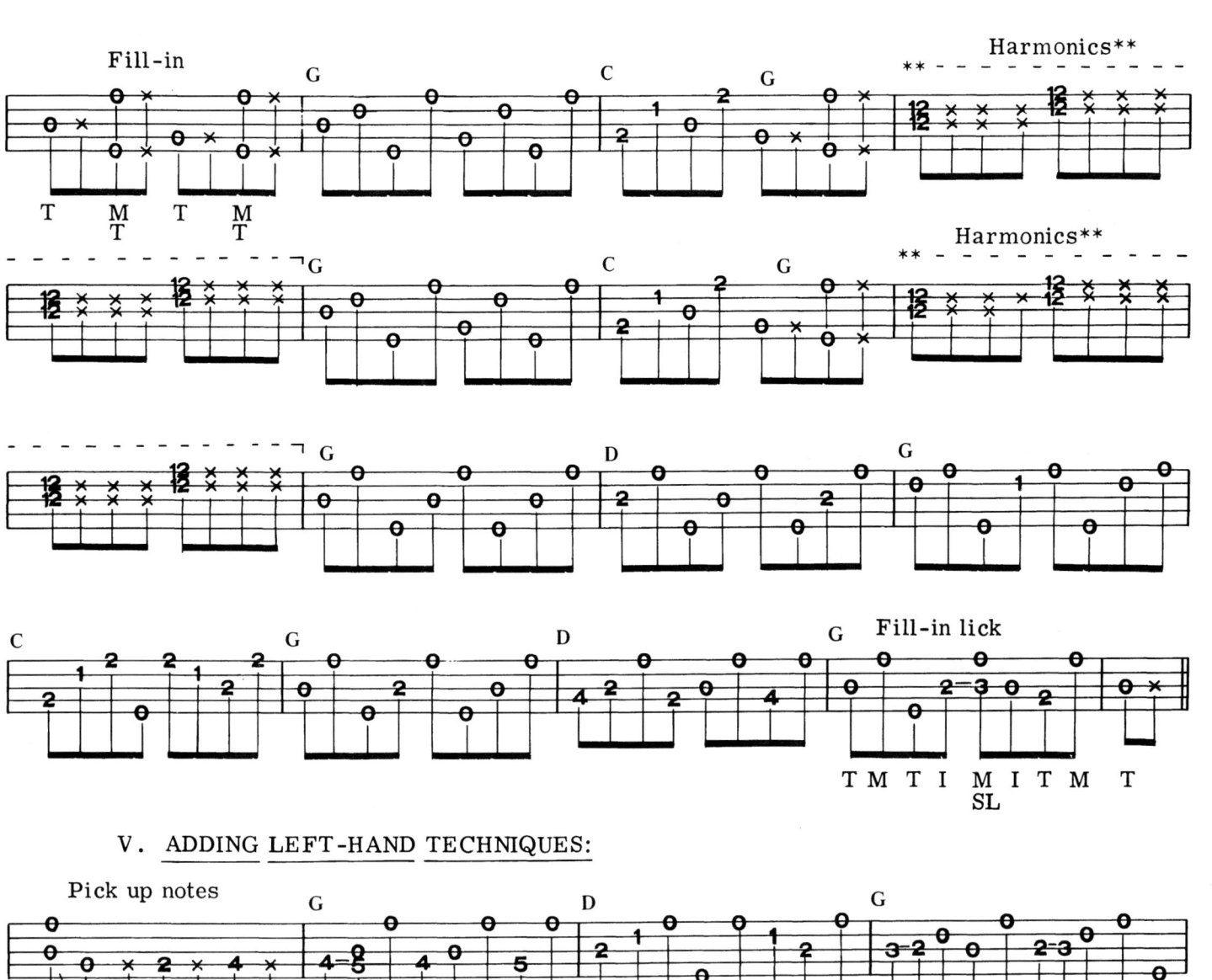

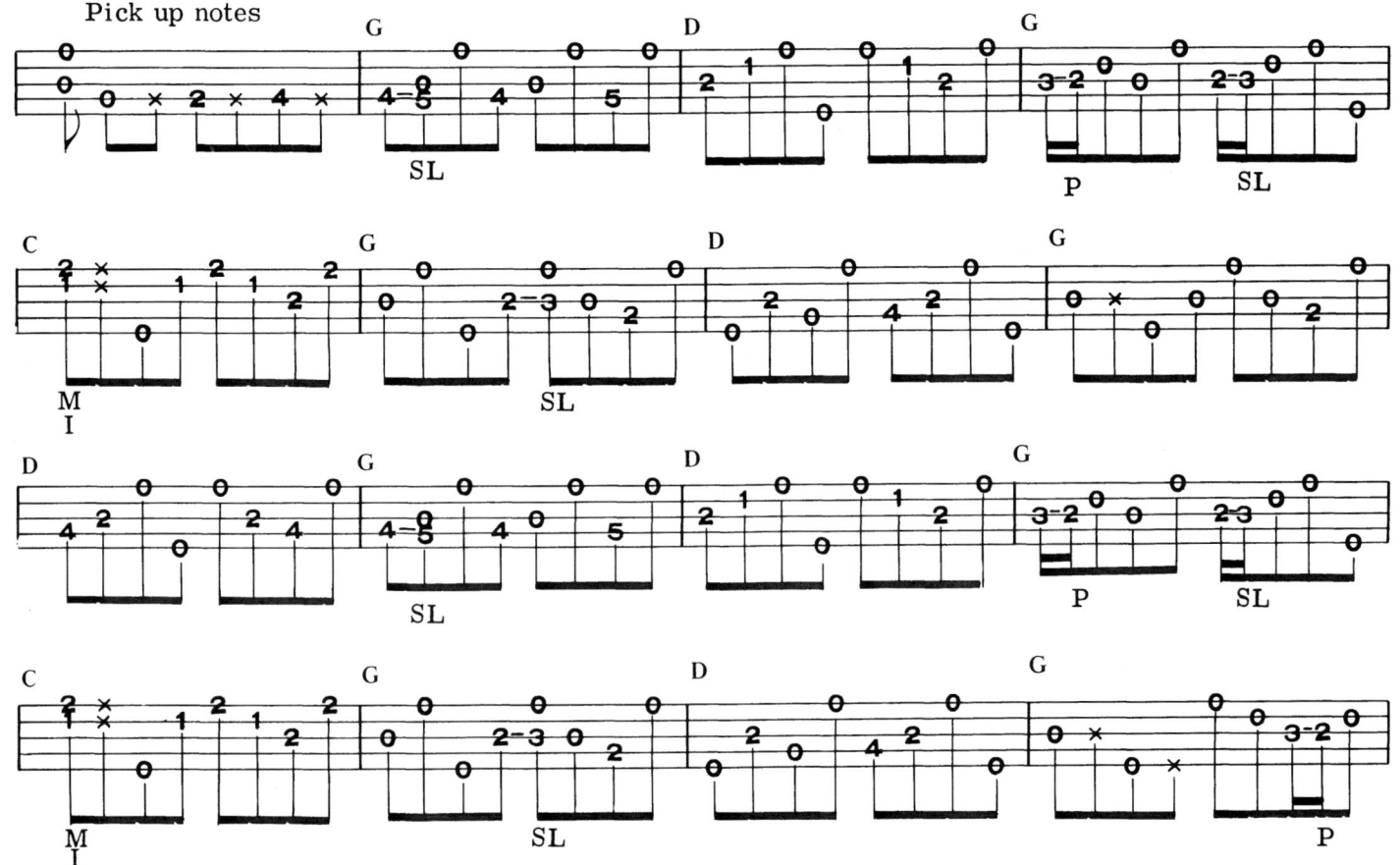

V. ADDING LEFT-HAND TECHNIQUES:

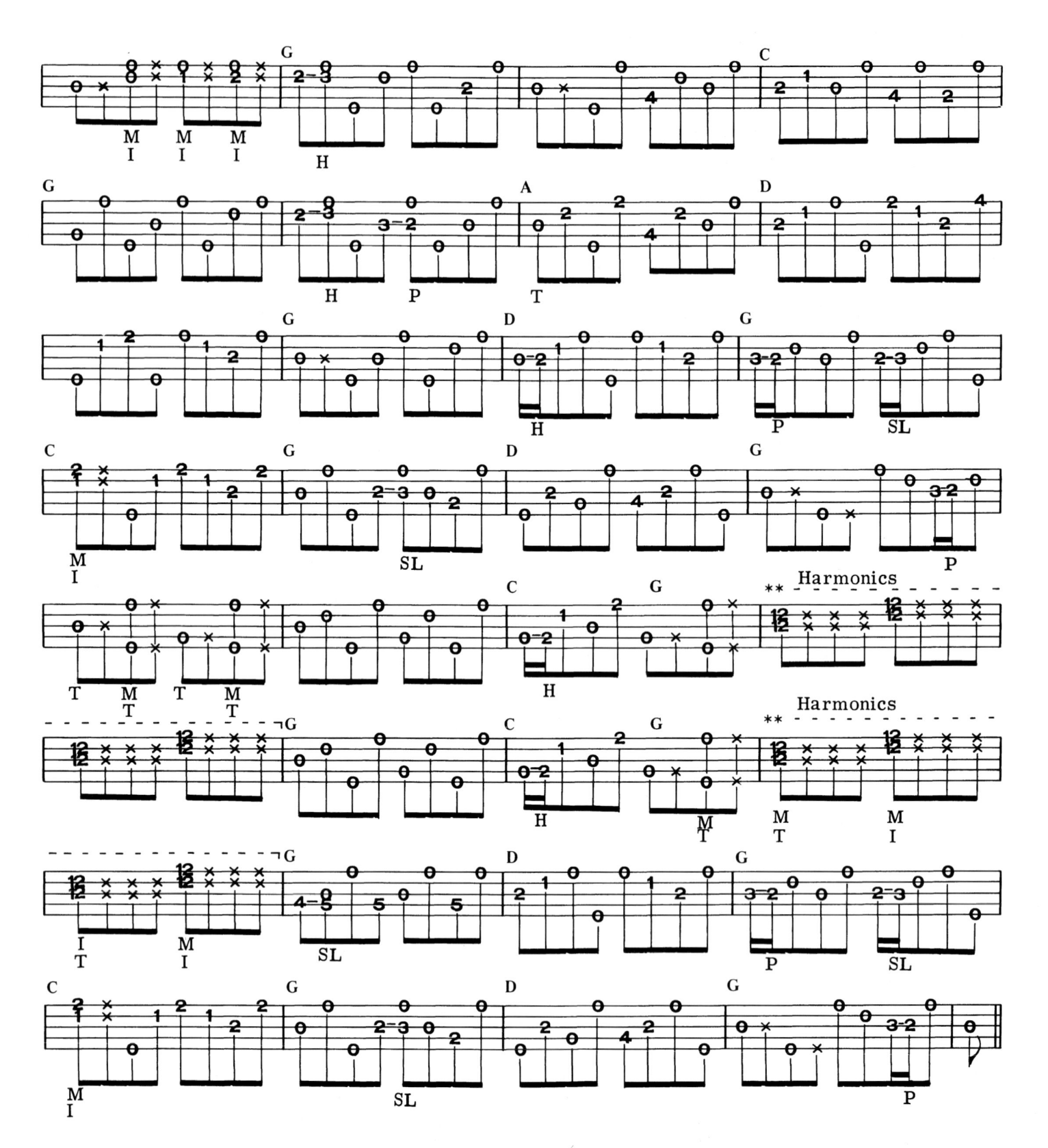

* Substituting different fill-in licks

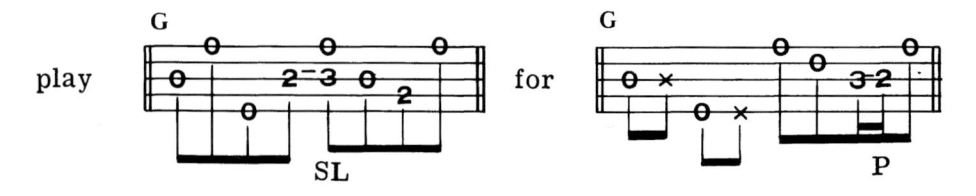

MELODIC/CHROMATIC STYLE

The following names have often been given to this style of playing: chromatic, melodic, Keith-style, and fiddle-style. The terms are interchangeable...chromatic is probably the most common; melodic is probably the most accurate...but they all refer to the same style of playing the banjo.

When playing this style, all three right hand fingers pick the melody, and the 5th string is used in the melody, rather than as a background drone. (Thumb, Index, and Middle fingers do the picking.) The accent or stress falls on every other note picked. As with Scruggs-style, there are eight notes per "roll", (all eighth notes,), and the notes should be picked consecutively without a pause.

Although this style of playing dates back to the playing of classical music on the banjo around 1900, Bill Keith and Bobby Thompson generally are credited with developing and popularizing it in the early 1960's. An entire song such as a fiddle tune or a hornpipe can be played in Melodic-style, or melodic "rolls" or "licks" can be inserted in a Bluegrass-style song. Fiddle tunes are easily reproduced on the banjo with this style.

Because melodies frequently work along scale lines, and because melodic "licks" are frequently derived from scales, the following exercises should ready your fingers for playing in this style. Each exercise should be learned up to tempo.

NOTE: Scales can also be played for chords. For example, the G scale can be played for the G chord, & the C scale for the C chord.

1. <u>CIRCULAR SCALE</u>: This scale consists of a four note pattern; the first note of each pattern is part of a scale line. (Play the first note of each four-note pattern, and notice that when played consecutively, they form the G scale.)
Many melodic licks are derived from this scale.

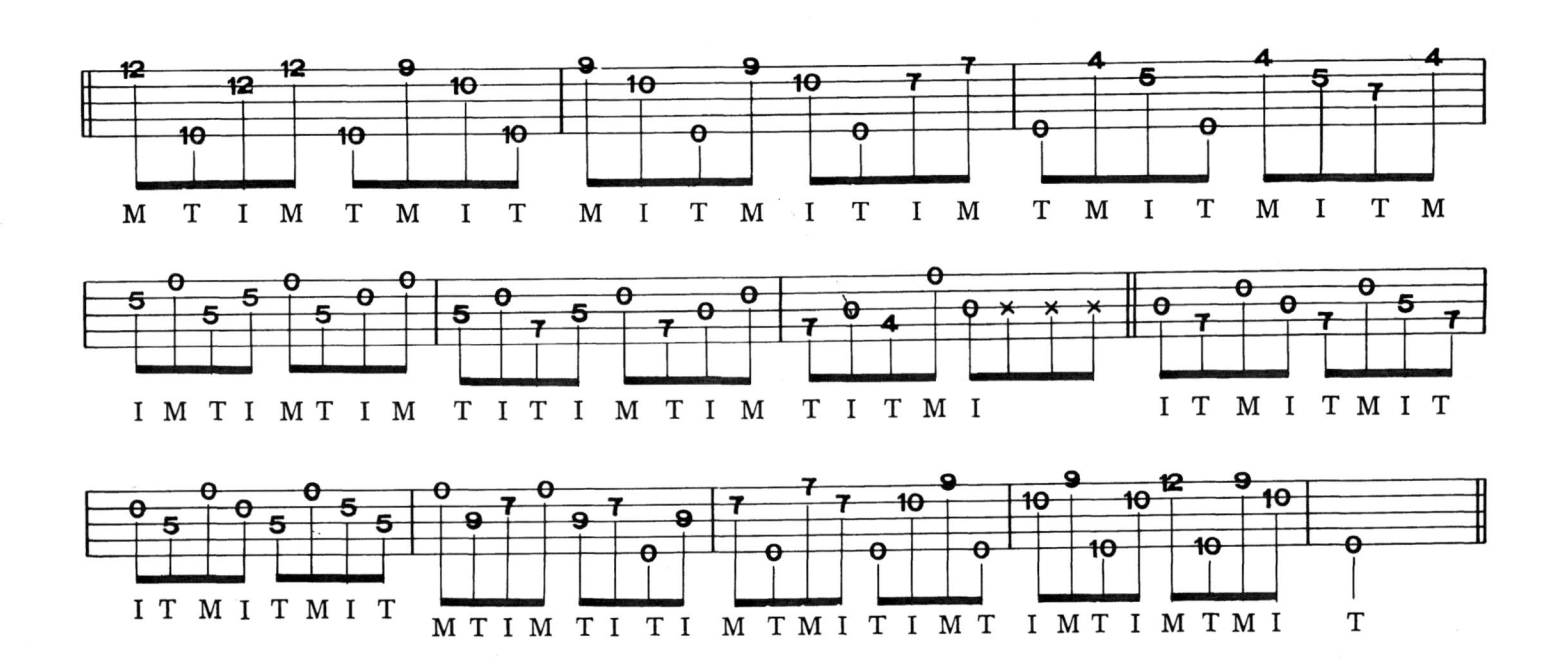

2. **G MAJOR SCALE EXERCISES:** (The tones which form the G chord are circled in the first example. The G scale can begin with any of these notes when it is used in a song for the G chord.)

   Basic 8 tone G Scale:

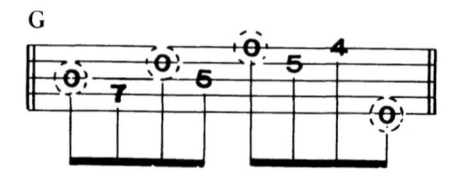

   Going up the fingerboard:

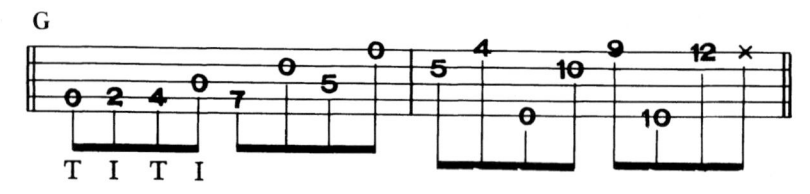

   T I T I

   From the open position to the 12th fret and back:

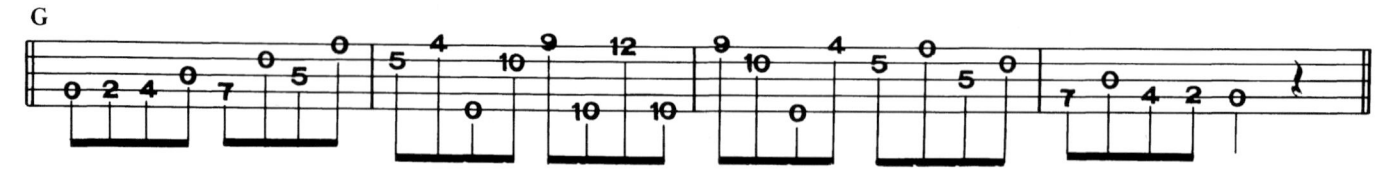

3. **C MAJOR SCALE EXERCISES:** (The C chord tones are circled in the first example.)

   Basic 8 tone C Scale:

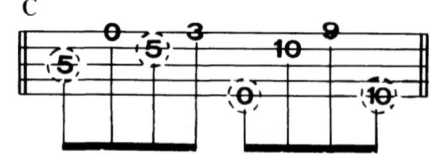

   Going up the fingerboard:

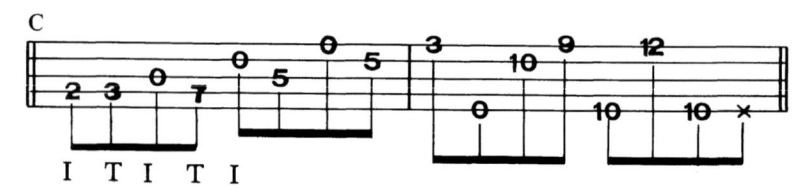

   I T I T I

   From the open position to the 12th fret and back:

50

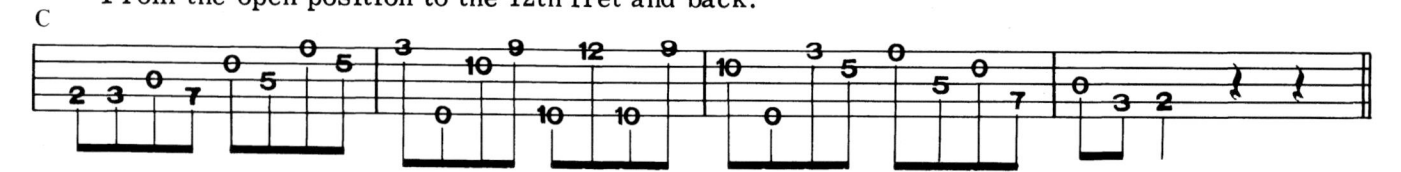

4. **D MAJOR SCALE EXERCISES:** (The D chord tones are circled in the first example. Locate these tones in the other D Scale exercises. The D scale can begin on any of these tones when it is played in a song for the D chord.)

Basic 8 tone D Scale:

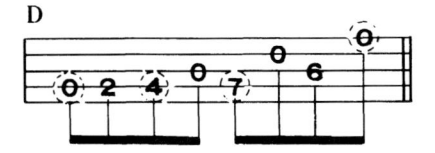

Basic 8 tone D Scale an octave higher:

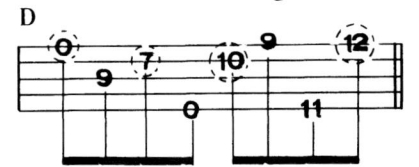

Going up the fingerboard:

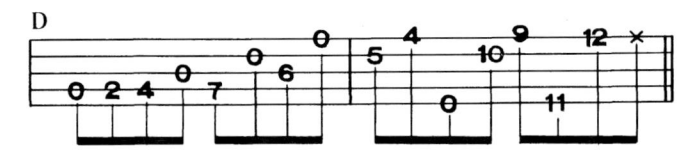

From the open position to the 12th fret and back:

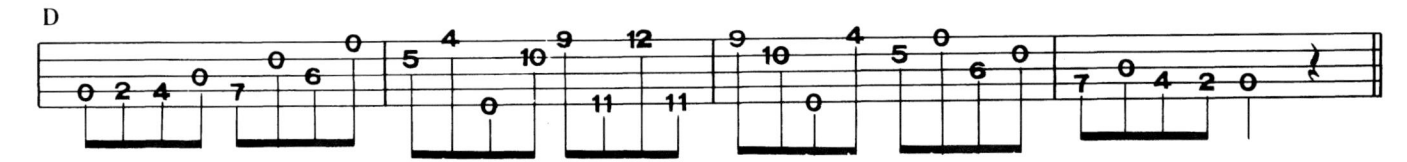

5. **A MAJOR SCALE:**

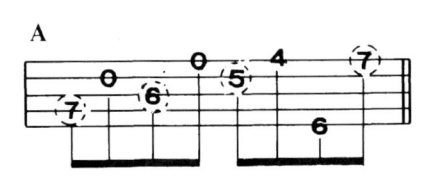

6. **F MAJOR SCALE:**

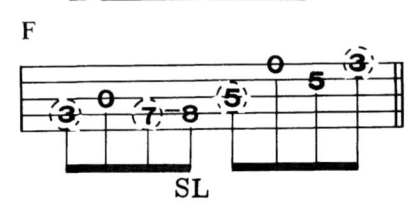

SL

7. **E MINOR SCALE EXERCISES:** (The Em chord tones are circled in the first example. This scale can be used not only for the Em chord, but also for the G chord. (Em is the relative minor of G major.)

Basic 8 tone Em Scale: (Natural)

Natural Em Scale up two octaves and back:

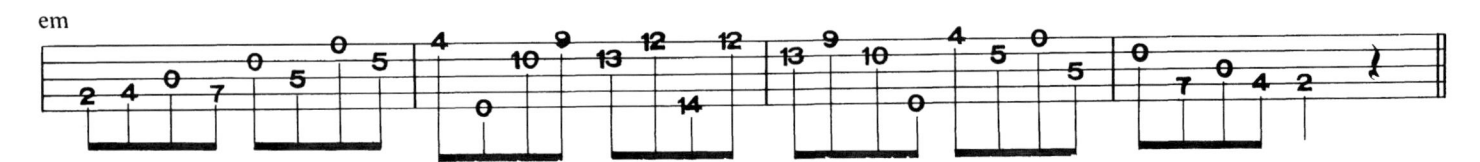

NOTE: There are three different forms of minor scales. The natural minor scale uses the key signature of the relative major scale, without alteration.

MELODIC STYLE FILL-IN ROLLS
FOR PAUSES, ENDINGS, AND CHANGING CHORDS

Most of the examples of fill-in rolls below consist of two measures, or sixteen counts. Each measure can be used alone, also, as an eight count fill-in roll for the chord written above it.

Each of these rolls is used in songs only for the specific chord indicated. As you learn the fill-in rolls, LEARN the chord to which each roll applies.

FILL-IN ROLLS FOR PAUSES AND FOR CHANGING CHORDS:

G CHORD LICKS:

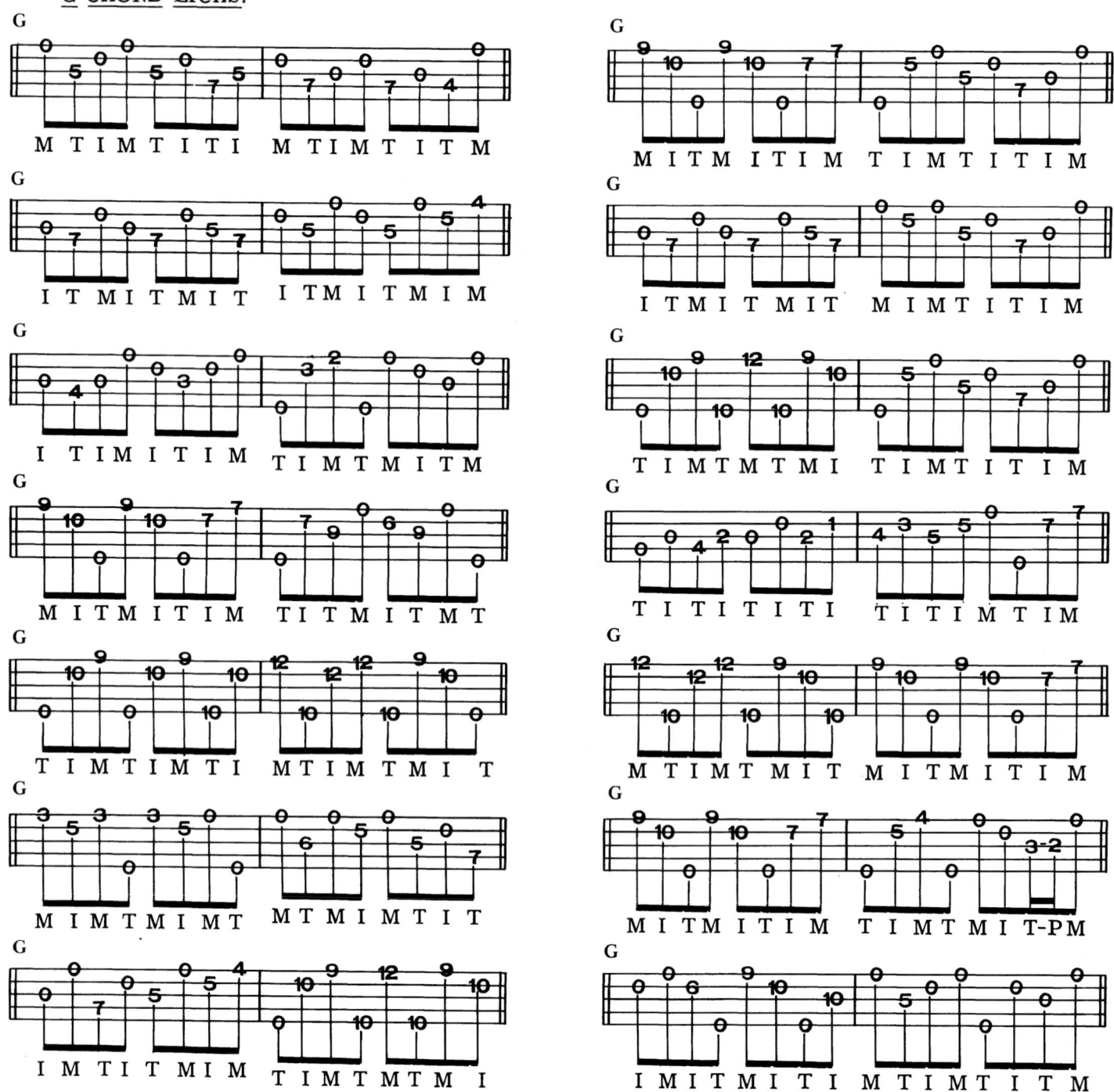

NOTE: The middle finger of the right hand occasionally must pick the inside strings, (2nd or 3rd string).

C CHORD LICKS:

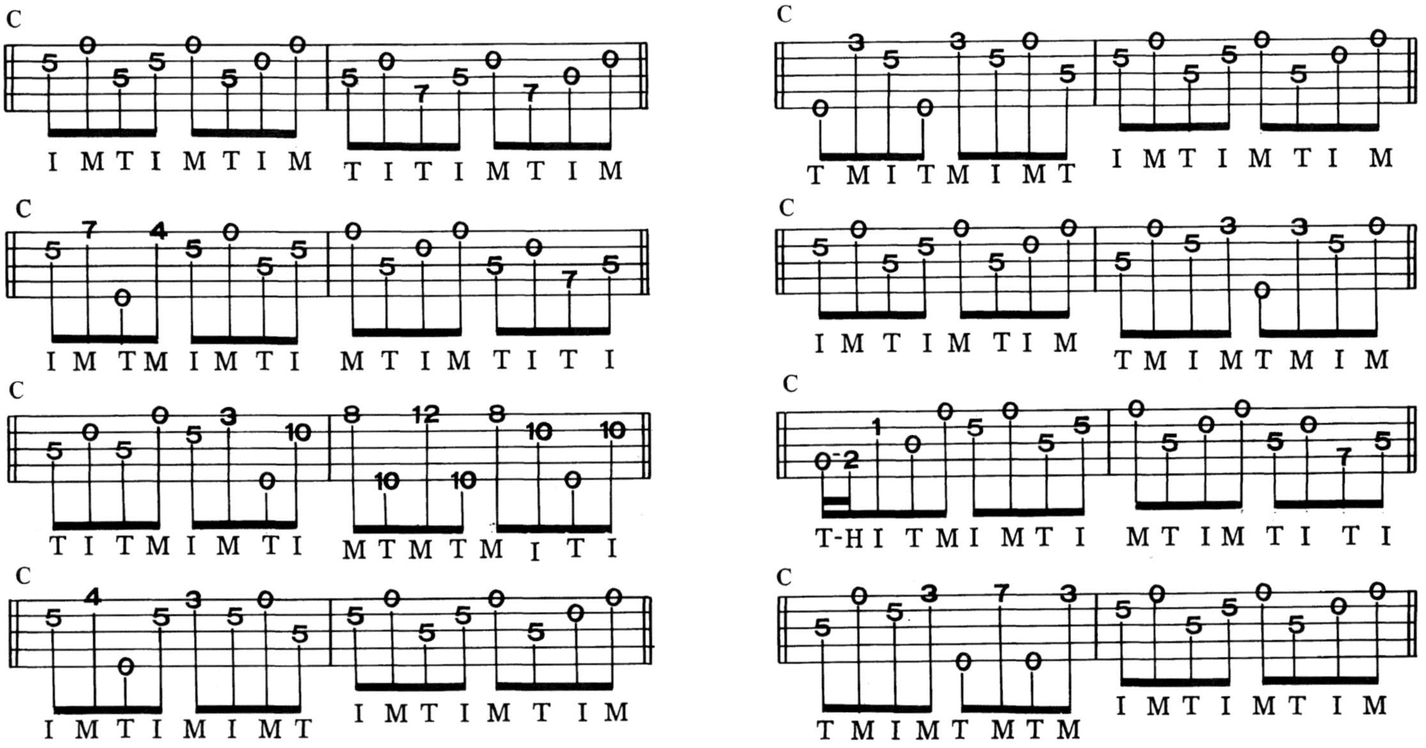

D CHORD LICKS:

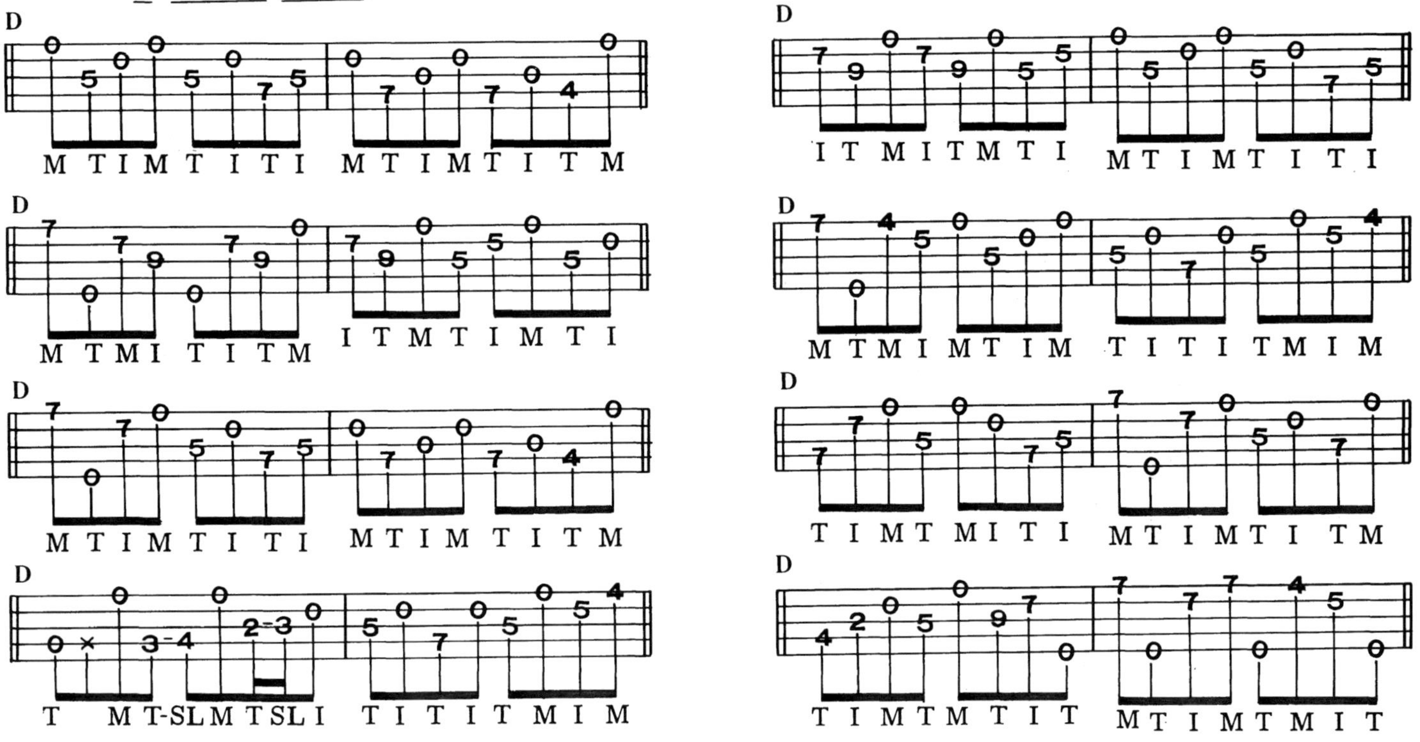

A CHORD LICKS:

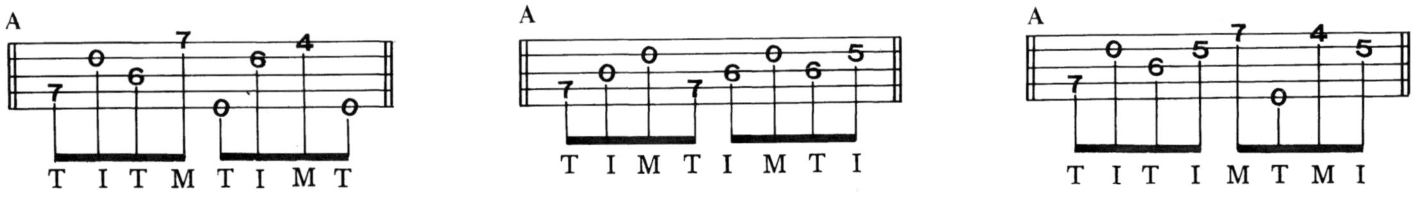

F CHORD LICKS:

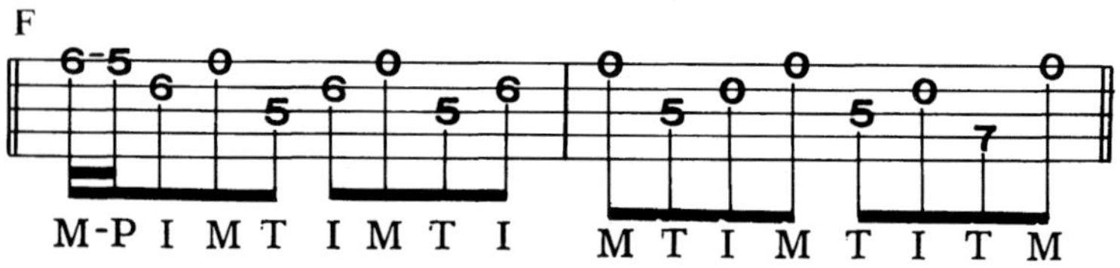

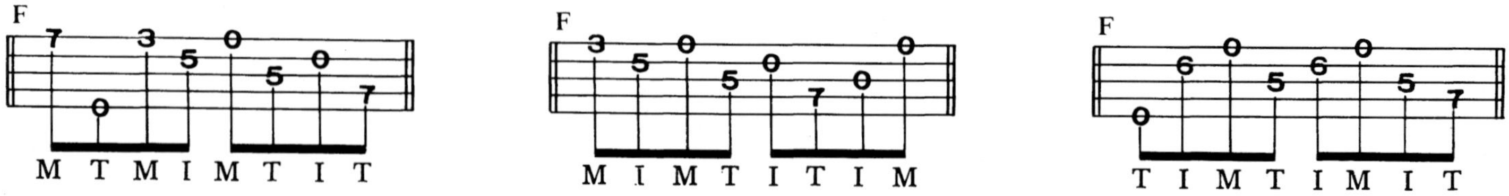

E Minor CHORD LICKS:

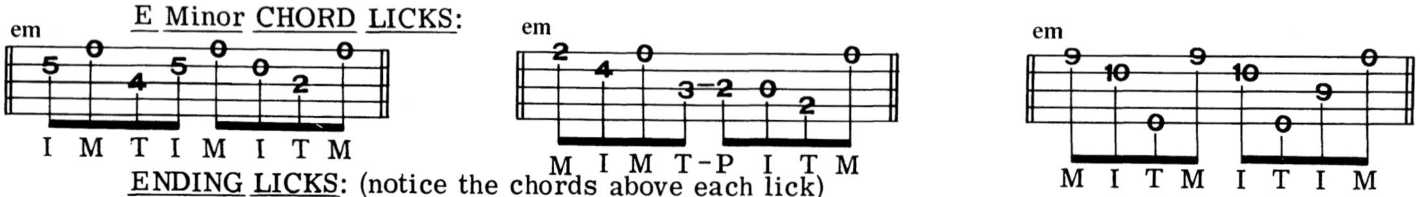

ENDING LICKS: (notice the chords above each lick)

G to D to G chord licks:

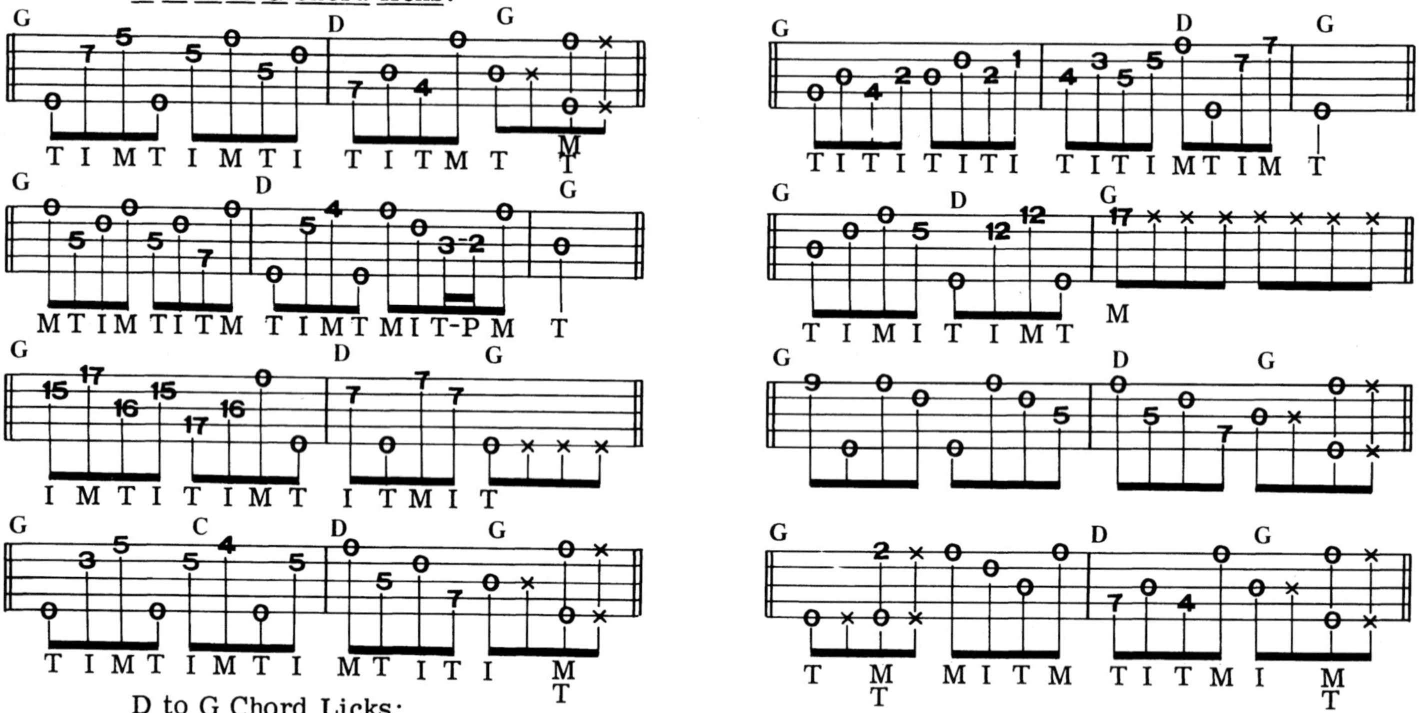

D to G Chord Licks:

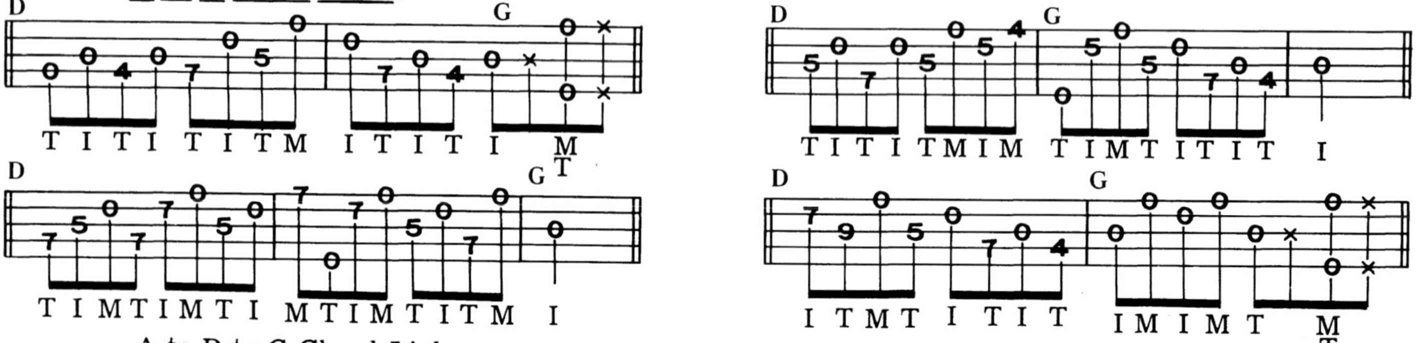

A to D to G Chord Lick:

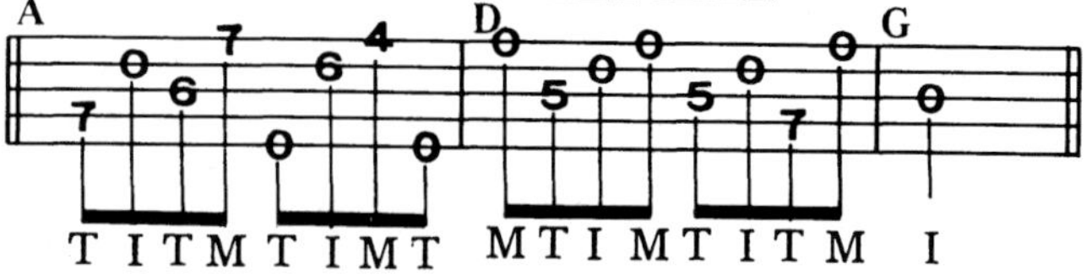

C to D to G Chord Lick:

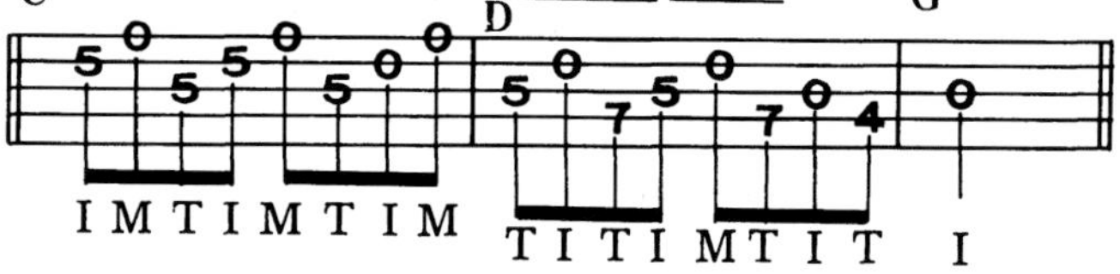

ARRANGING SONGS FOR THE BANJO
MELODIC/CHROMATIC STYLE

Before arranging a song in this style, review the section on styles-melodic and the exercises. Also you should know several songs in this style from tablature. Keep in mind that generally each note plucked is a melody note (see EIGHTH OF JANUARY for an example), and that when it isn't a melody note, it is usually very close in sound to the note just before and after it. (See OLD JOE CLARK for an example of this.) Also keep in mind that the accent or stress falls on every other note.

STEPS FOR ARRANGING A SONG IN MELODIC STYLE:

1.) Learn the chords to the song you want to play. Although your left hand doesn't actually form chords, you must choose the correct rolls for the appropriate chords in the song.

2.) Review the exercises and melodic rolls in the section on styles. Concentrate on the chord name applicable to each roll.

3.) Decide exactly which notes or tones you will play. Try singing it. If you run into difficulty in keeping it moving along, use tones that are right next to it in sound. (Insert the tone that is next to that tone on the fingerboard of your banjo.) In the following examples the first two measures show the melody of a song that is not moving along and needs extra notes, The second two measures show how to add notes next to those melody notes.

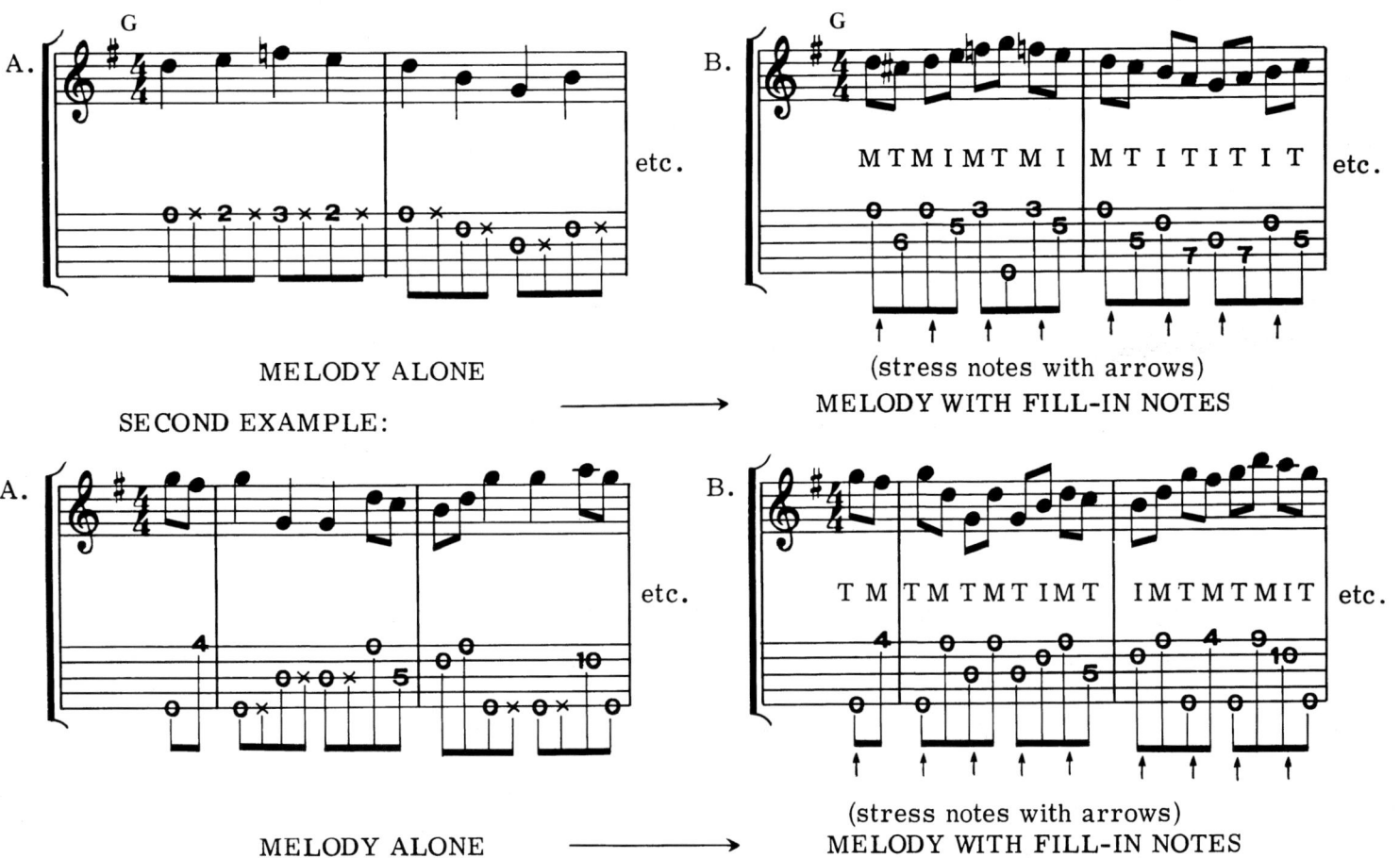

FIRST EXAMPLE:

A. MELODY ALONE

B. MELODY WITH FILL-IN NOTES
(stress notes with arrows)

SECOND EXAMPLE:

A. MELODY ALONE

B. MELODY WITH FILL-IN NOTES
(stress notes with arrows)

NOTE: If the song you are arranging is a fiddle-tune or a hornpipe, it will be easier to pick out the melody and arrange in this style, as most of the notes will be melody notes... refer to the second example in Step 3 above.

4.) After you have decided what notes you will play, you must <u>find the notes on the banjo</u>.
NOTE: You must arrange the song so that you do NOT pick the same string twice in a row, or use the same finger of the right hand twice in a row. (Most tones which are close together in sound, are also close together on the fingerboard on different strings.) For example:

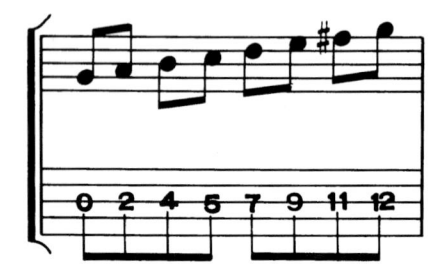

should be played like: (Notice that each note is picked on a different string with a different finger from the note next to it, and that except for the open strings, most notes occur around the same area of the fingerboard (around the 5th fret.))

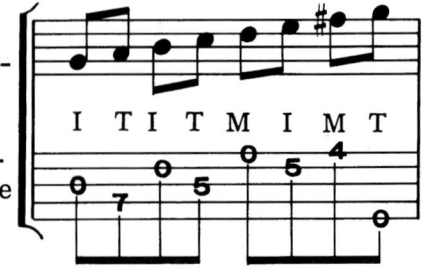

NOTE: Use as many open strings as possible.

NOTE: Begin picking out the melody by locating the notes around the 5th fret as in the above example. Usually you can find the melody using the 4th through 7th frets plus open strings.

NOTE: If you find that you are having to play the same string twice at times, try to play those notes around frets 8 through 10 without playing the same string two times.

NOTE: If the same tone is repeated without another tone in between, find the tone on two different strings. Keep in mind that the 5th fret of the 1st string and the 5th string open play the same tone. You should use the 5th string often.

The reason you should not play the same string twice in a row, or use the same finger twice in a row is that you can play faster and smoother if you use a different finger on a different string each time you pick.

Exception: There is a style of playing called "Single String Picking" where you do pick the same string twice in a row or even more often. I don't advocate it's use frequently, but there are times when it is necessary. However there are rules governing it's use in the technique of playing: Alternate the fingers of the right hand to pick them, TITITI. You should NOT use the same finger to play them. The only place you <u>generally</u> might need this is on the 4th string.

Not: T T T T   But: T I T I

Because most of the notes are melody notes or notes filling in around the melody notes, there is not that much to say about arranging songs in the melodic style. The main thing to keep in mind is locating the notes on different strings and using different fingers to pick them. If, however, there is a long pause in the melody and you don't know exactly what to play there, refer to the fill-in licks. That is what they are for. You can also use some Bluegrass-style fill-in licks in a melodic arrangement.

THE EIGHTH OF JANUARY

G Tuning

I. MELODY and CHORDS ONLY: (PAUSE FOR X'S)

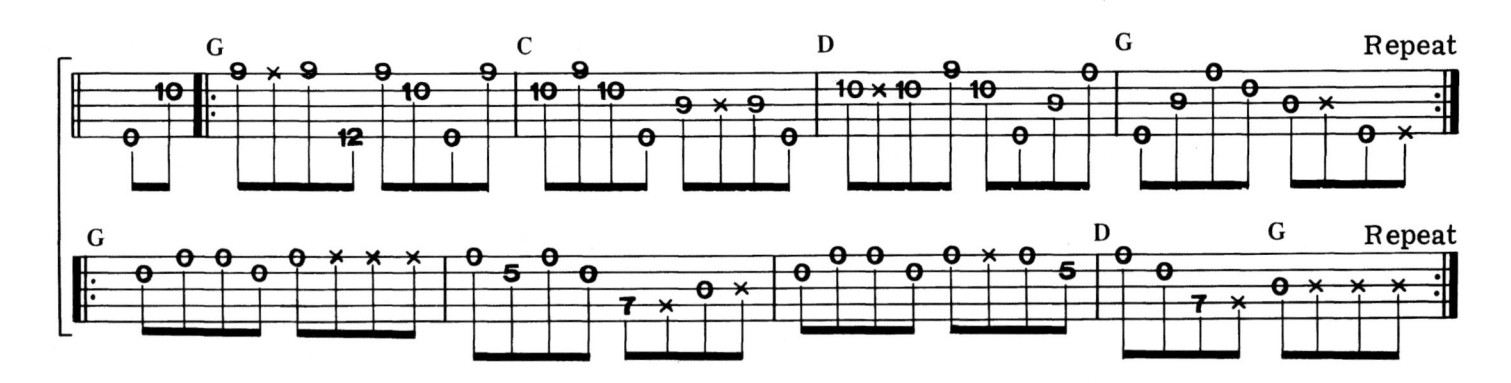

II. MELODIC/CHROMATIC VARIATION: (X'S ABOVE REPLACED WITH NOTES)

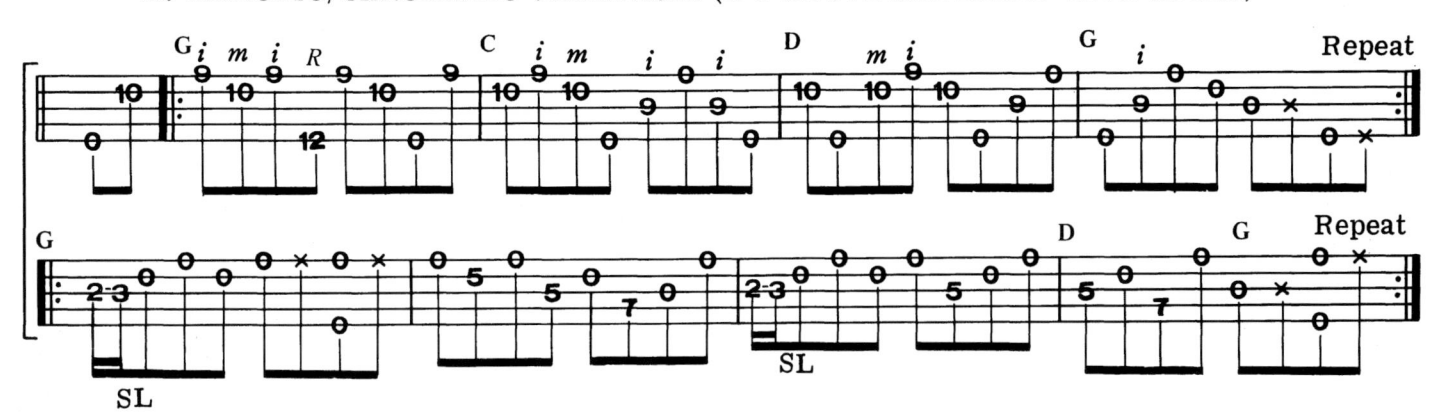

BANJO JOE

(This tune is often played in the Key of C, with the capo on the 5th fret.)

I. MELODY and CHORDS ONLY:

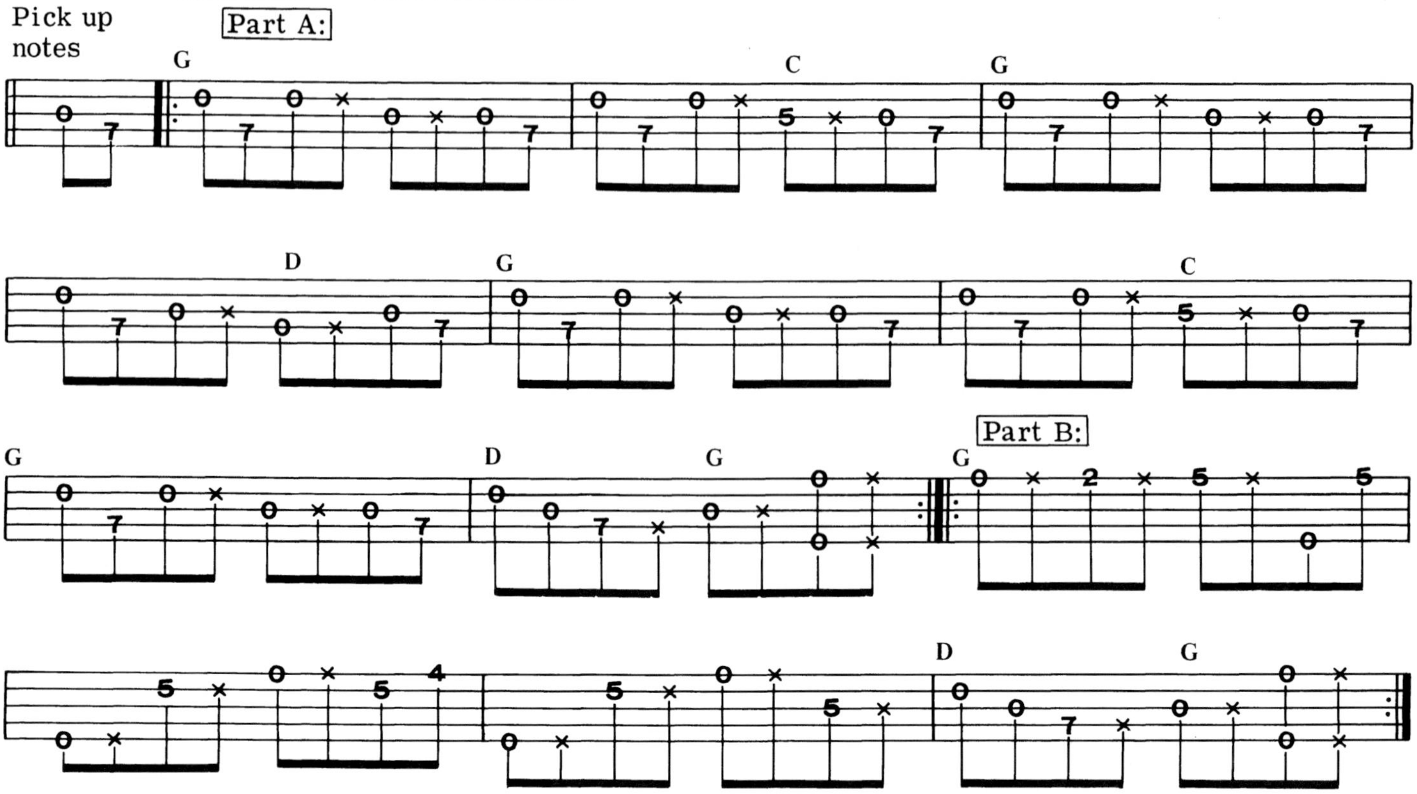
Pick up notes
Part A:
G
C
G
D
G
C
G
D
G
Part B:
G
D
G

II. MELODIC-STYLE VARIATION: Replacing many of the x's above, with notes: (The right Middle finger picks the 2nd string in the following arrangement.)

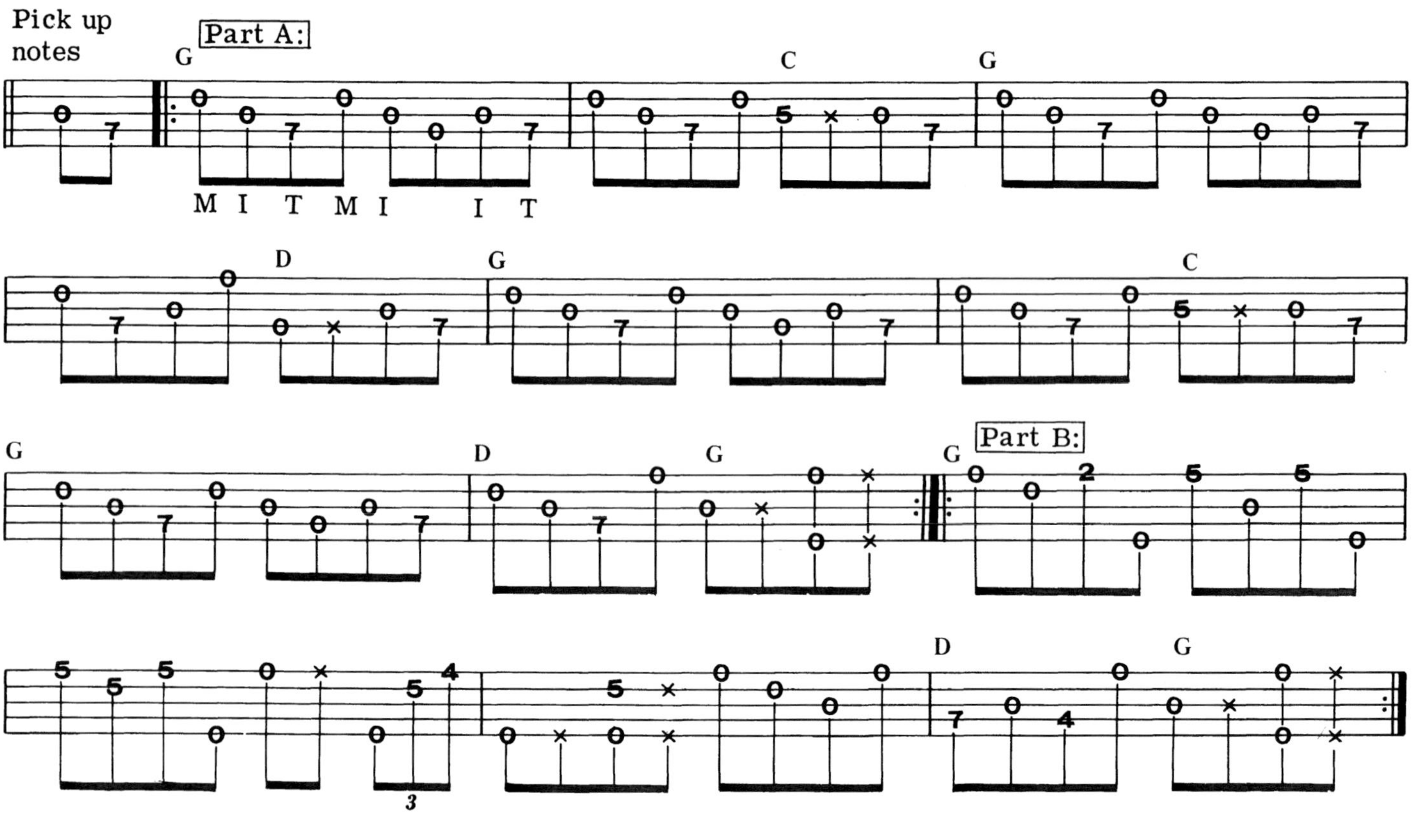
Pick up notes
Part A:
G
C
G
M I T M I I T
D
G
C
G
D
G
Part B:
G
D
G

BILL CHEATHAM

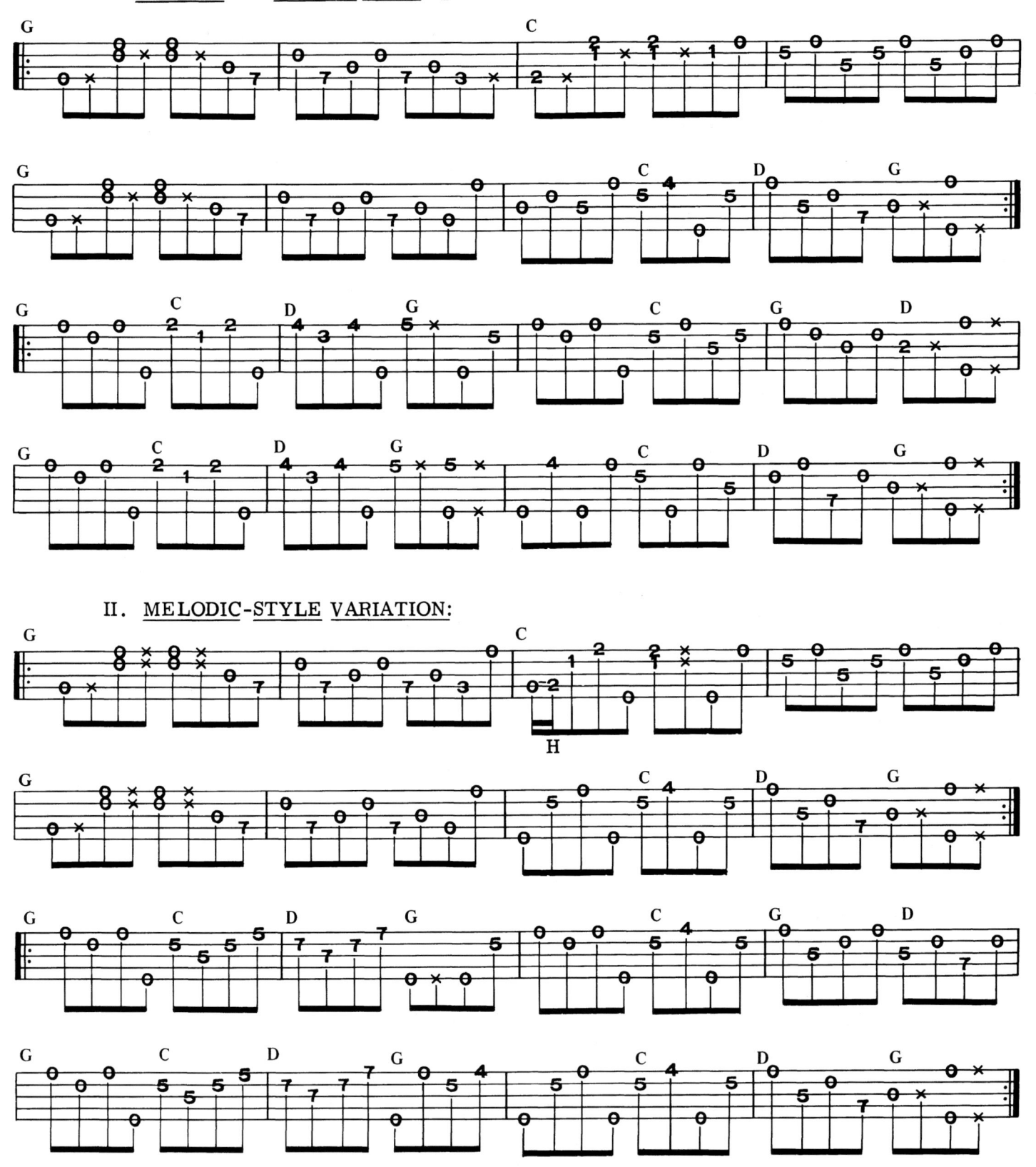

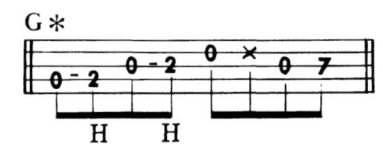

DEVIL'S DREAM

I. MELODY and CHORDS ONLY: (This tune is usually played with the capo on 2, in the key of A.)

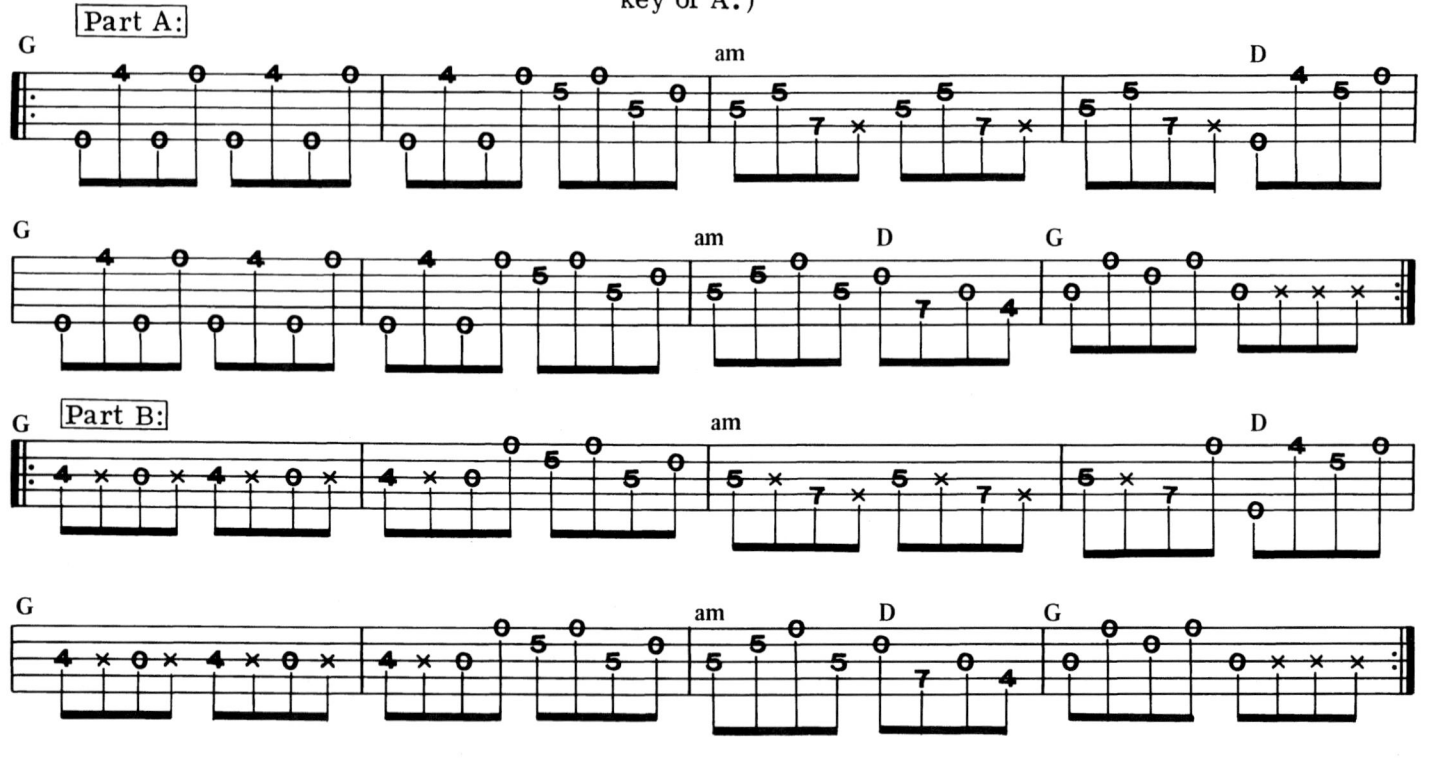

II. MELODIC VARIATION: (The x's above are replaced with notes.)

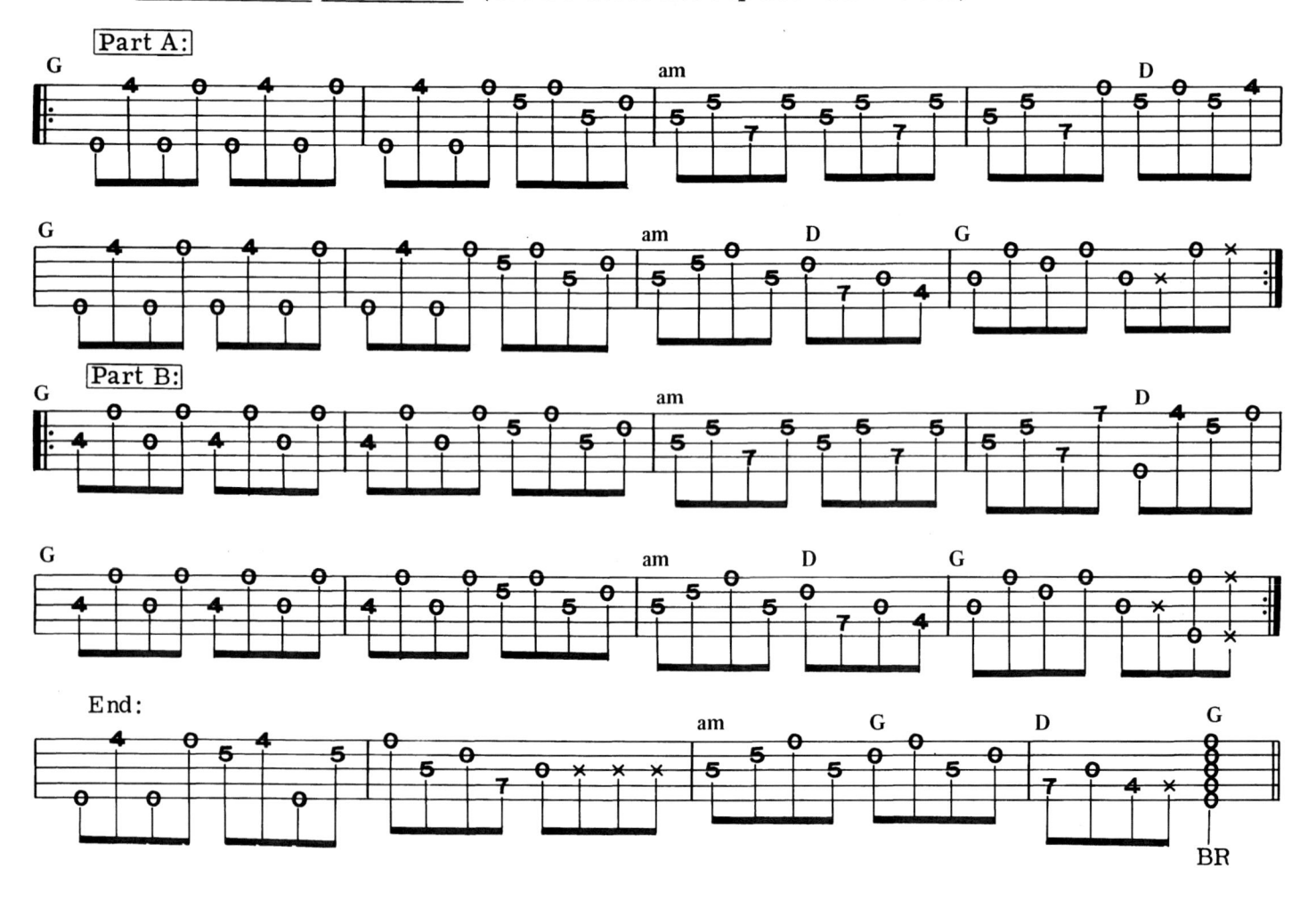

BLACKBERRY BLOSSOM

I. <u>MELODY</u> and <u>CHORDS</u> ONLY: (The melody is based upon the circular scale.)

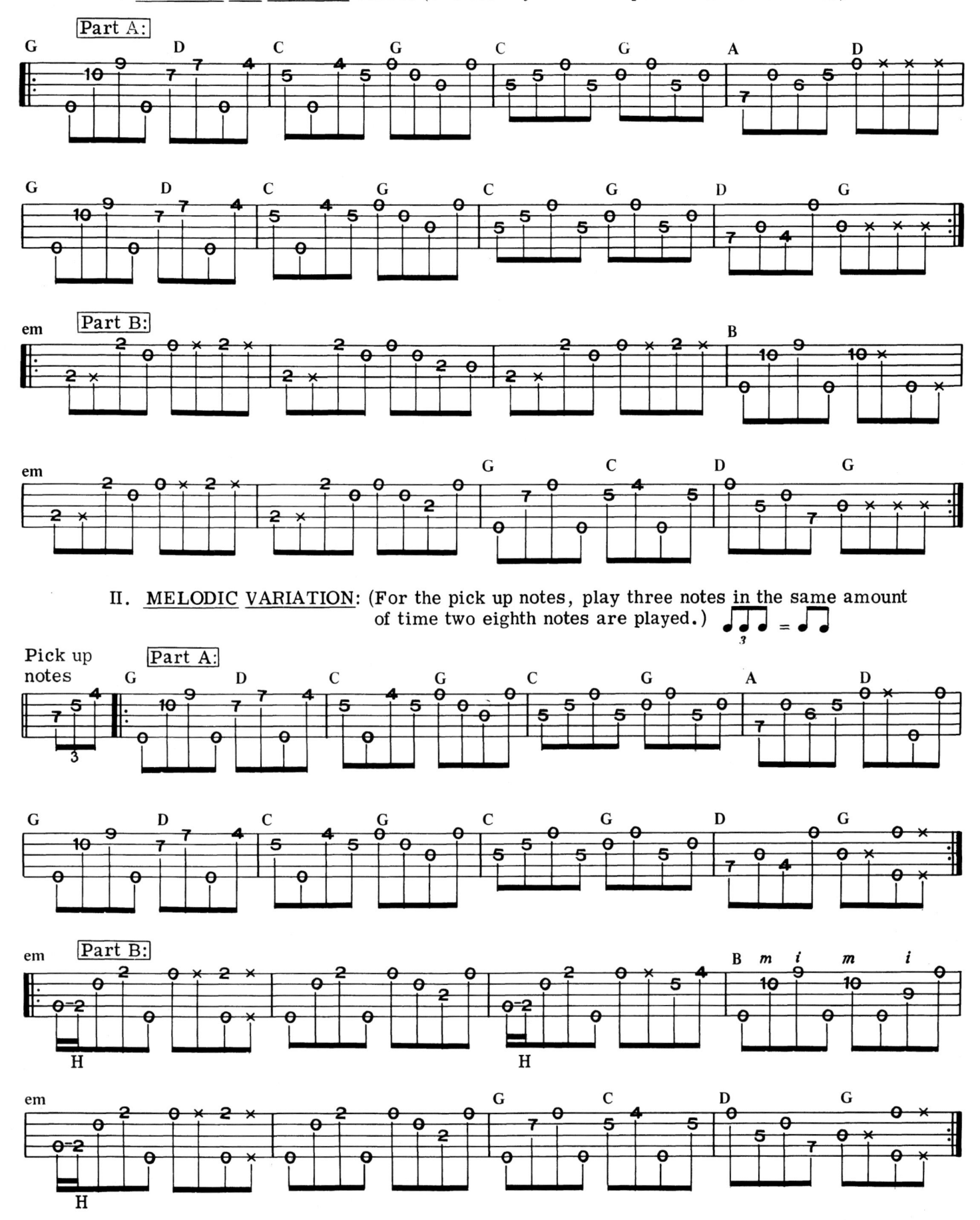

II. <u>MELODIC VARIATION</u>: (For the pick up notes, play three notes in the same amount of time two eighth notes are played.)

SAILOR'S HORNPIPE

The melody for this tune is divided into two parts:
an A Part, which is repeated, and a Part B, which is also repeated.
NOTE: This is often played in the key of A, (place capo on 2nd fret).

I. <u>MELODY</u> and <u>CHORDS</u> ONLY: (Pause for the x's)

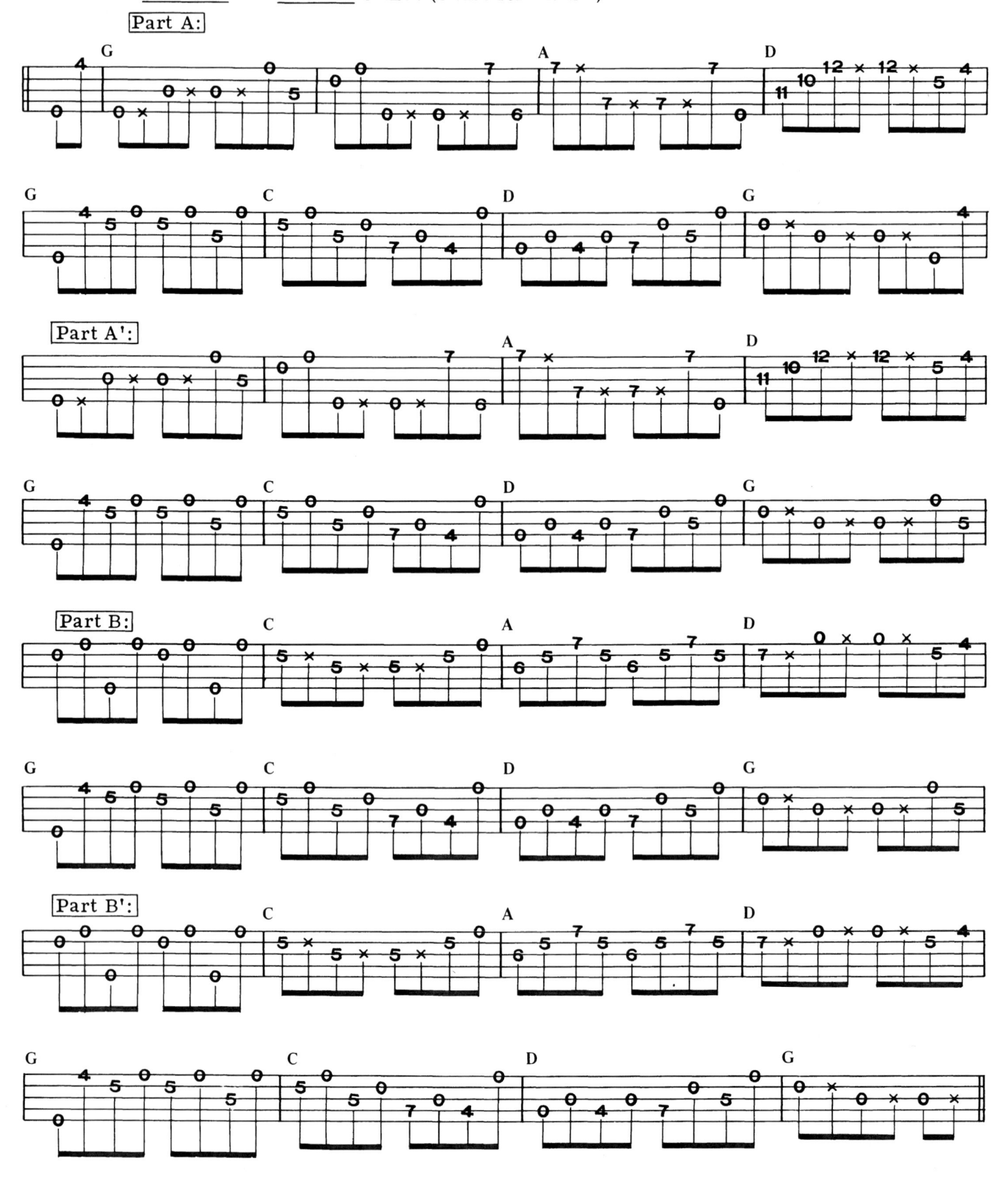

II. **MELODIC VARIATION:** (x's in I. are replaced with notes)

   NOTE: Several x's remain in the following arrangement for the purpose of emphasizing certain parts of the melody. You should pause for the x's.

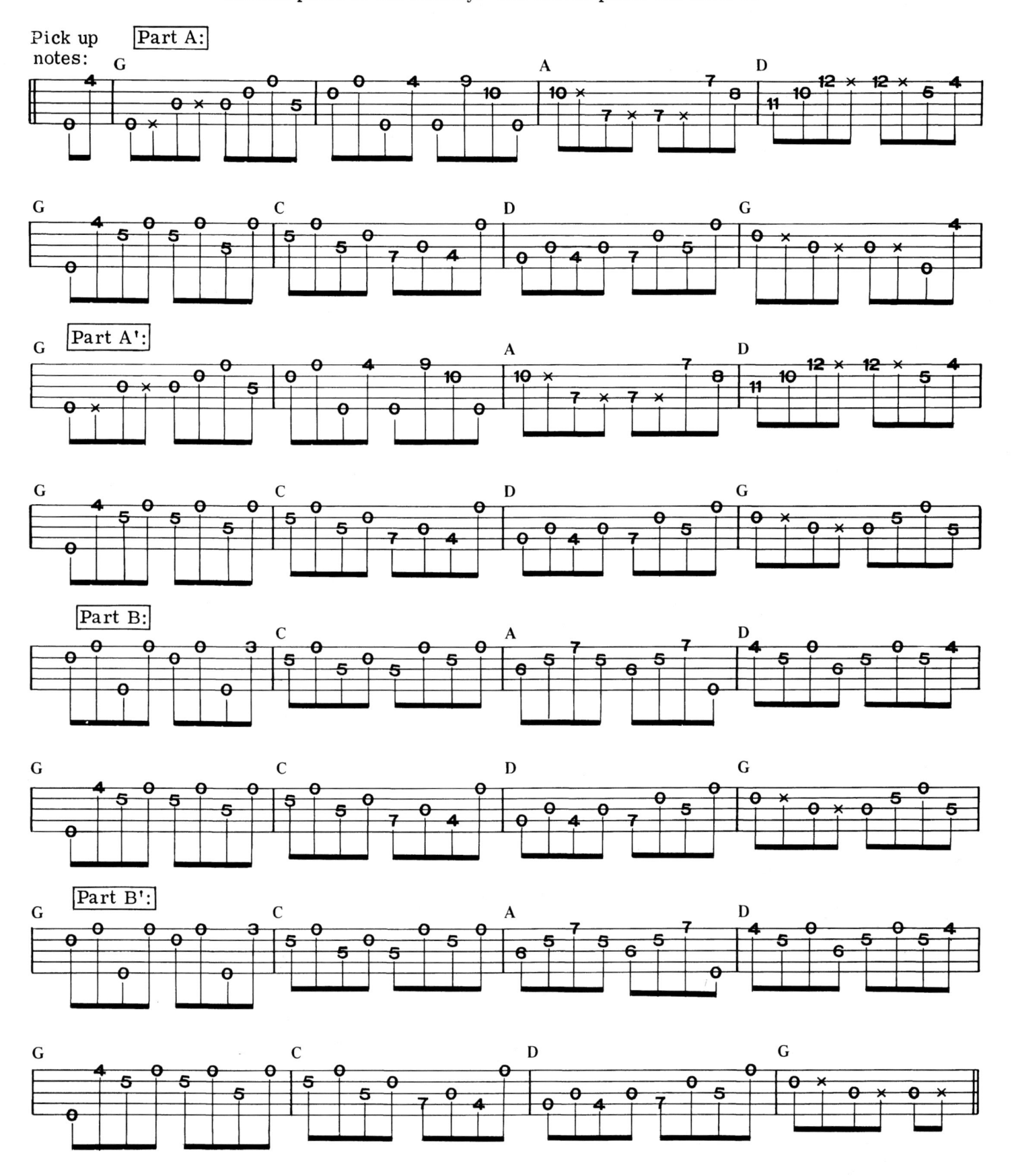

RED HAIRED BOY

I. **MELODY** and **CHORDS ONLY**: (Place capo on 2nd fret to play in key of A.)

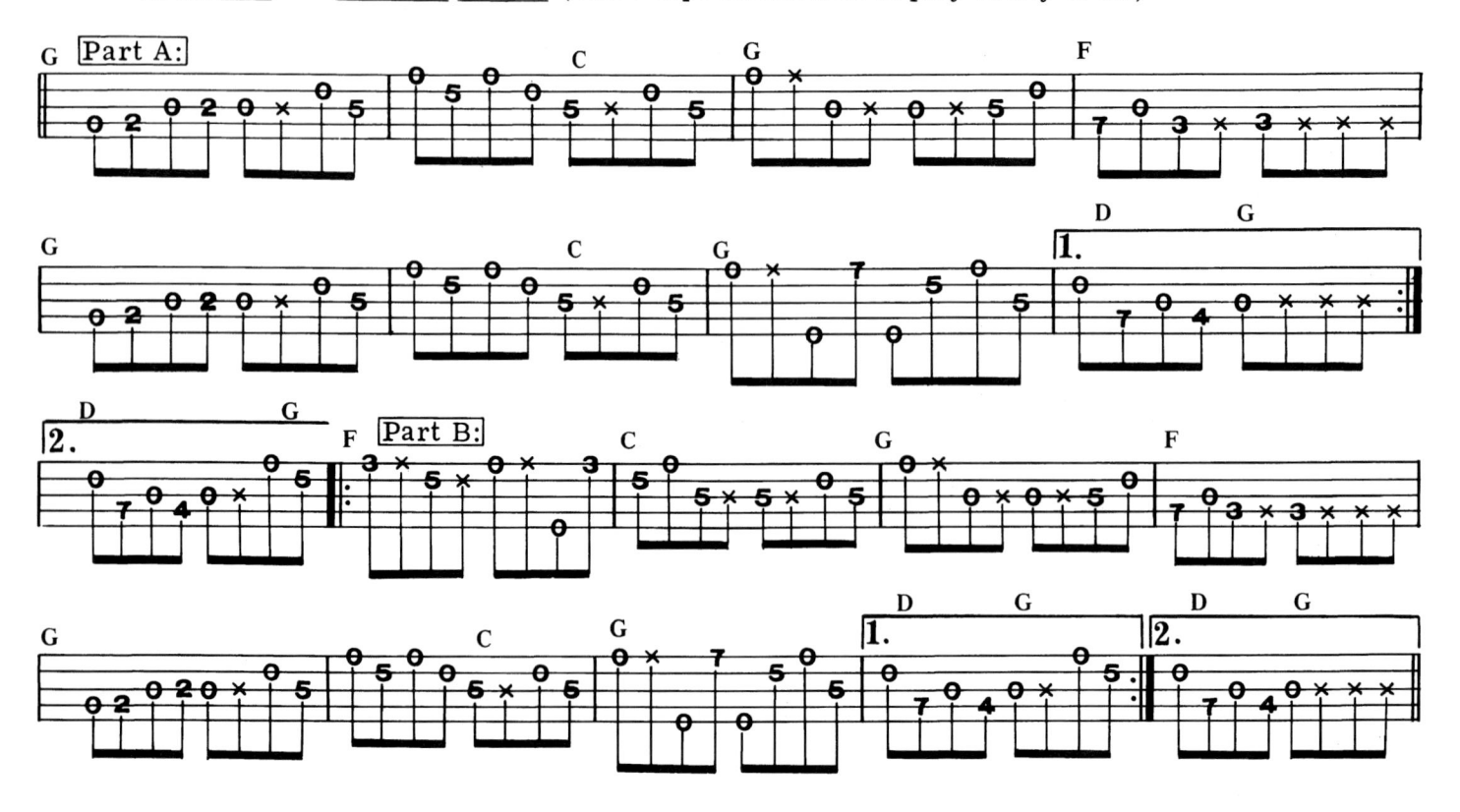

II. **MELODIC VARIATION**: The x's in I. are replaced with notes, except where melody notes are emphasized by pauses. (Notes can also replace these x's if desired; this will add drive to the arrangement.)

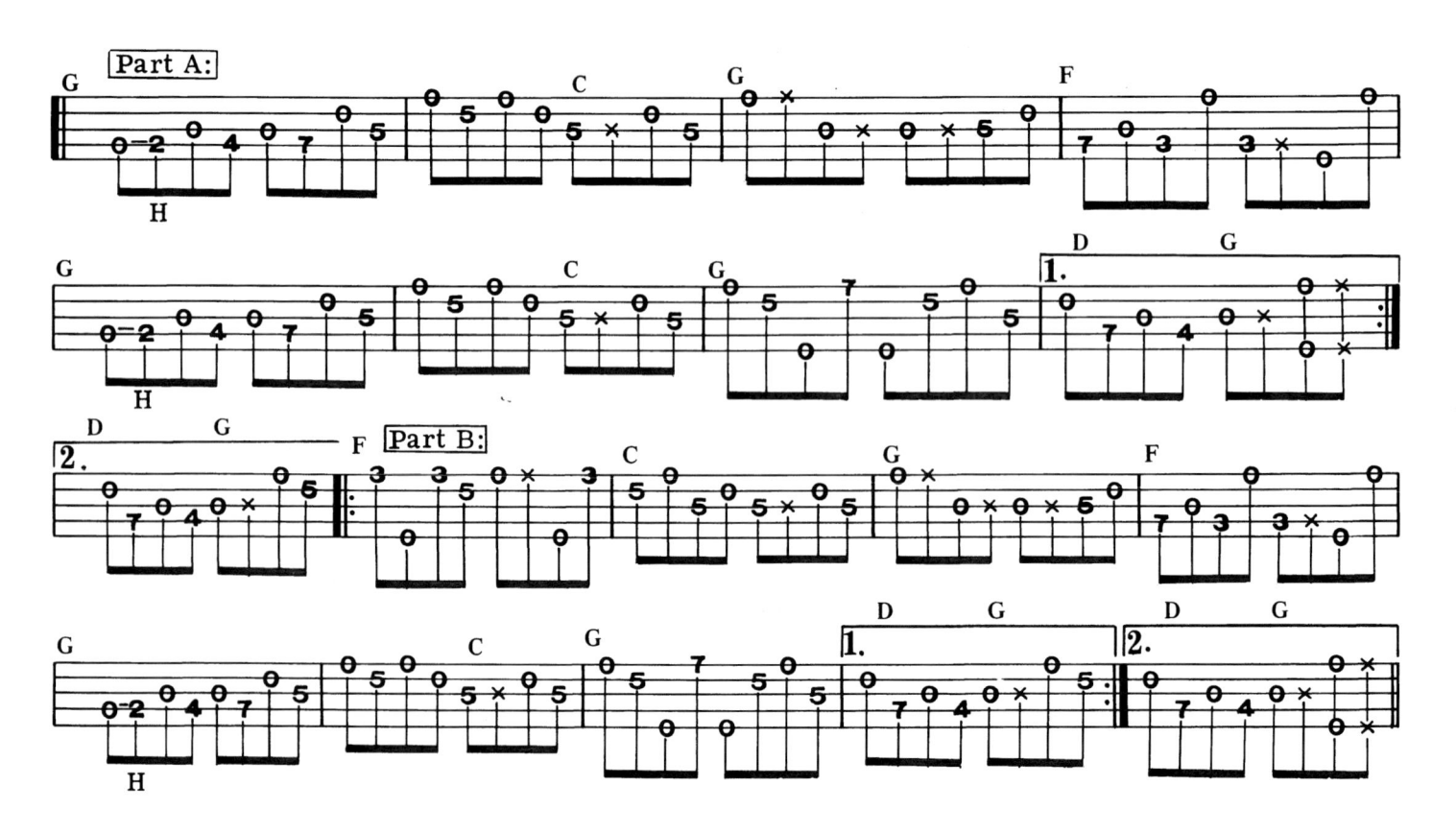

TURKEY IN THE STRAW
EXERCISE: WORKING OUT A SONG IN MELODIC STYLE

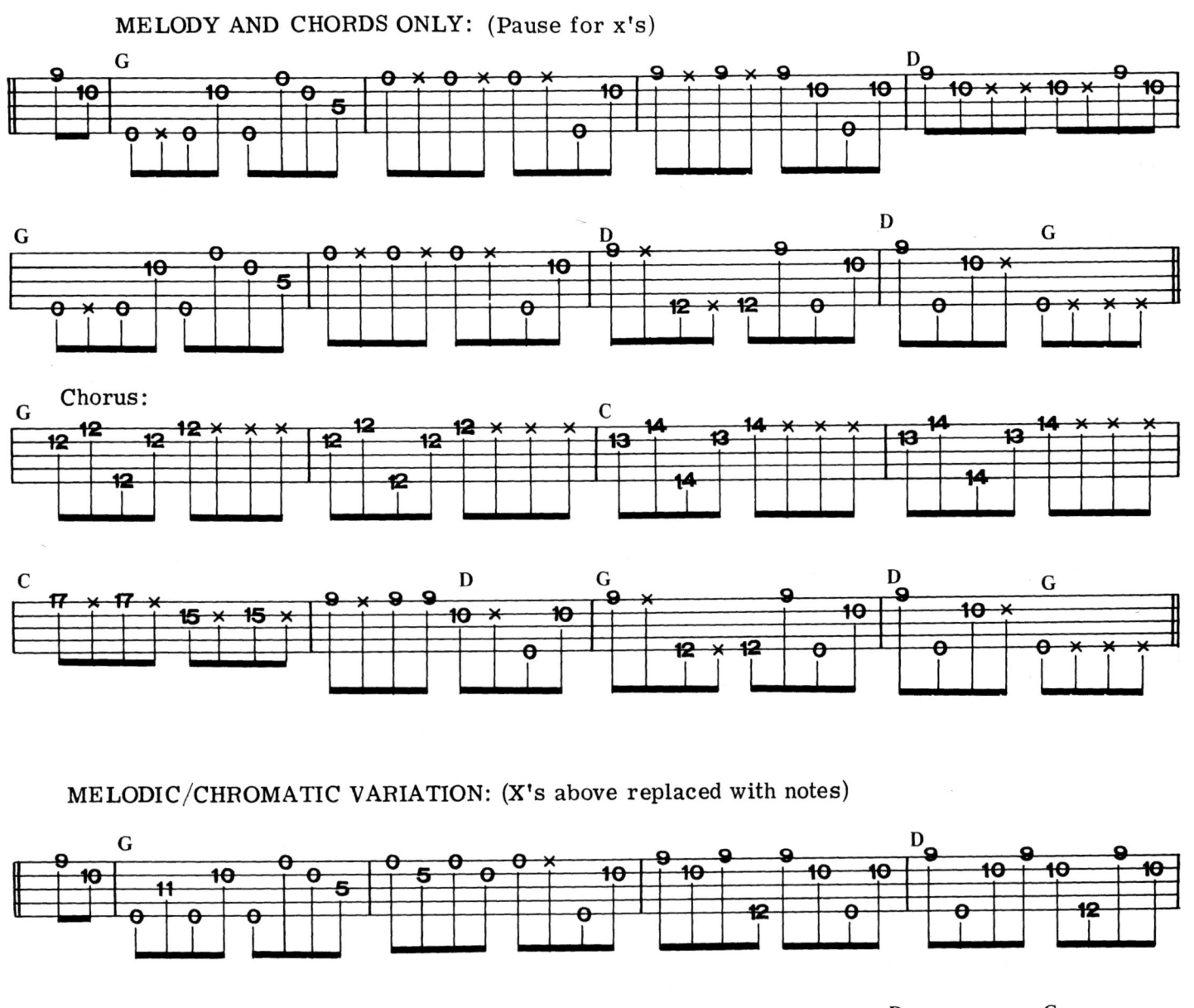

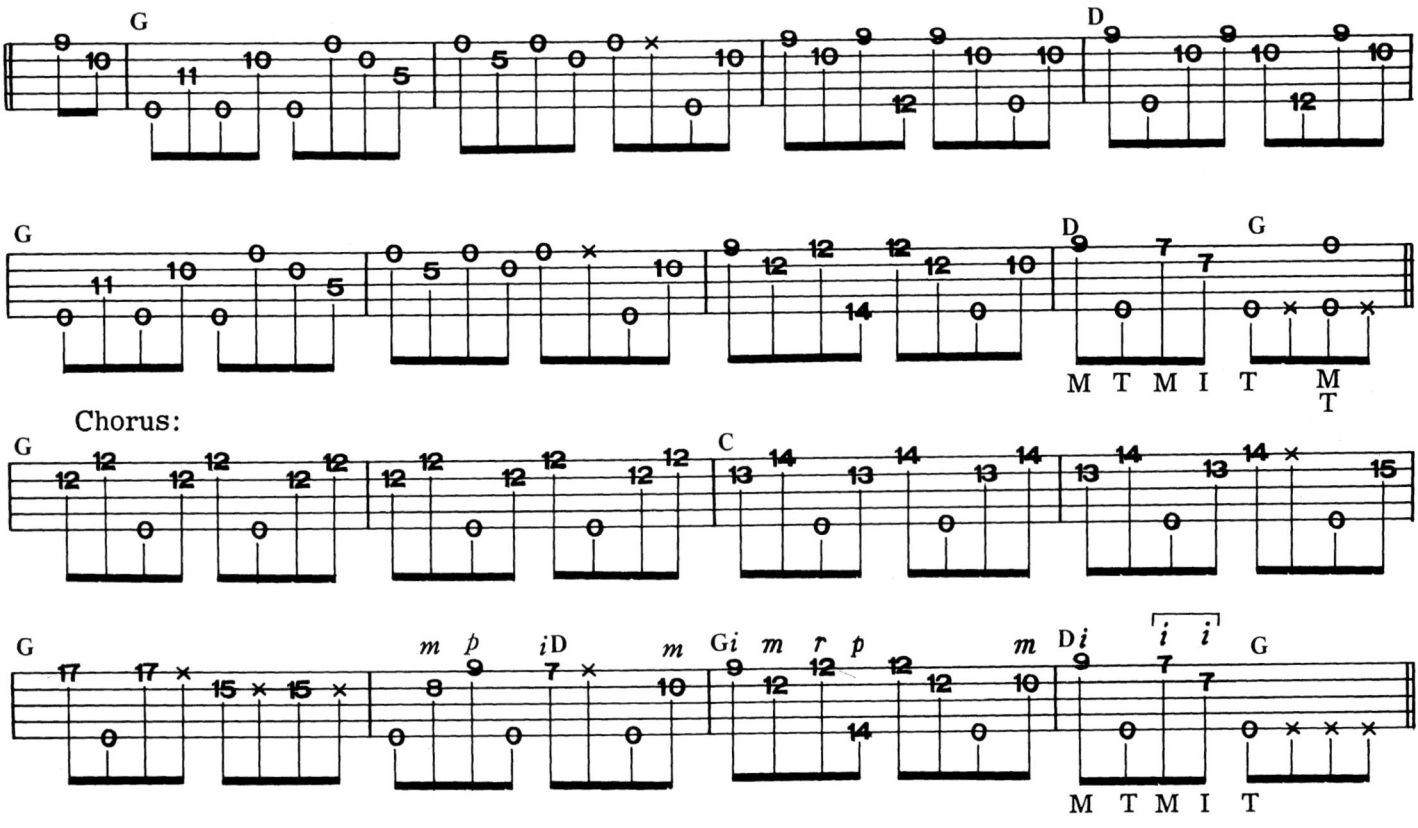

FIRE ON THE MOUNTAIN

Part A: (Key of G)

Part B: (Key of C)

Part C: Key of G

Ending:

An introduction (play to begin song).

SL

Note:

1. Play part A 4 times (the 1st 3 times play ending |1.2 and 3. ; the 4th time, skip |1.2. 3.| & play |4. instead.)

2. Play part B twice (1st time, play |1. |; 2nd time skip|1. |& Play |2. .)

3. Play part C once.

NOTE: This tune is usually played with the capo on the 2nd fret, (in the key of A & D).

CRIPPLE CREEK

The melody for this tune can be found in the section on Bluegrass-style.
NOTE: This song is often played in the key of A, with the capo placed on the 2nd fret of the banjo.

I. <u>MELODIC-STYLE</u> VARIATION:

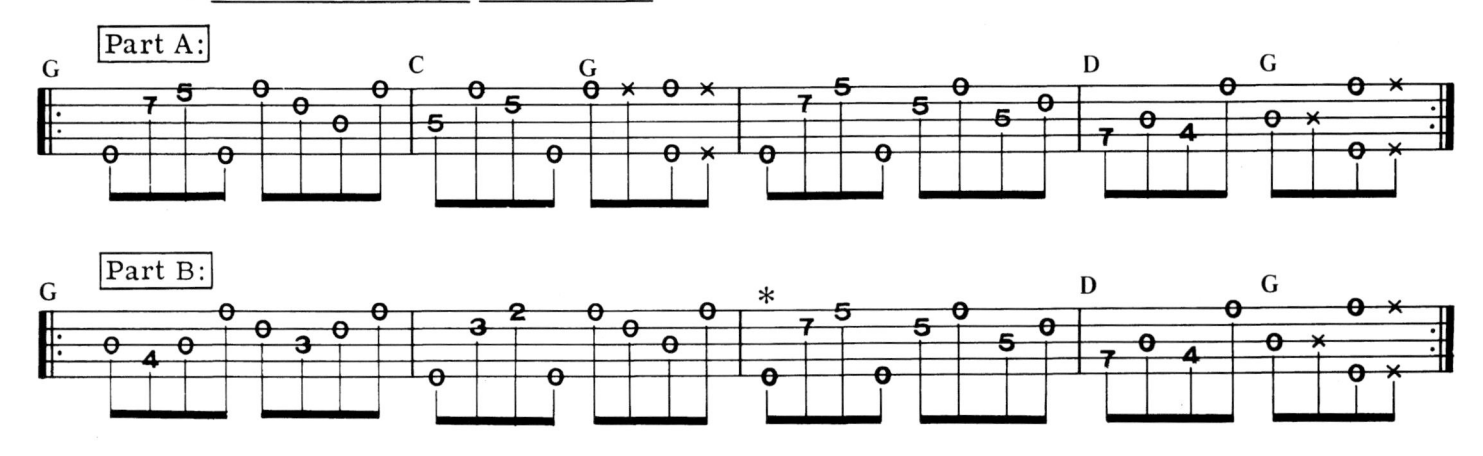

Part A:

Part B:

II. <u>MELODIC-STYLE</u> VARIATION: (using different licks from I)

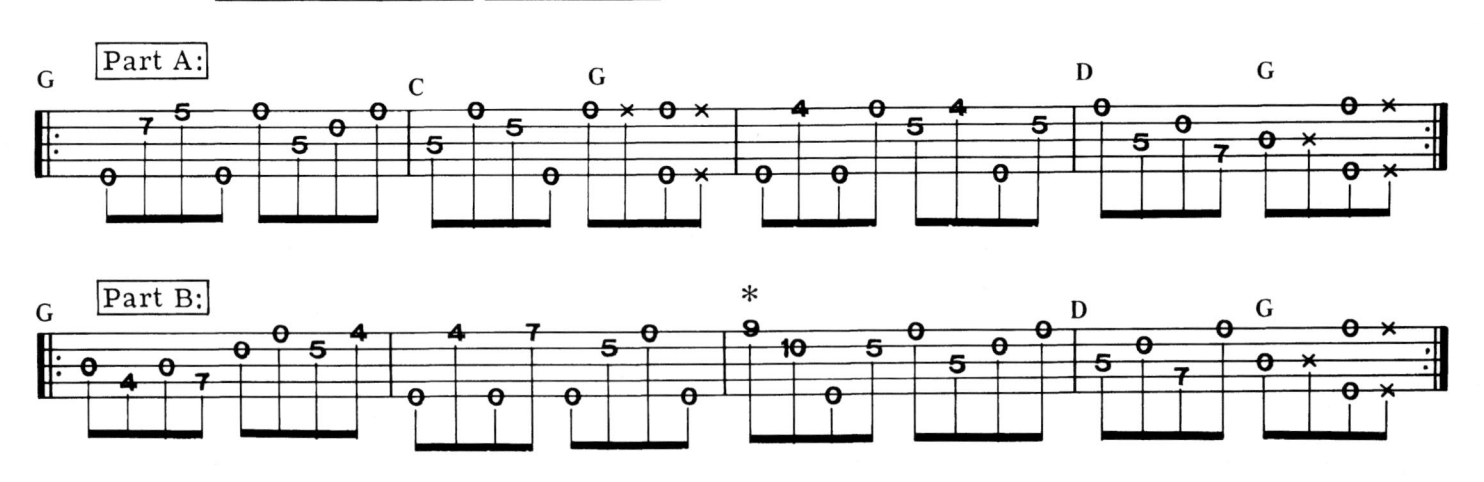

Part A:

Part B:

<u>FOR PRACTICE</u>: Substitute each of the following alternate licks for the last two measures in each of the above variations.

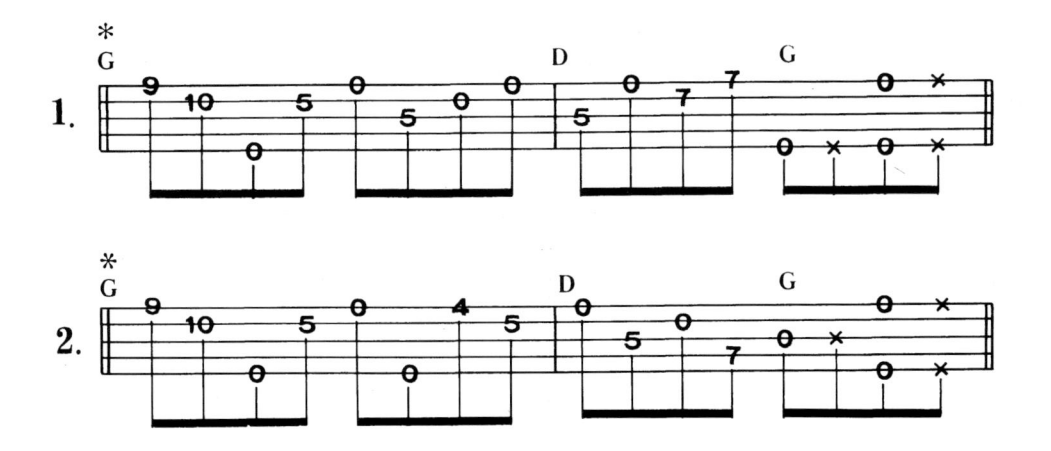

1.

2.

A COMPARISON
OF BLUEGRASS-STYLE & MELODIC STYLE

    Almost any song can be arranged for the banjo so that it can be played either in "Bluegrass-Style", (which is based upon roll patterns and licks, with one right hand finger emphasizing the melody notes while the other fingers play background notes), or in "Melodic-Style", (where almost every note played is a melody note, or a note which is a neighbor tone to the melody note).

    The songs, JOHN HARDY and OLD JOE CLARK, are arranged in Bluegrass-Style and in Melodic-Style, so that you can compare the two styles when they are used for the same song. Try, first, to work out your own arrangements from the basic melody, using the principles for each style which were discussed in the section on each style of playing. Keep in mind, that the left hand works primarily out of chord positions in Bluegrass-Style arrangements, while it works primarily with scale patterns, which are played for the chords to the song, in Melodic-Style.

NOTE: Also, see "Cripple Creek", pp. 35 & 67, for comparison.

JOHN HARDY

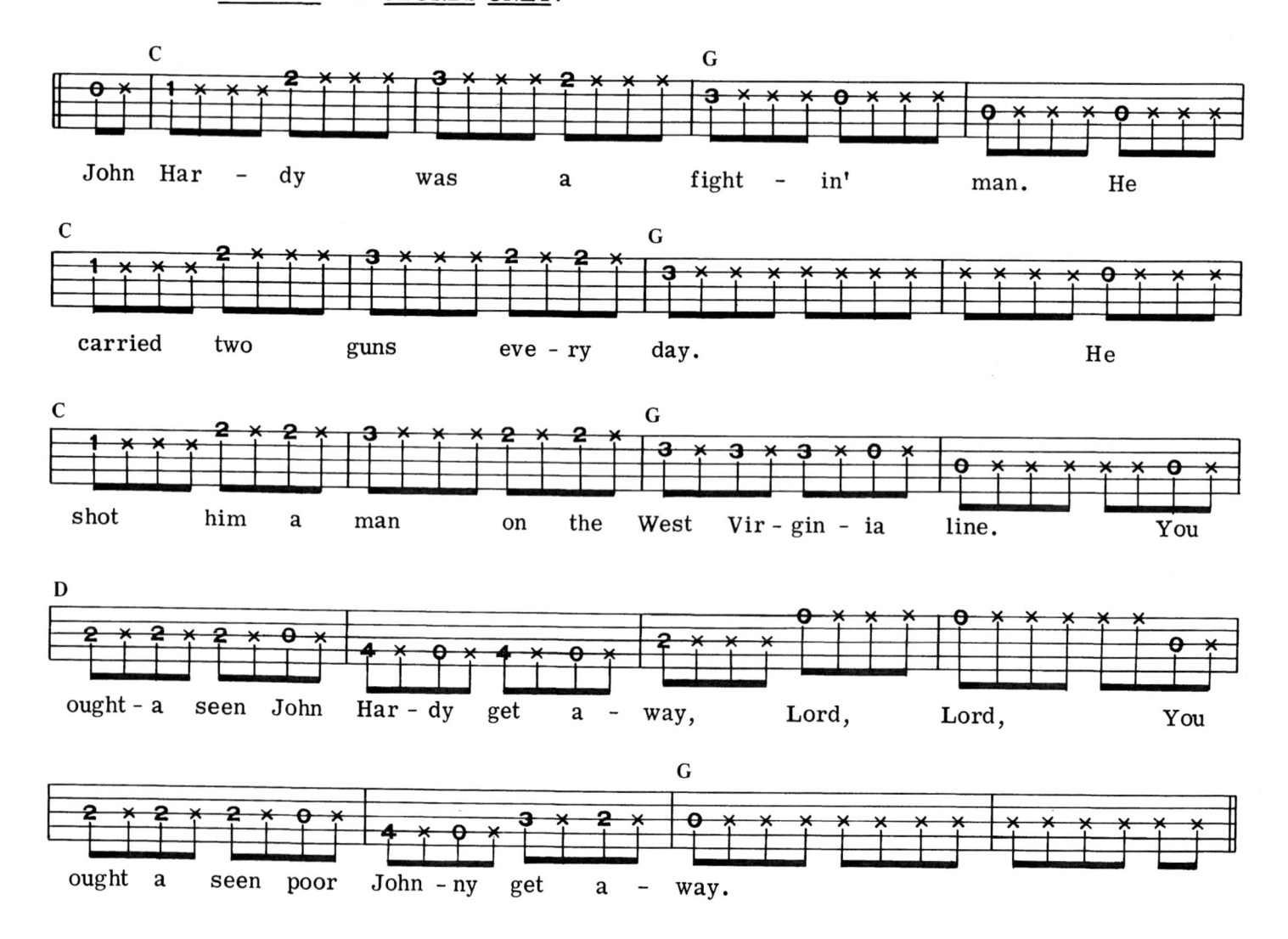

I. <u>MELODY</u> and <u>CHORDS</u> <u>ONLY</u>:

II. **BLUEGRASS-STYLE** **VARIATION**: (Using all techniques of this style).

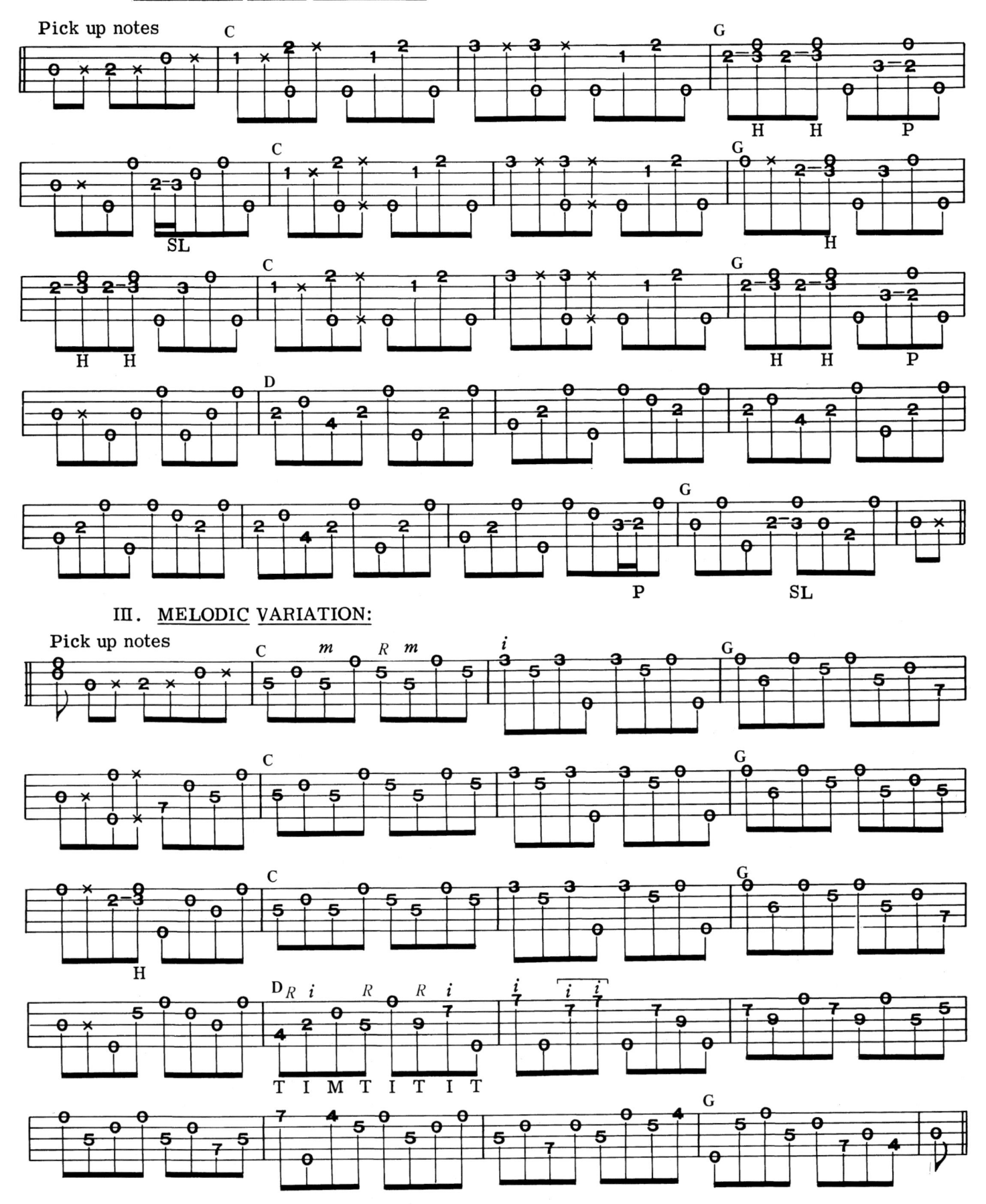

III. **MELODIC** **VARIATION**:

OLD JOE CLARK

NOTE: Place capo on 2nd fret to play in Key of A.

I. <u>MELODY</u> and <u>CHORDS</u> <u>ONLY</u>:

Part A: (Verse)

Old Joe Clark's a mean old man, Mean as he can be...

Knocked me down with his right hand, Walked all ov-er me.

Part B: (Chorus)

Round and round, Old Joe Clark, round and round I say...

Round and round, Old Joe Clark, Ain't got long to stay.

II. BLUEGRASS-STYLE VARIATION:

Part A: (Verse)

Part A':

Part B: (Chorus)

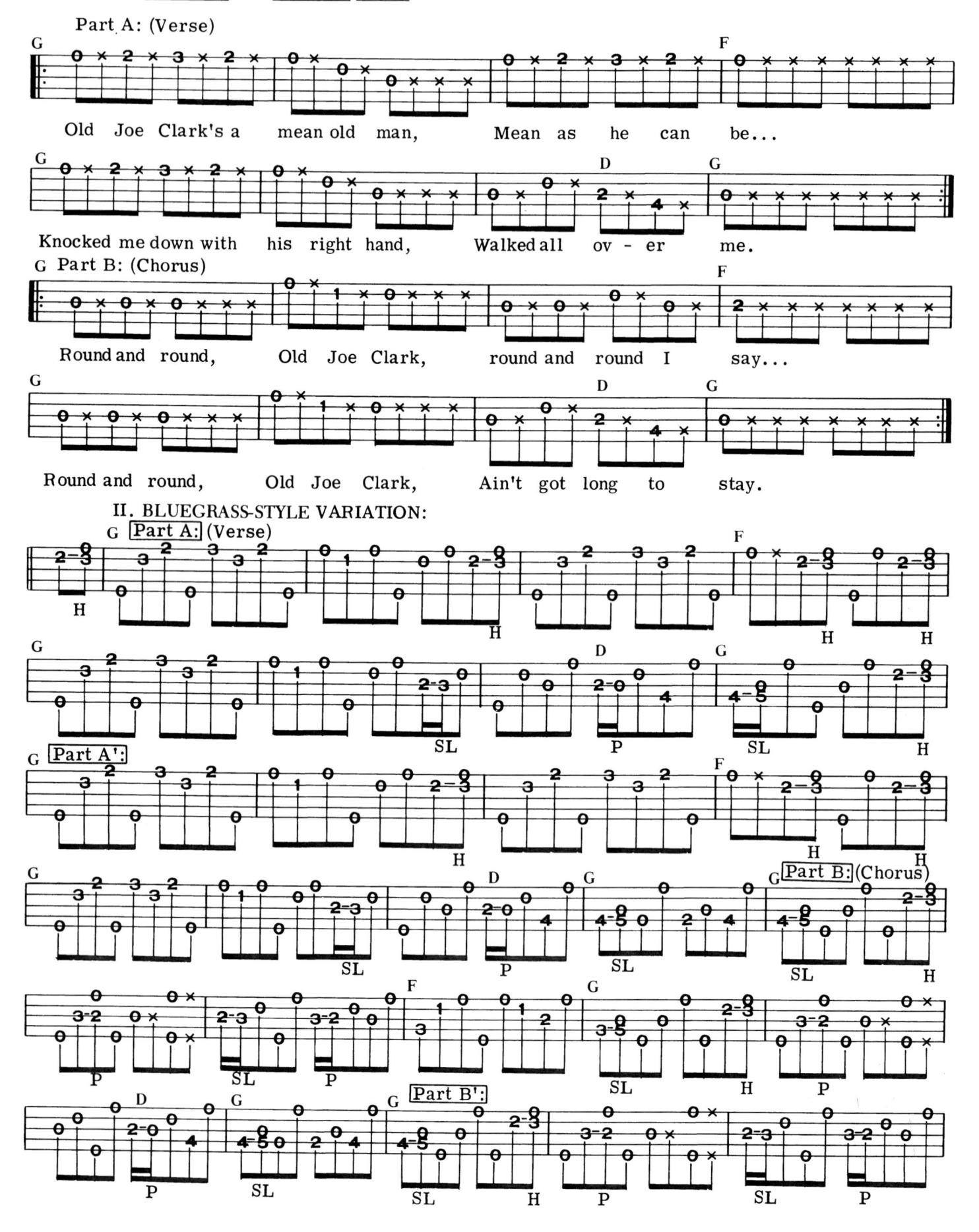

Part B':

III. MELODIC-STYLE VARIATION:

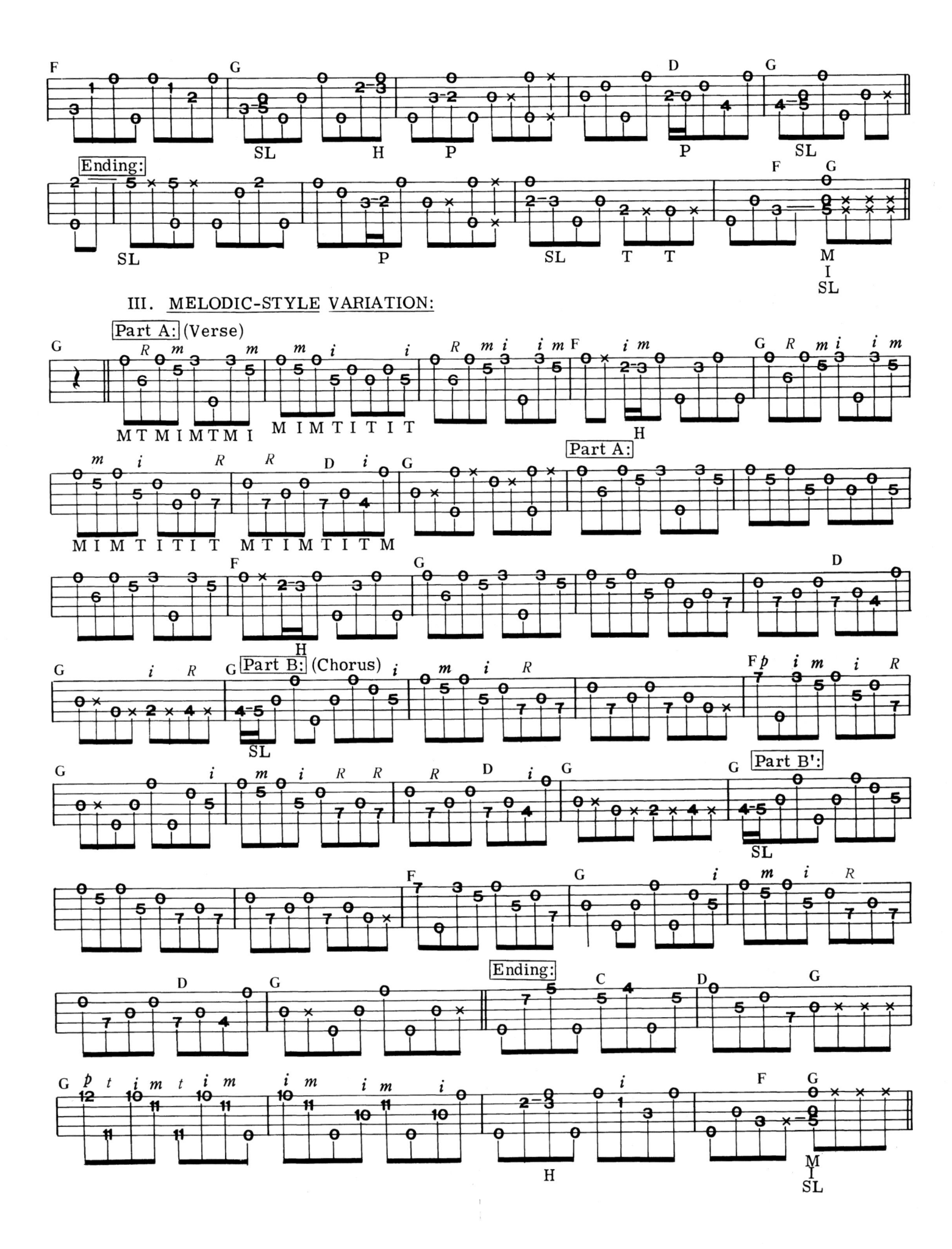

COMBINING STYLES OF PLAYING
IMPROVISING WITH ADVANCED FILL-IN LICKS

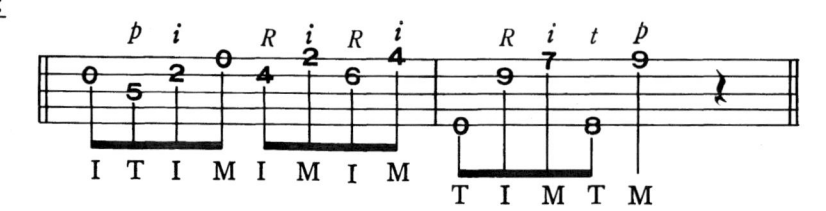

Advanced fill-in licks are variations of the standard fill-in licks, and may be substituted for the standard fill-in licks in a song, as long as the chords correspond, and as long as each lick uses the corresponding number of measures or beats. Advanced licks may be Bluegrass-style licks, Melodic-style licks, or they may be a combination of styles. Each lick has a little something "unique" or unusual to make it interesting. (For example, the 5th string may begin the lick, or the lick may involve playing a progression of several chords with the left hand, even though it is applied to only one chord in a song.)

The following exercise should help the left fingers become fairly adept at changing chord positions, in order to play the licks of the latter type described above. This exercise involves changing chord positions with the left hand every four notes.

EXERCISE:

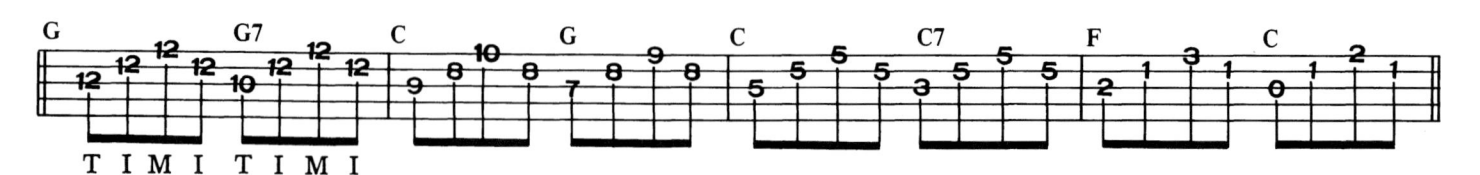

Many advanced fill-in licks are derived from the chromatic scale. This scale consists of twelve tones, (the eight tones of the diatonic scale, plus each tone in between those tones). If the B chromatic scale were played up the banjo fingerboard on only one string, it would be played as follows:

The following exercise demonstrates one way the above scale can be played for an octave up the fingerboard, without picking the same string twice in a row with the right hand. The licks which are derived from this scale, often use the Bluegrass-style roll patterns with the right hand, while the left hand holds the notes in a manner similar to the melodic-style, (i.e. two notes at a time.)

EXERCISE:

ADVANCED FILL-IN LICKS

Each of the following examples may be substituted for a standard fill-in lick in a song, as long as the chord is the same, and as long as the licks are the same number of measures, (or have the same number of counts--i.e. a sixteen count lick (two measures) must be replaced by a lick with sixteen counts, (two measures).

G CHORD LICKS:

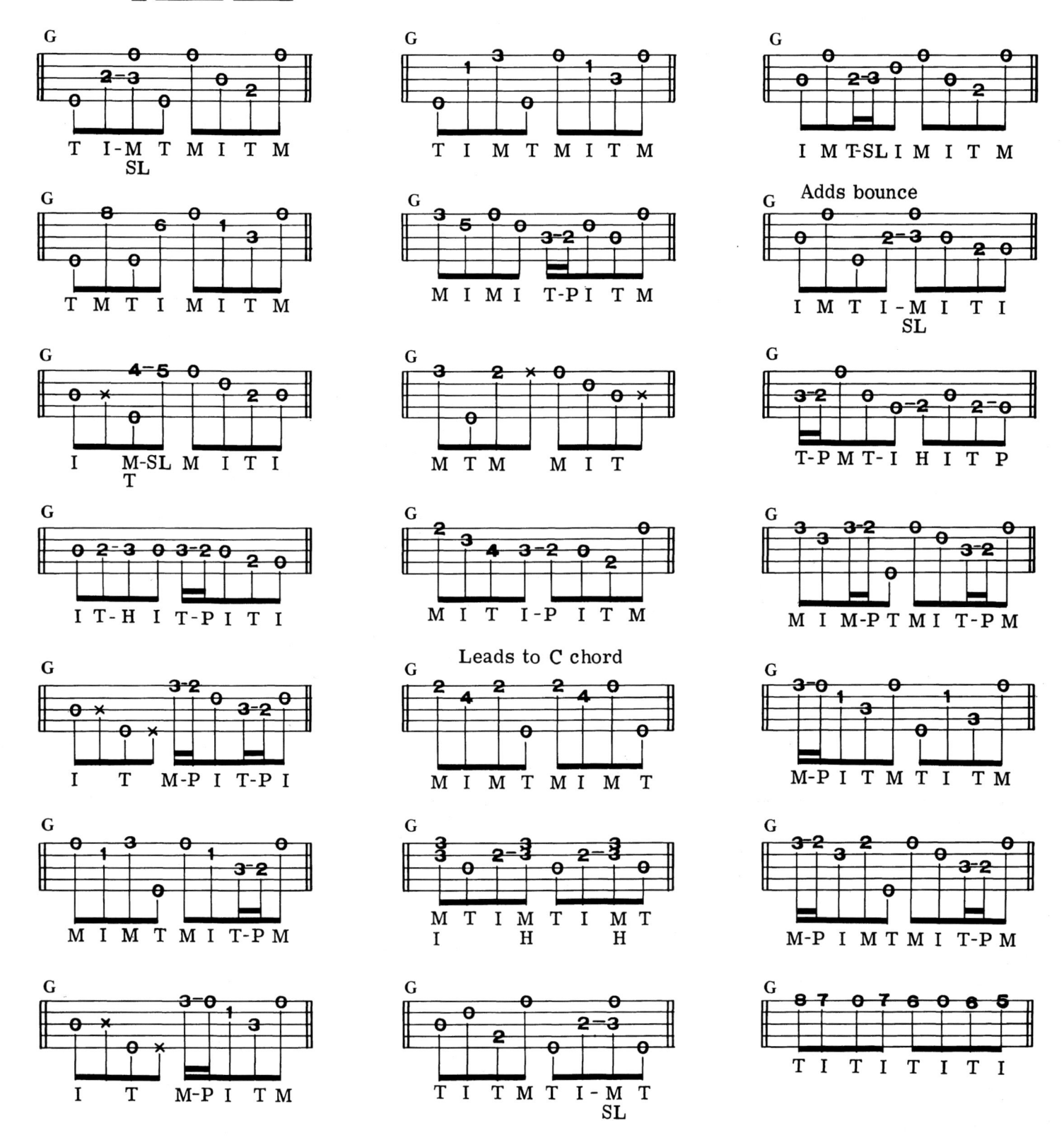

G Chord Licks consisting of two measures (16 counts):
(Each of the following licks is actually a combination of two one-measure licks.)

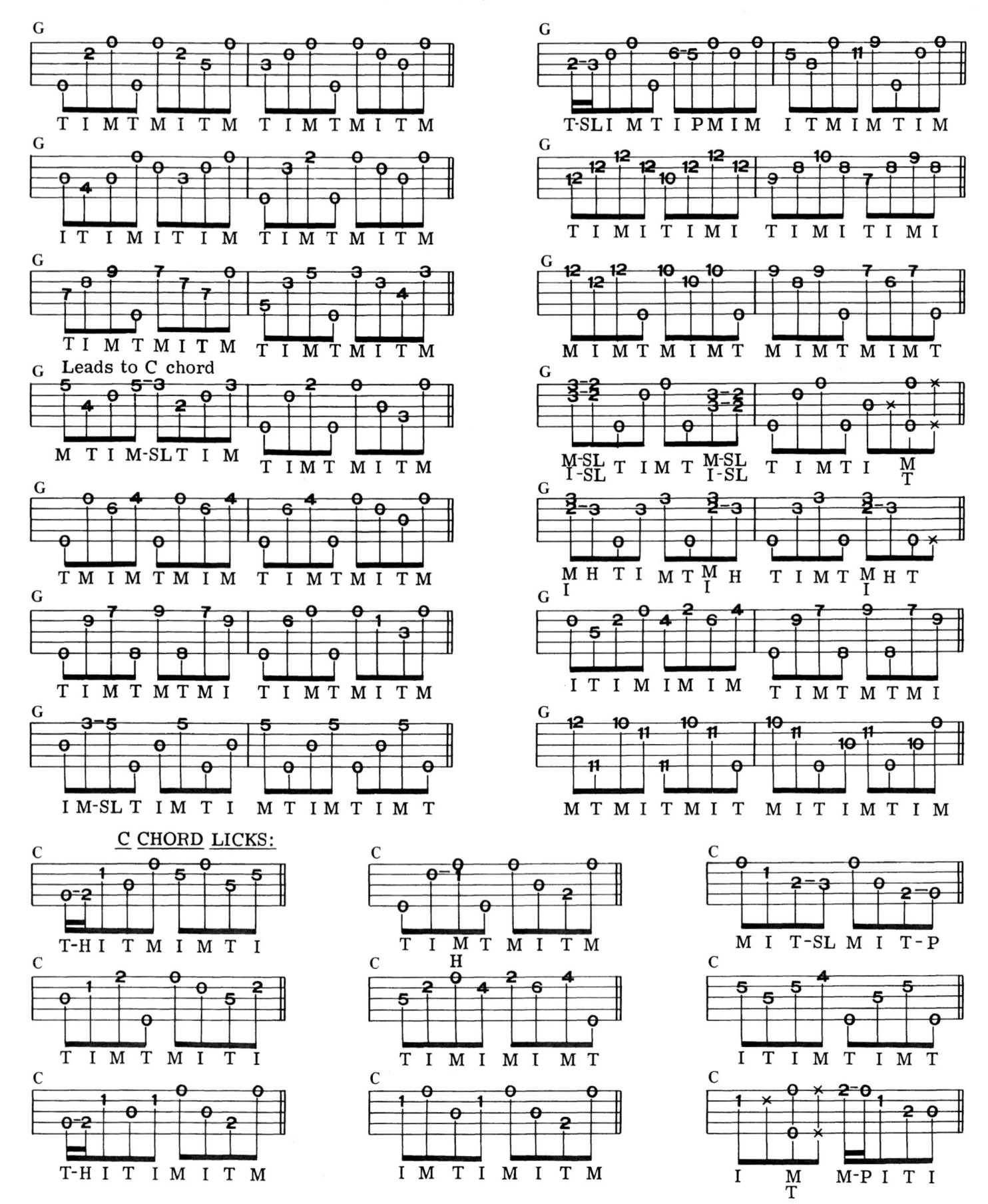

C CHORD LICKS:

C Chord Licks consisting of two measures:

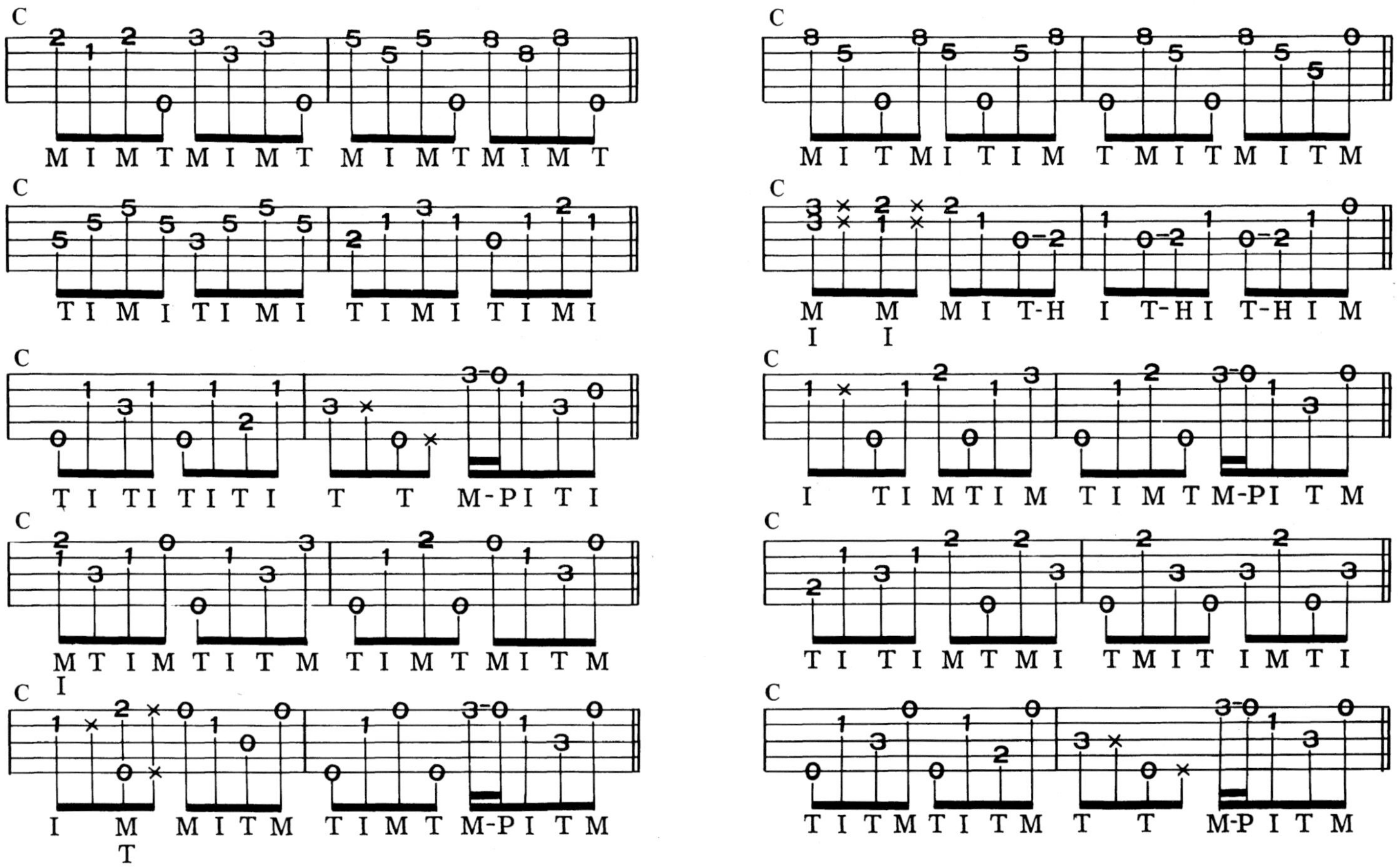

D CHORD LICKS:

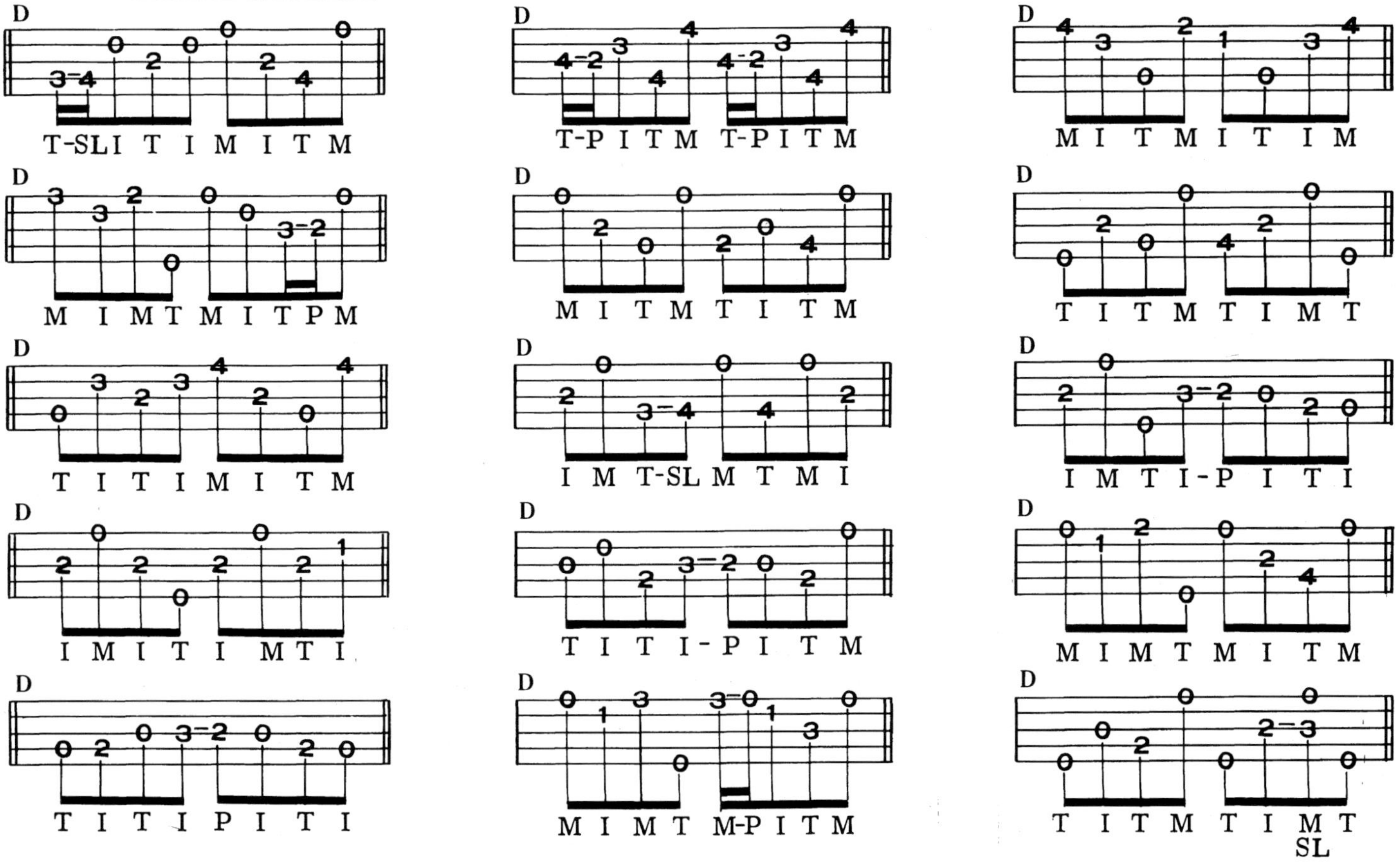

D Chord Licks (two measures): Each of the following examples can be used either during the pauses, when a vocalist might take a breath, or as an ending lick, just before the final G chord of a song.

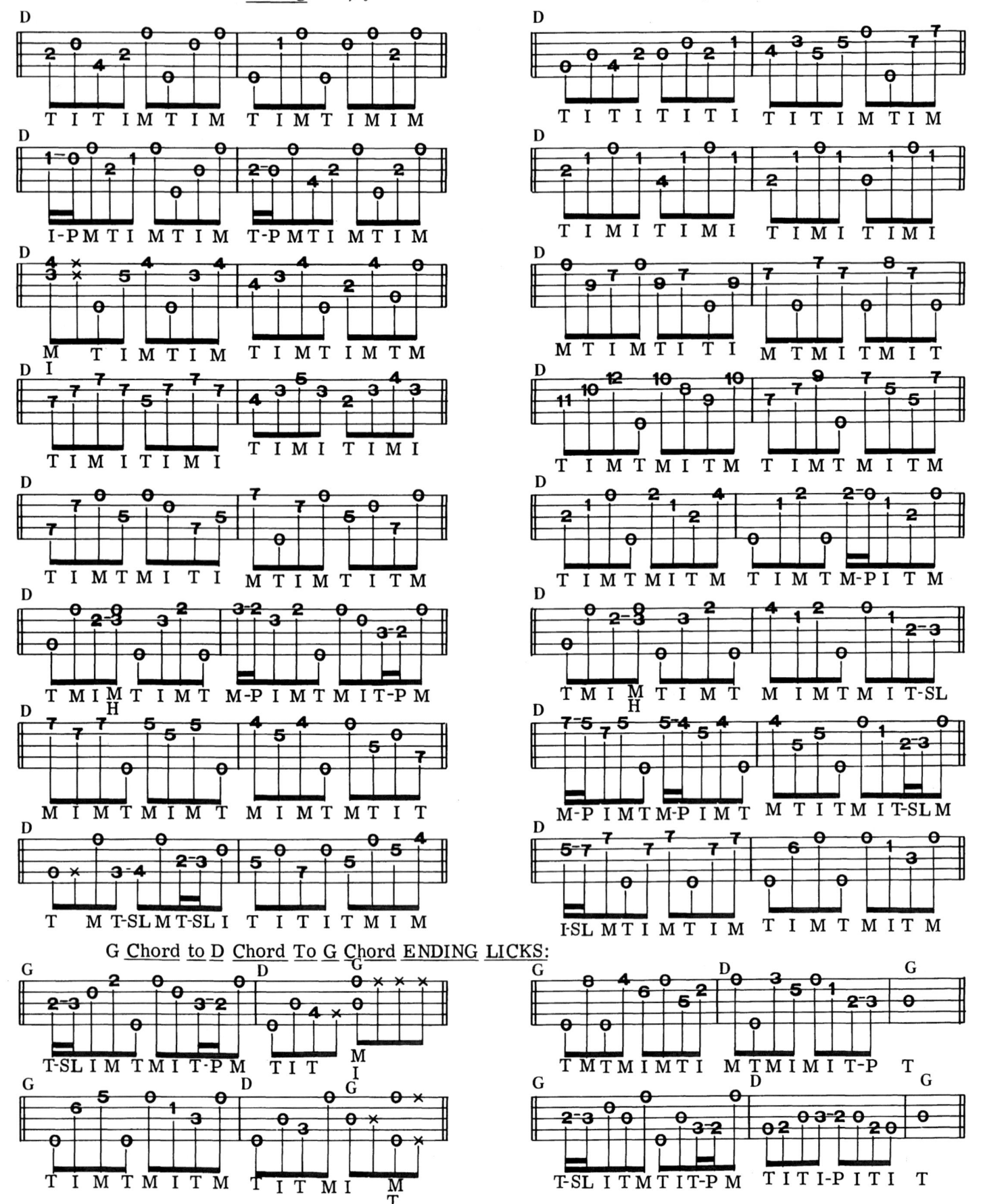

G Chord to D Chord To G Chord ENDING LICKS:

ARRANGING SONGS FOR THE BANJO
USING ADVANCED FILL-IN LICKS

Before you work on arranging and improvising with the advanced fill-in licks, you should be thoroughly familiar with the standard fill-in licks of both Melodic and Bluegrass-styles of playing. Practice substituting specific licks from the sheet of advanced fill-in licks for fill-in licks in songs you already know, once you are comfortable with the standard fill-in licks. Remember that the chords must correspond when substituting licks.

PROCEDURE FOR ARRANGING SONGS USING ADVANCED FILL-IN-LICKS:

1.) Work out a song using the steps described in the section on arranging songs-- Bluegrass-style. (These licks are usually used in Bluegrass-style arrangements, so this discussion will be centered around this style of playing. However, they are also used in Melodic-style songs...and the same procedure for using them applies in that style of playing.)

EXAMPLE: "WORRIED MAN BLUES"
(STANDARD FILL-IN LICKS)

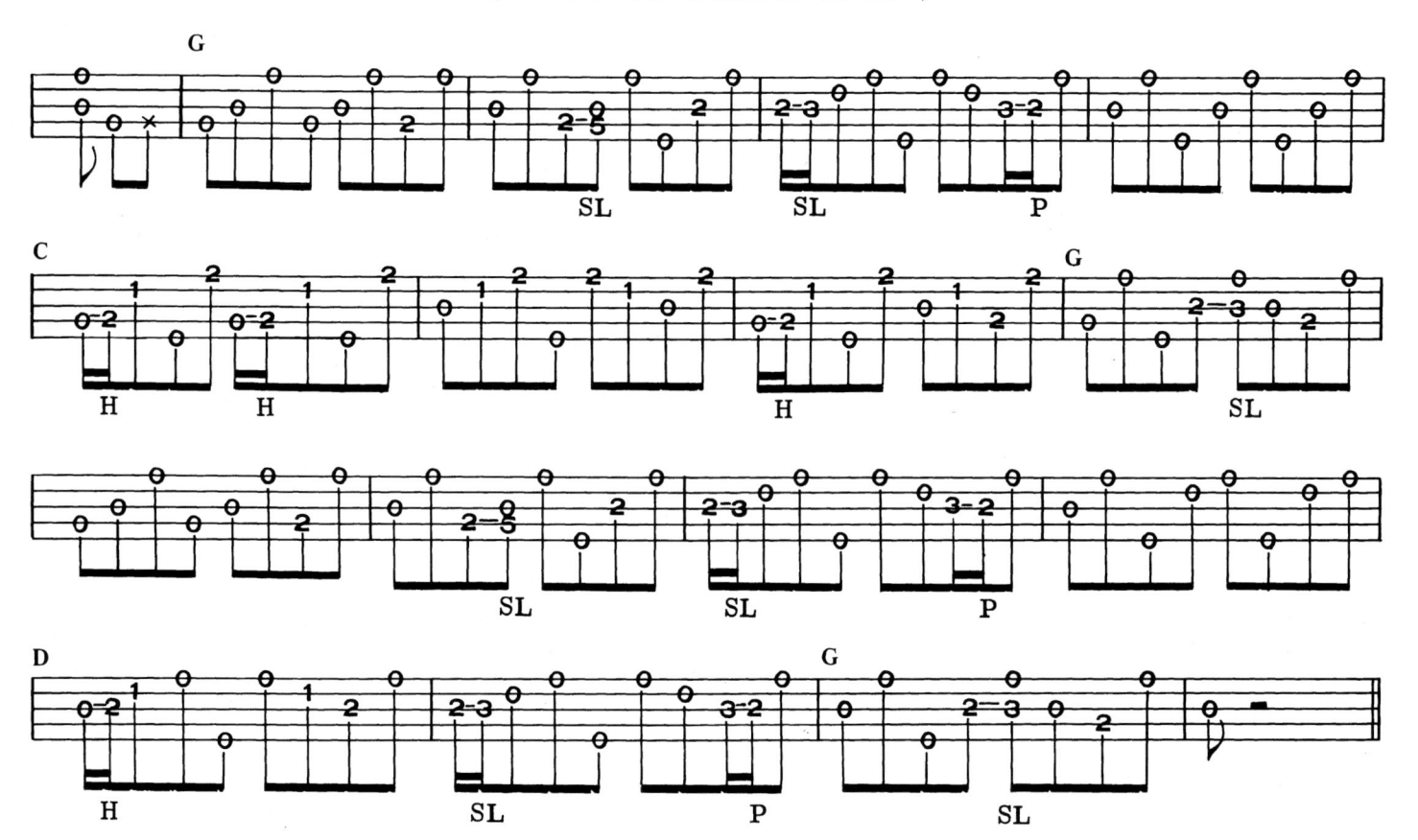

2.) After you have completed using the standard fill-in licks and feel you have a smooth arrangement of the song, substitute advanced fill-in-licks for some of the standard fill-in-licks.
   a. Begin with the ENDING LICKS--when you find the one that you feel sounds right, or that is fun to play, that may be the only substitution your arrangement needs.
   b. If you want to use more licks in the same variation, substitute an advanced lick for a standard "Pause" lick.

In the following example, an advanced fill-in lick for a G chord has been substituted for the lick which leads into the final D chord, and an advanced ending lick for a D chord has been substituted for the D chord ending lick.

EXAMPLE: "WORRIED MAN BLUES"
(ADVANCED FILL-IN LICKS)

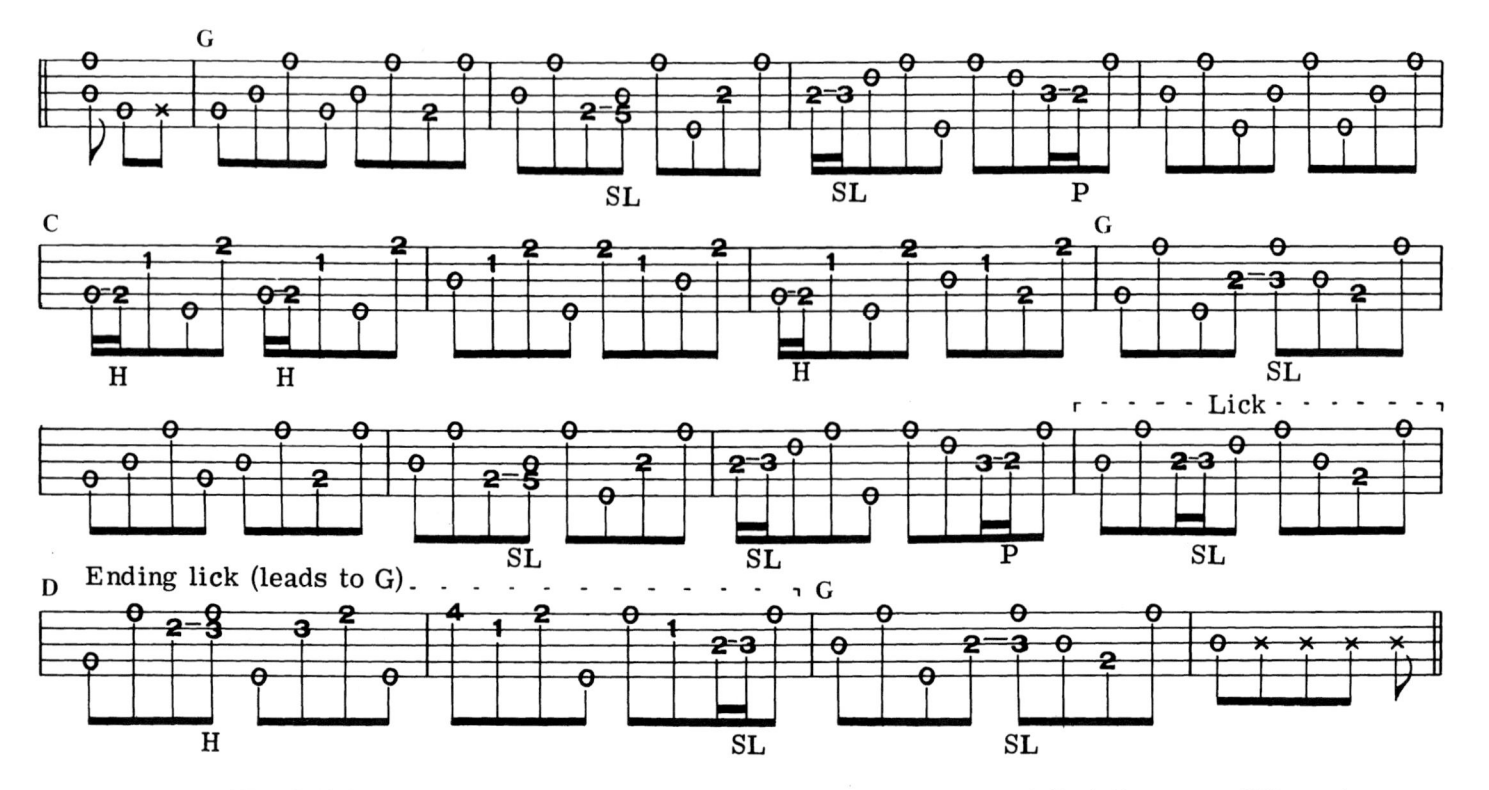

The following example is the same as the one above, except that it uses a different advanced ending lick for the D chord, and for the final G chord. Notice that although only three measures of the music are changed, the overall effect of each arrangement is quite different.

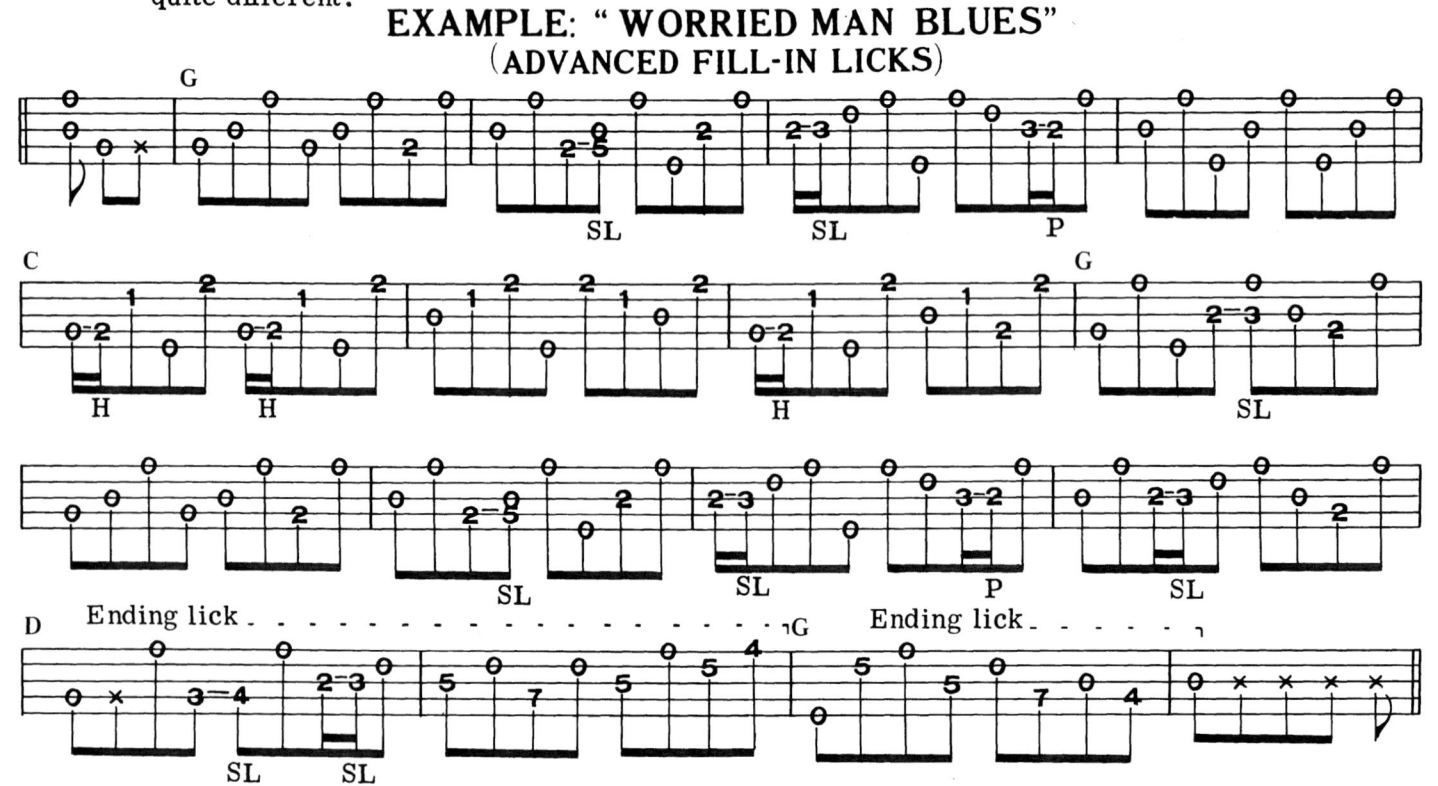

EXAMPLE: "WORRIED MAN BLUES"
(ADVANCED FILL-IN LICKS)

3.) You can combine advanced licks according to the correct chords of a song like a chain, until you have an entire arrangement of a song from fancy licks. I have found, however, that in most songs, this tends to replace taste with technique. Taste should generally come first. If you use just enough of these advanced licks to add interest to the song, the arrangement should sound clever, difficult, and above all--pleasing.

EXCEPTION: If you are playing three or four lead breaks to the same song, the last variation you play can go completely beserk and sound fine, or you may prefer to play this type of arrangement in the middle, and reestablish the melody for the last variation.

In the following example, advanced fill-in licks have been substituted for the C chord, and also for the G chord at the end of each phrase, including the final G chord lick. Only the first line of G chord licks is left unchanged from the example in step 1.

EXAMPLE: "WORRIED MAN BLUES"

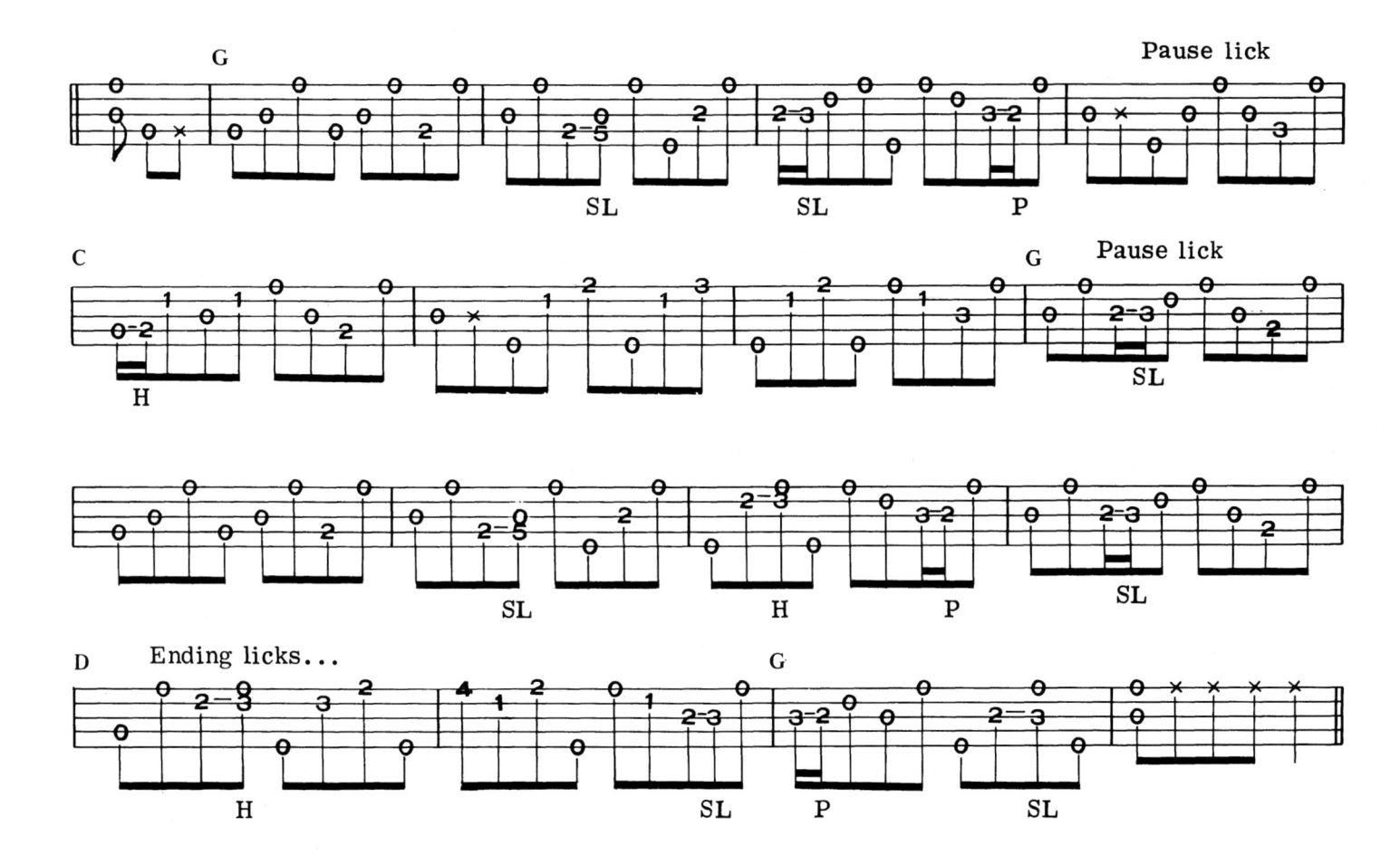

ROLL IN MY SWEET BABY'S ARMS

I. BLUEGRASS-STYLE ARRANGEMENT using STANDARD FILL-IN LICKS:

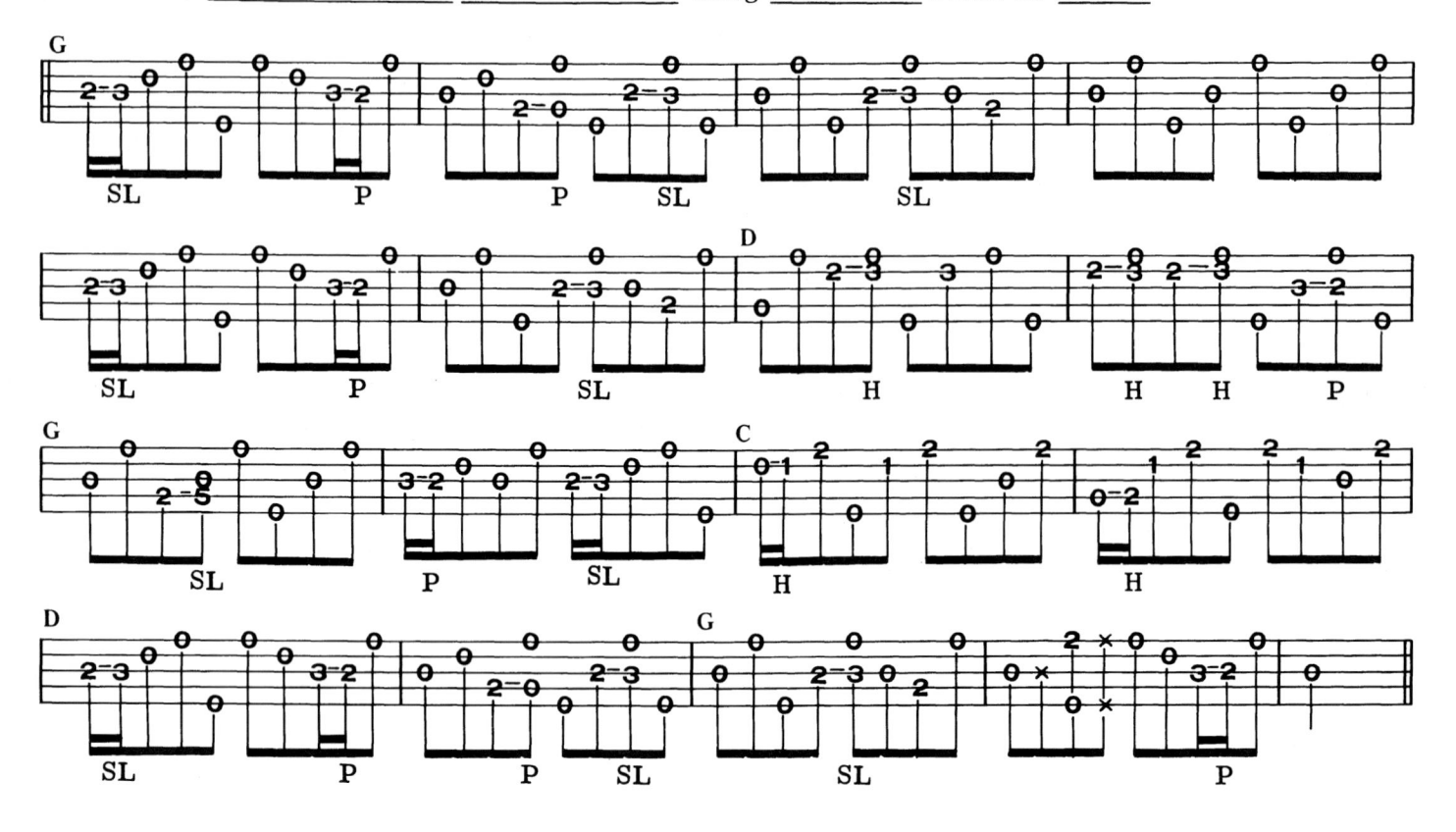

II. BLUEGRASS-STYLE ARRANGEMENT USING ADVANCED LICKS:
(Notice that the C chord lick(s) is based on the "Backward Roll".)

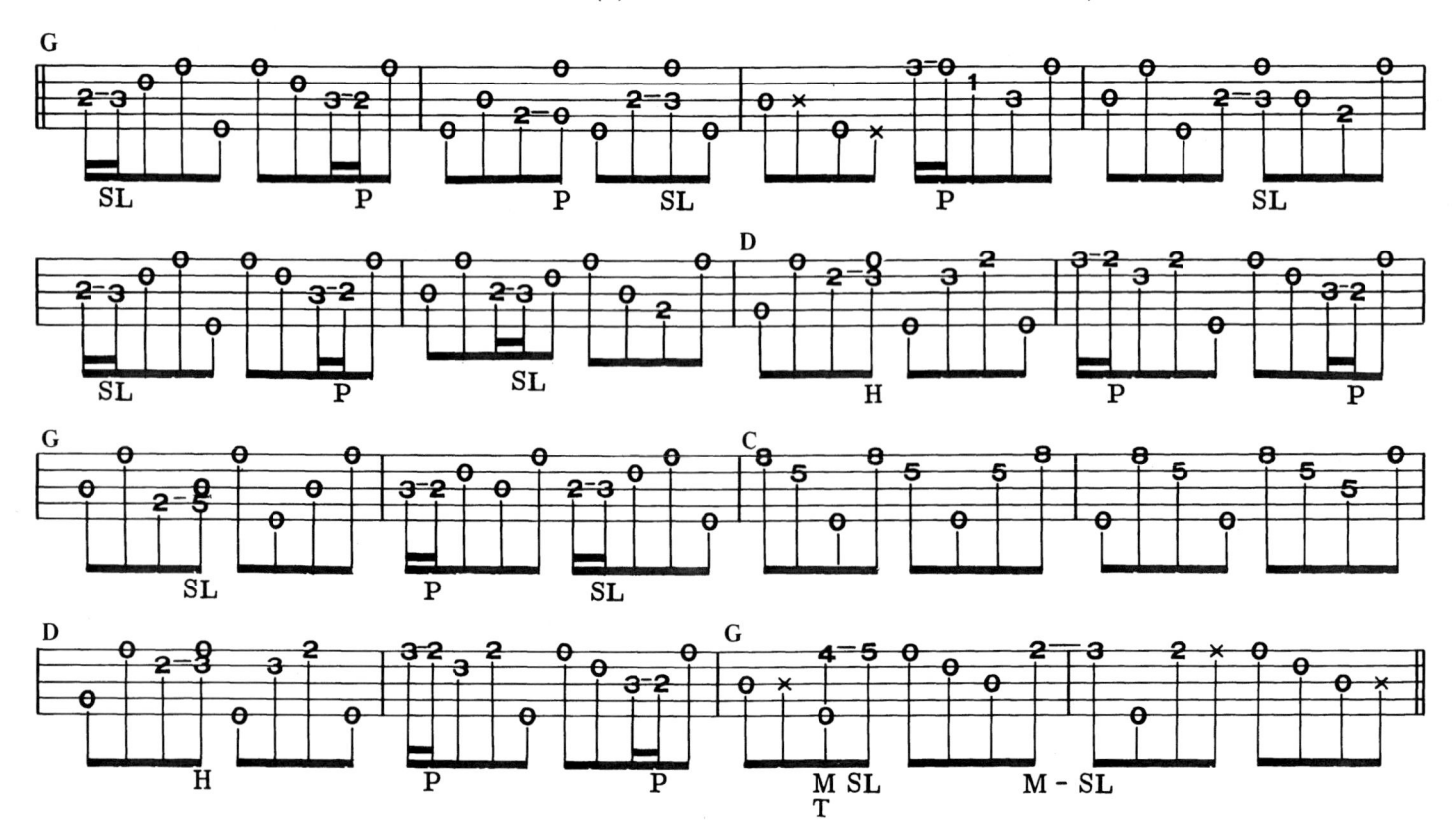

III. <u>SUBSTITUTING</u> <u>DIFFERENT</u> <u>ADVANCED</u> <u>LICKS</u> for those used in II:
(Remember that <u>each lick must be used only for a specifc chord</u>.)

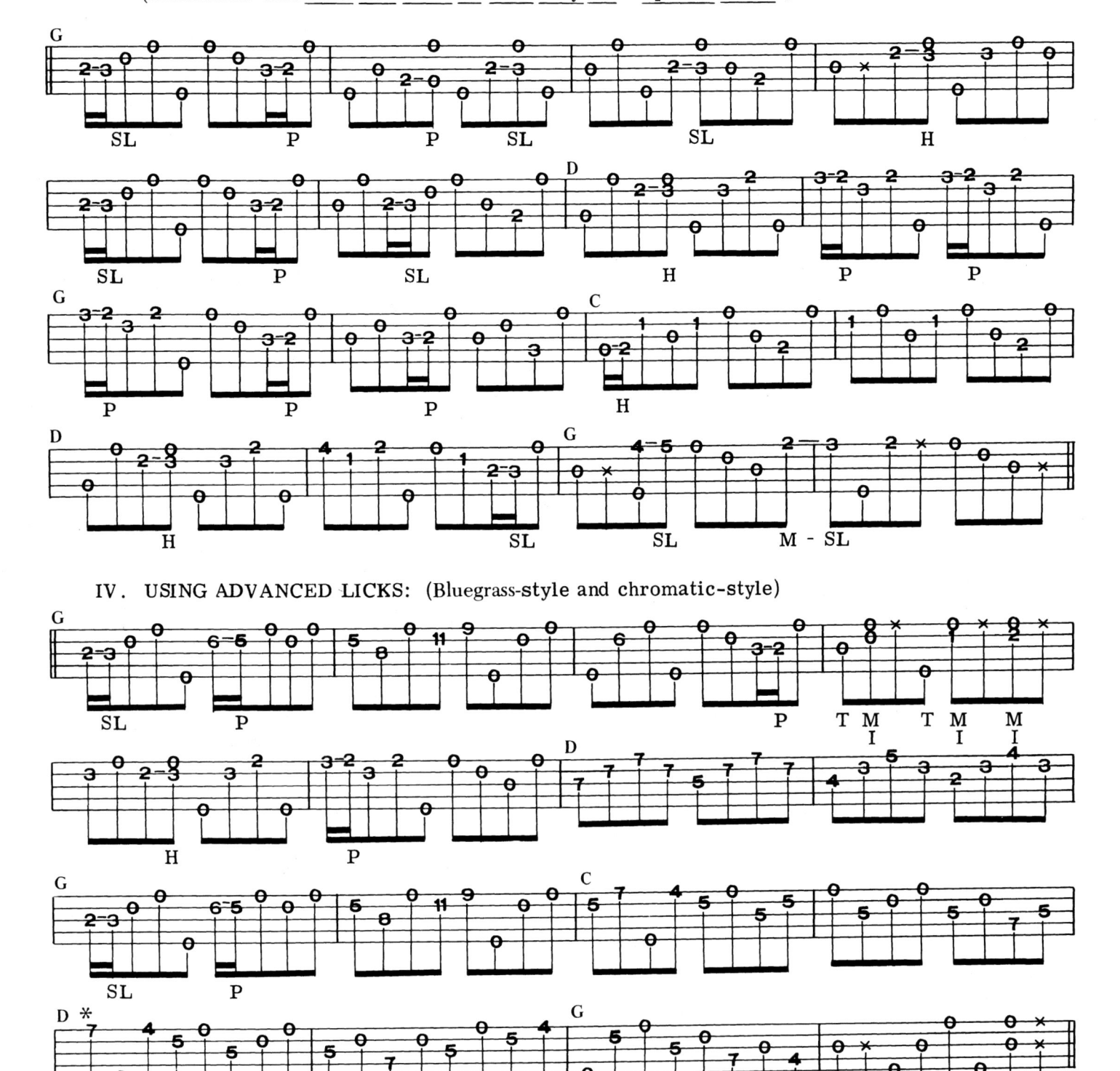

IV. USING ADVANCED LICKS: (Bluegrass-style and chromatic-style)

FOR PRACTICE: Substitute the following ending lick for the final D chord in the above arrangement (IV):

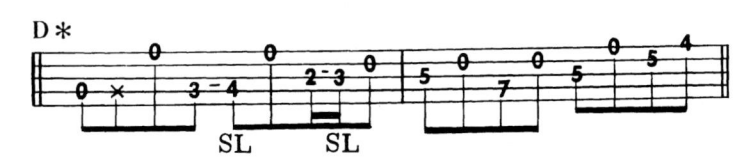

GOIN' DOWN THAT ROAD FEELIN' BAD
(ALSO "LONESOME ROAD BLUES")

Each of the following arrangements builds upon the Bluegrass-style arrangements presented earlier in this book. (See pp. 28, 29).

I. ADDING ADVANCED LICKS for the PAUSES and ENDING LICKS ONLY:

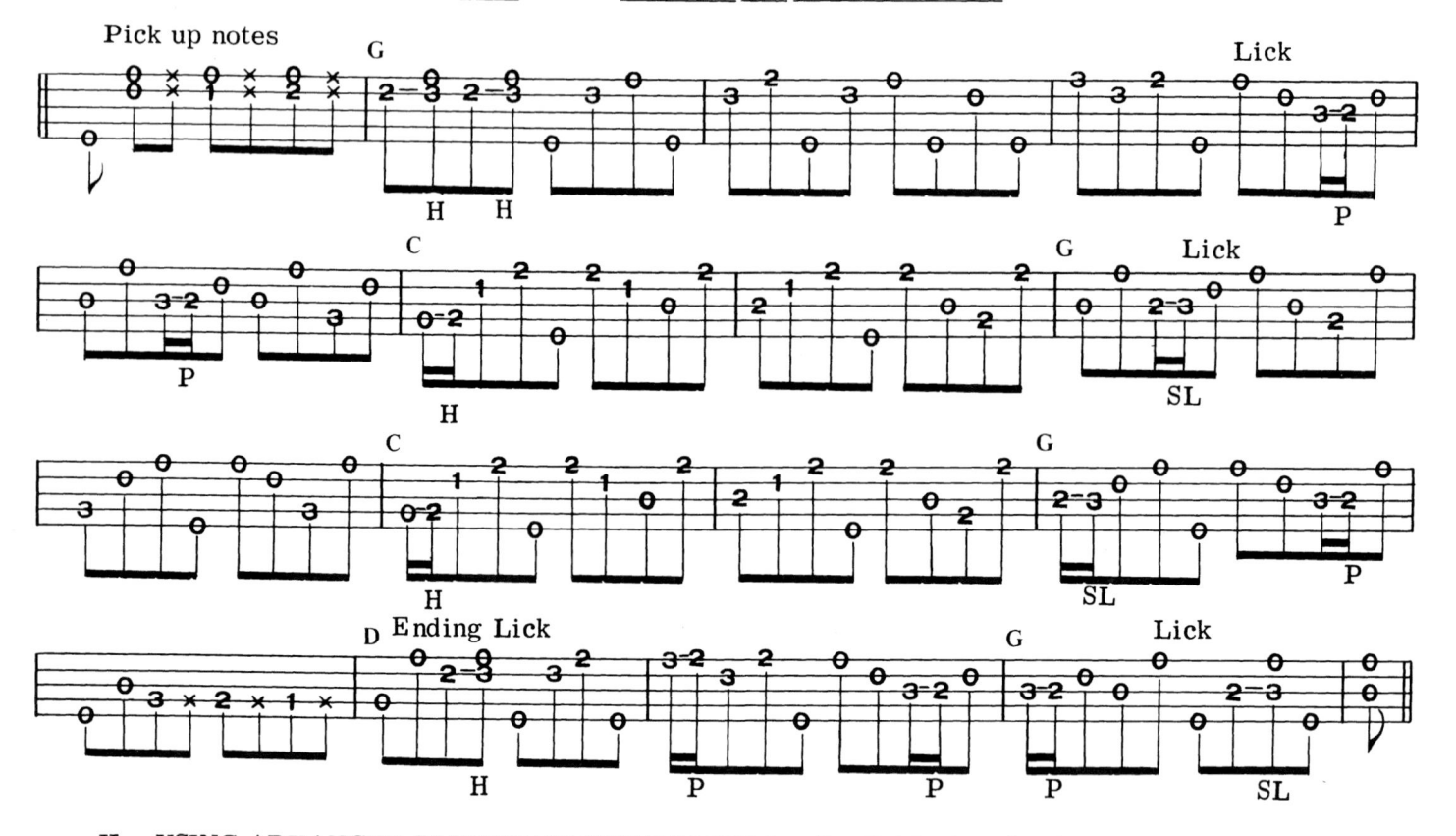

II. USING ADVANCED BLUEGRASS-STYLE LICKS for the ENTIRE VARIATION:

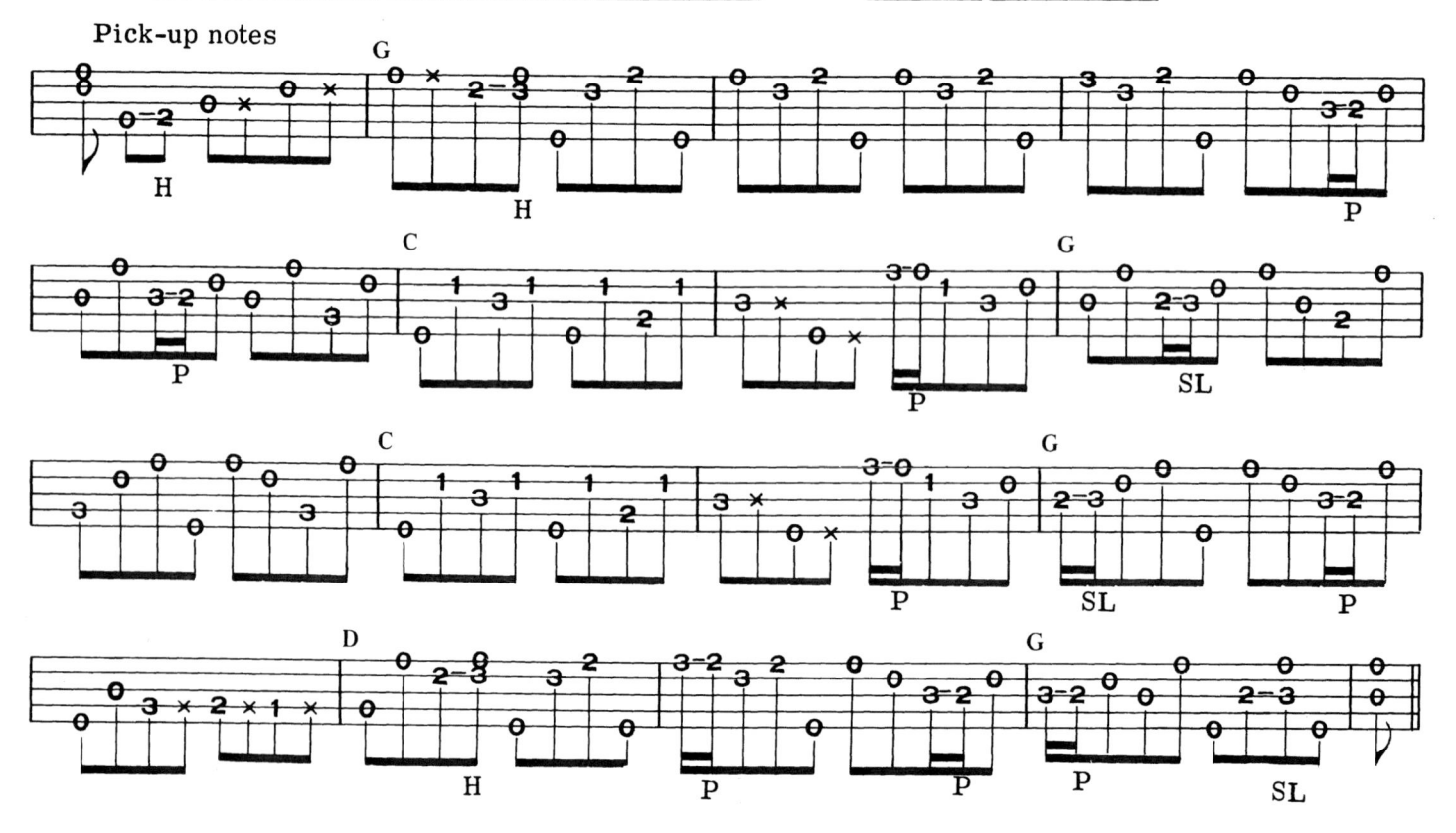

III. ADDING ADVANCED BLUEGRASS-STYLE & MELODIC-STYLE LICKS for the PAUSES and the ENDING LICKS:

(NOTE: This arrangement is the same as I, on the previous page, except that different licks are used for the pauses and for the ending.)

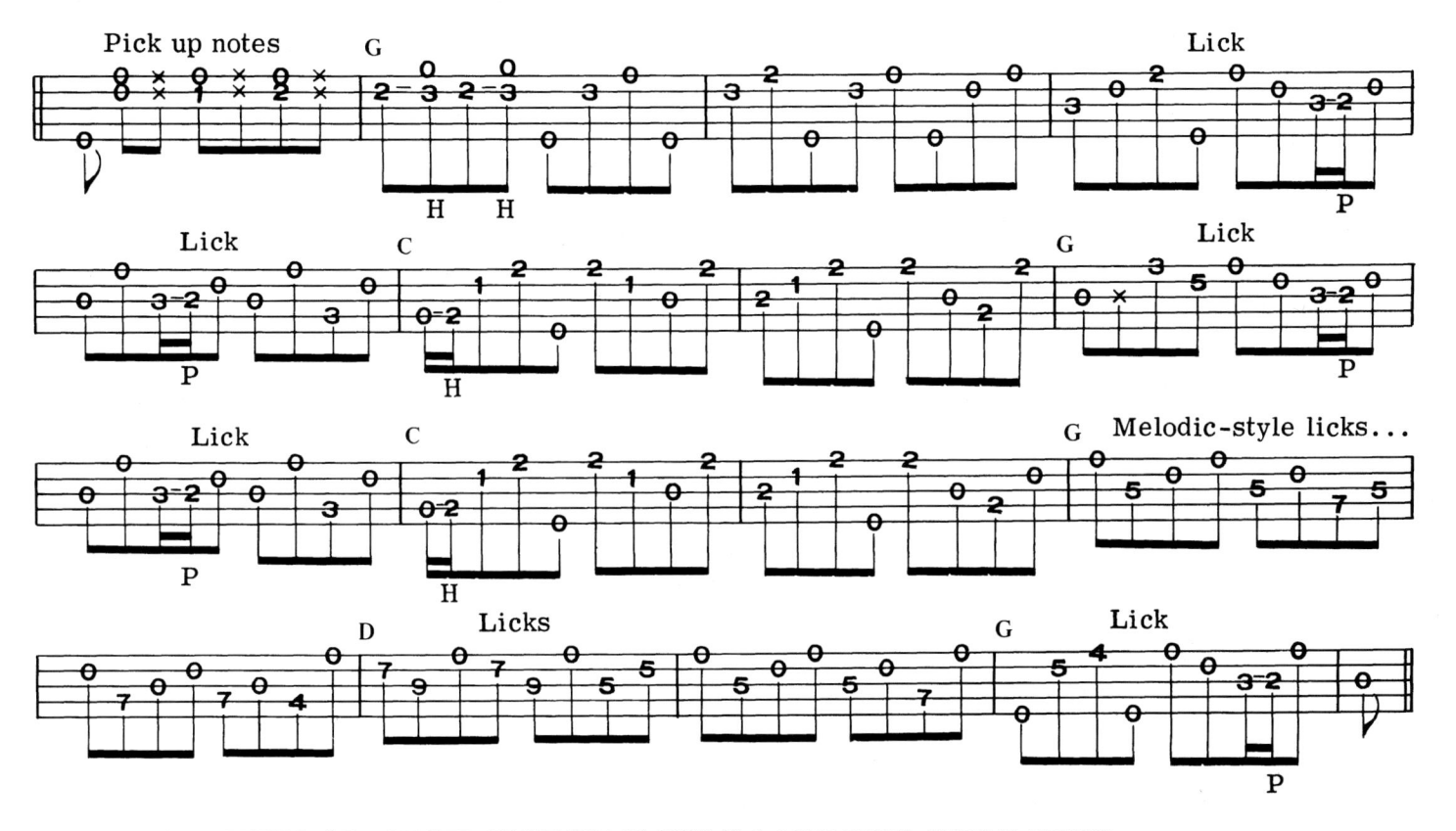

IV. USING ADVANCED BLUEGRASS-STYLE & MELODIC-STYLE LICKS for the ENTIRE VARIATION:

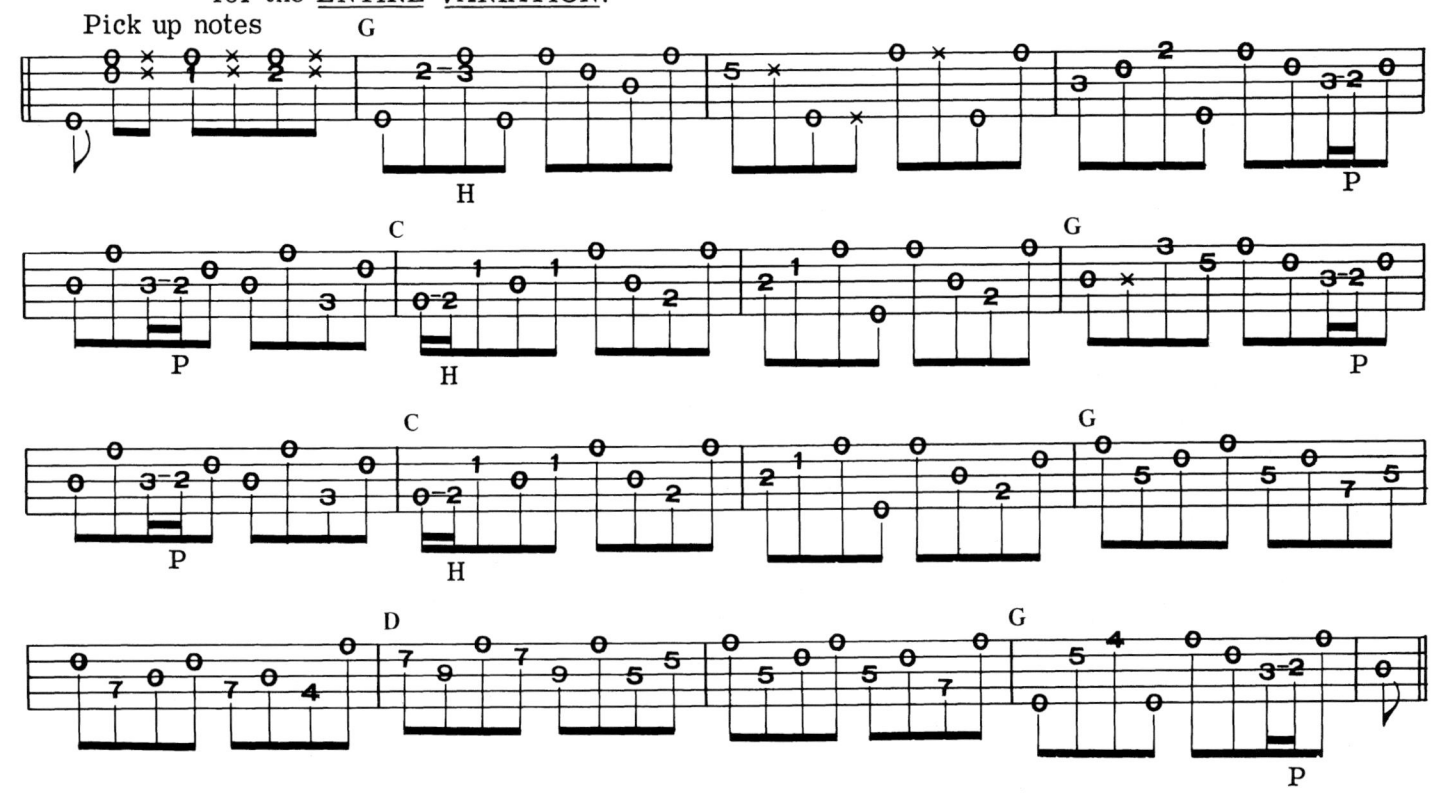

WHOA MULE

This tune is often played in the key of C, with the capo on the 5th fret.

I. MELODY and CHORDS ONLY:

Verse:
Grandma had a mu-ley cow, mu-ley when she's born,.... It took a jay bird for-ty years to fly from horn to horn.

Chorus:
Whoa Mule, Whoa, Whoa Mule I say, I ain't got time to kiss you now my mule has run a-way.

II. VARIATION USING BLUEGRASS-STYLE LICKS:

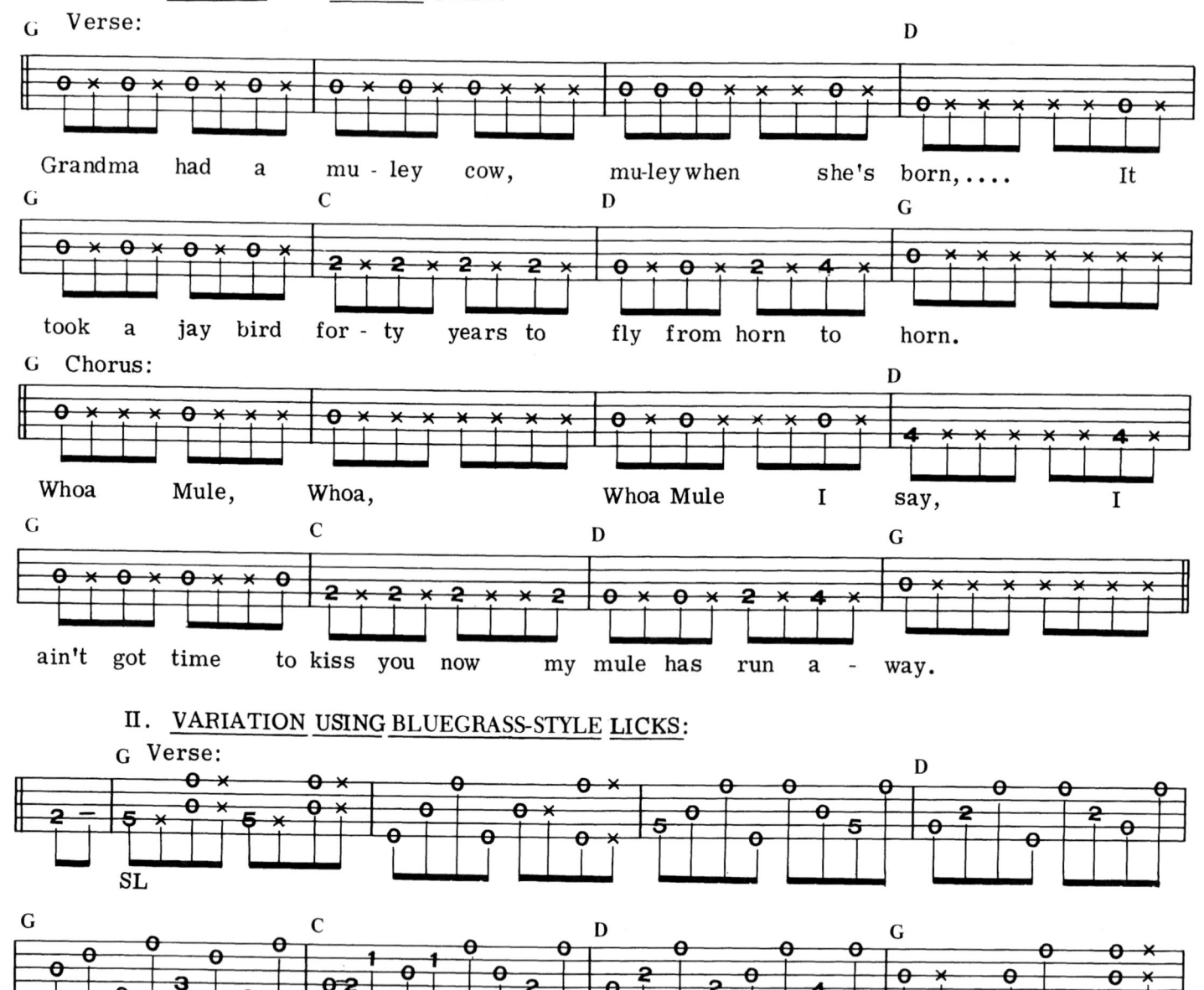

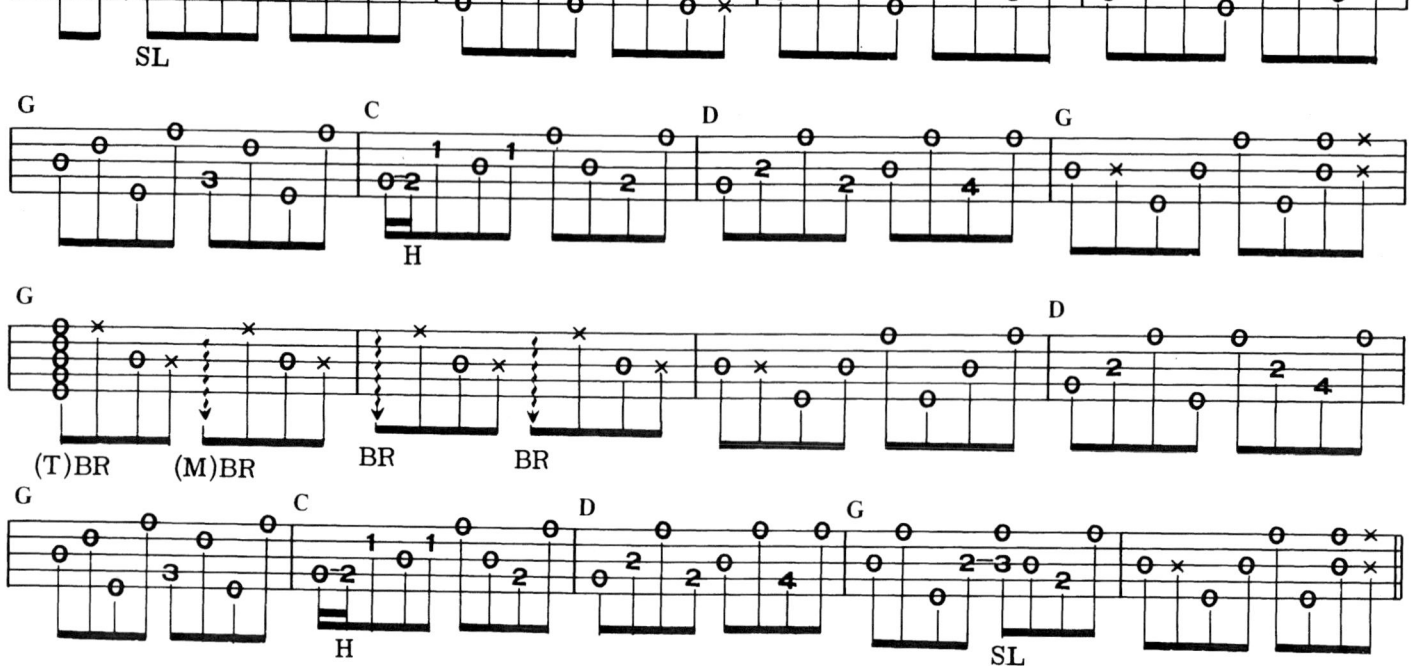

TABLATURE EXPLANATION: ↓ means to BRUSH across all 5 strings, (beginning with the 1st string), with your middle finger in the area of your banjo BETWEEN THE BRIDGE AND THE TAILPIECE! (with your right hand)

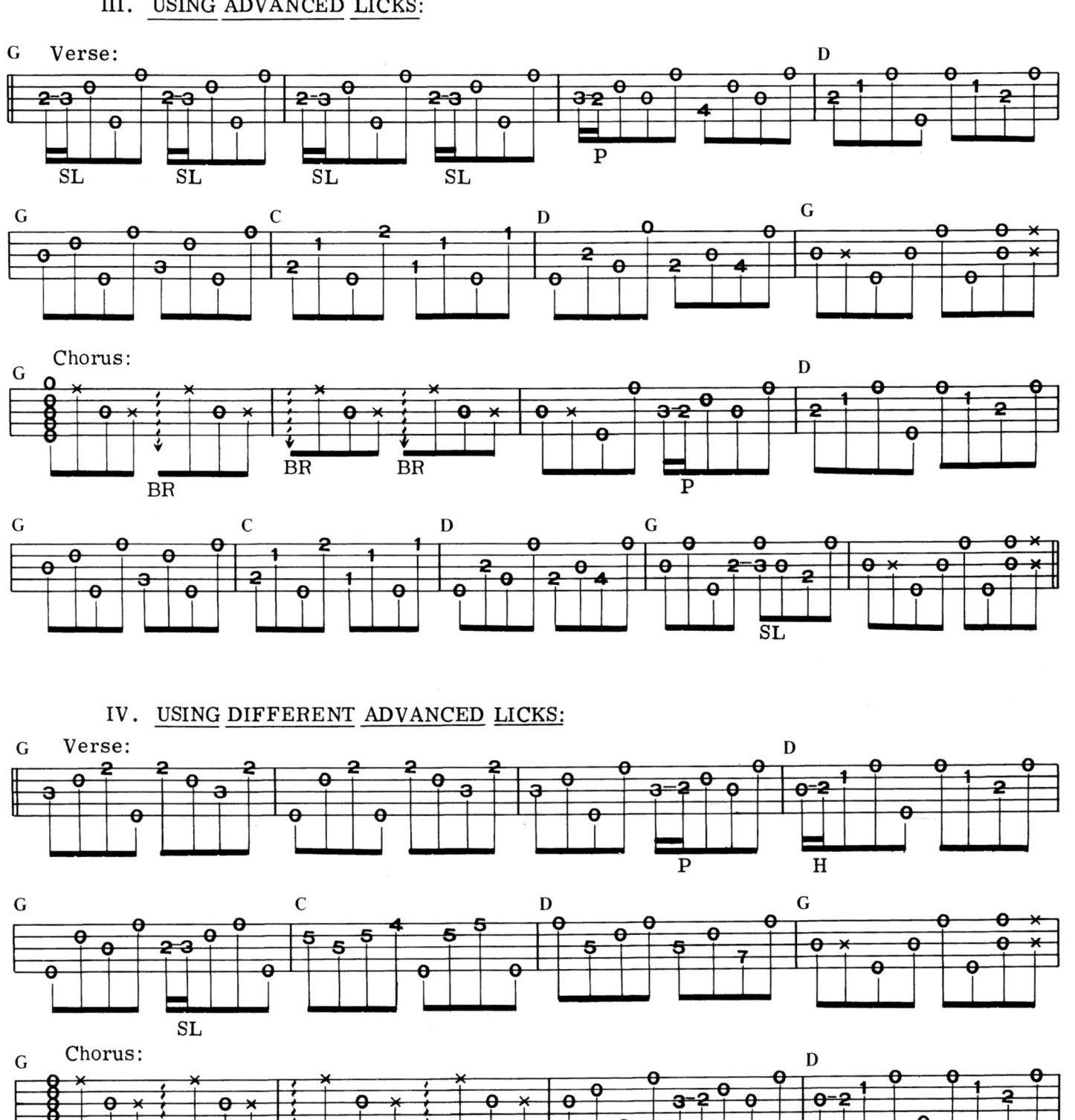

III. USING ADVANCED LICKS:

IV. USING DIFFERENT ADVANCED LICKS:

WABASH CANNONBALL

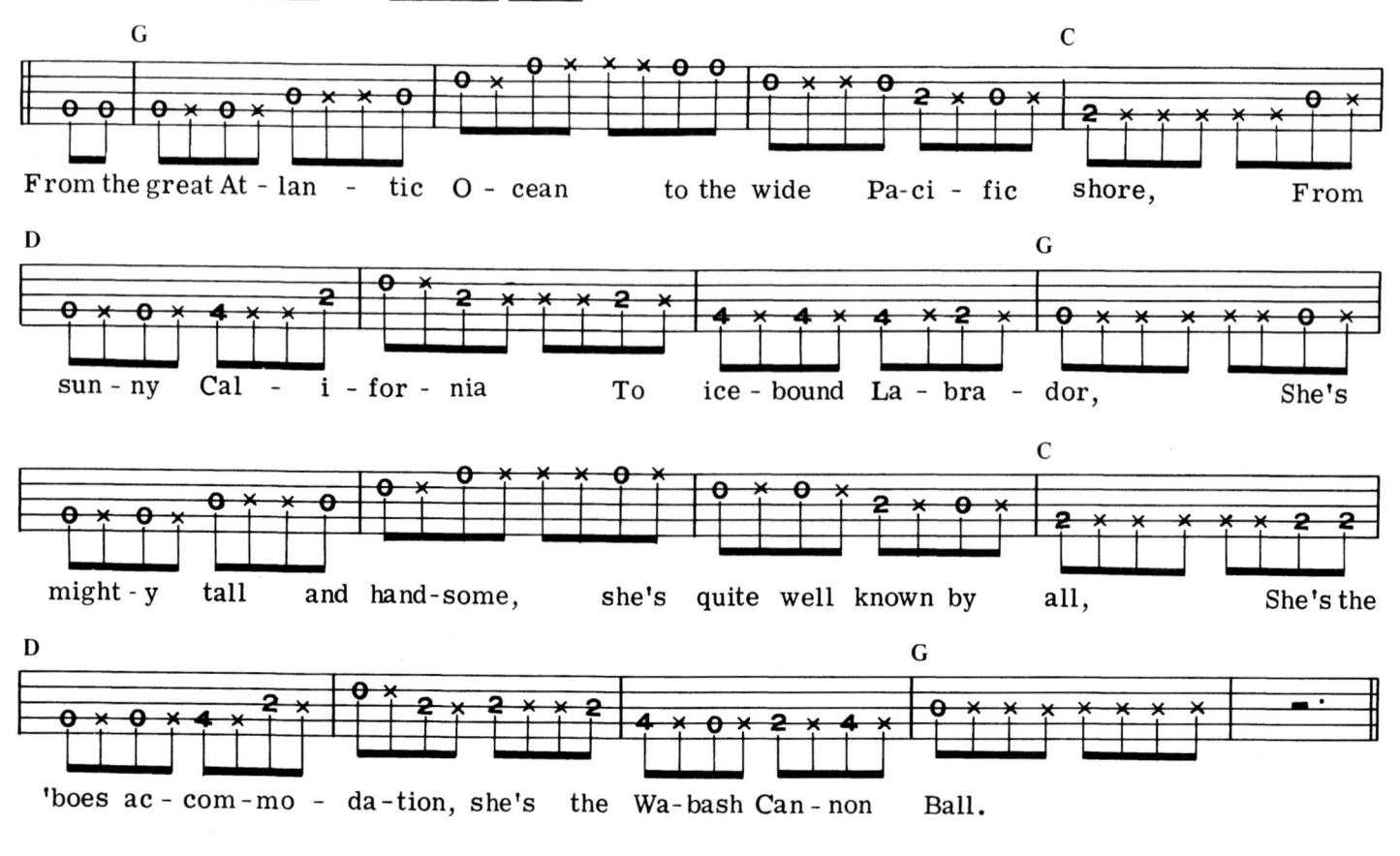

I. <u>MELODY</u> and <u>CHORDS</u> <u>ONLY</u>:

From the great At-lan-tic O-cean to the wide Pa-ci-fic shore, From sun-ny Cal-i-for-nia To ice-bound La-bra-dor, She's might-y tall and hand-some, she's quite well known by all, She's the 'boes ac-com-mo-da-tion, she's the Wa-bash Can-non Ball.

II. <u>BLUEGRASS-STYLE</u> ARRANGEMENT USING <u>ADVANCED LICKS</u>:

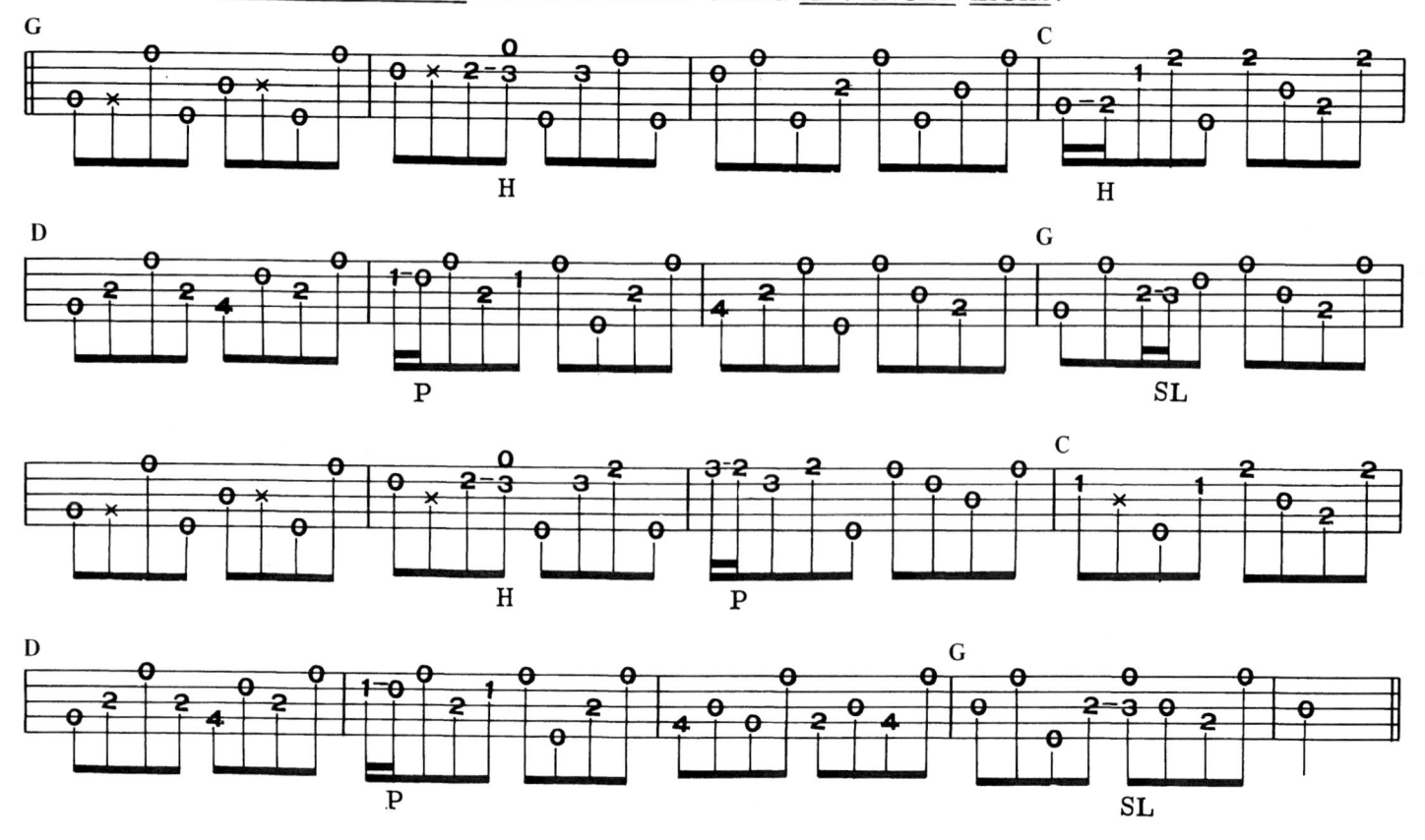

III. USING ADVANCED LICKS: (Bluegrass-style and melodic)

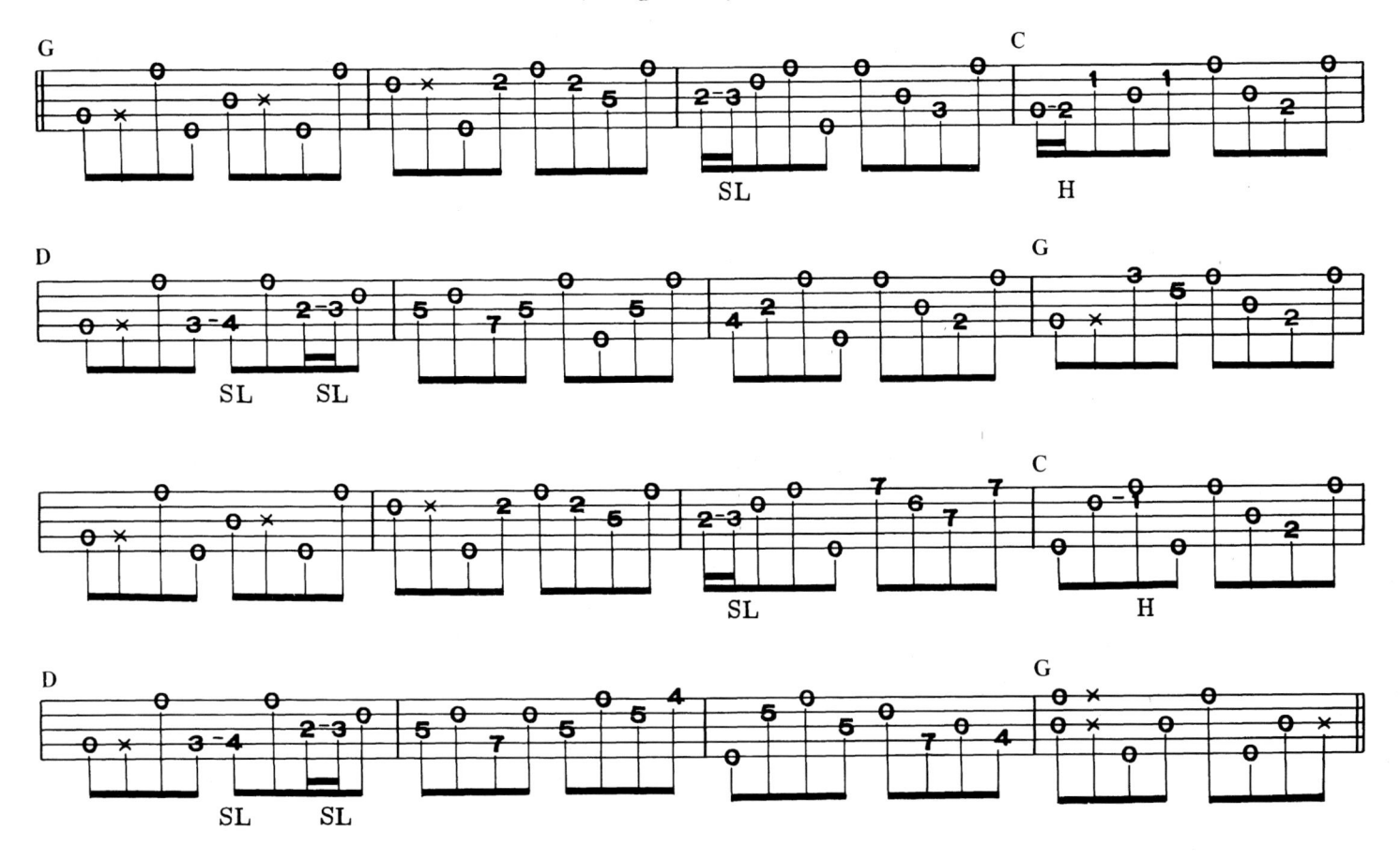

FOR PRACTICE: Try to reverse the arranging process--locate the advanced licks, and substitute standard licks.

Also, try to replace some of these licks with other advanced licks. Try to create some of your own advanced licks.

REMEMBER: The more you play with licks and chords, the easier it becomes to work out songs.

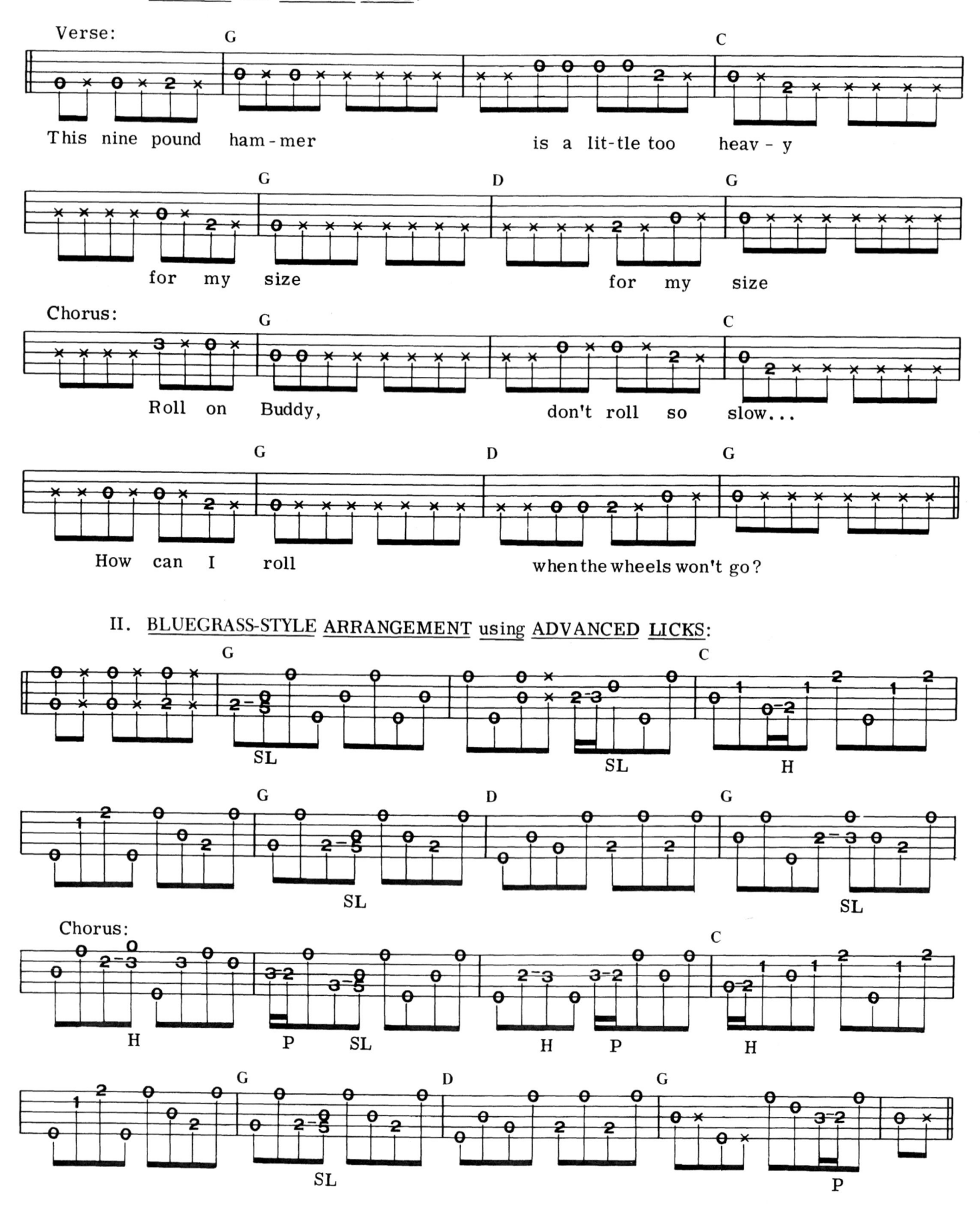

NINE POUND HAMMER

I. <u>MELODY</u> and <u>CHORDS</u> <u>ONLY</u>:

Verse:
This nine pound ham-mer is a lit-tle too heav-y
for my size for my size

Chorus:
Roll on Buddy, don't roll so slow...
How can I roll when the wheels won't go?

II. <u>BLUEGRASS-STYLE</u> <u>ARRANGEMENT</u> using <u>ADVANCED LICKS</u>:

Chorus:

88

III. <u>USING</u> <u>ADVANCED</u> <u>LICKS</u>: The chorus part of the following arrangement uses the technique of repeated tones. This is very effective for a second or third variation, and is a technique to which listeners frequently respond with enthusiasm. The key to the technique of playing repeated tones, is to play them long enough for the listener to wonder if you can get out of them smoothly, but not so long that the listener becomes bored.

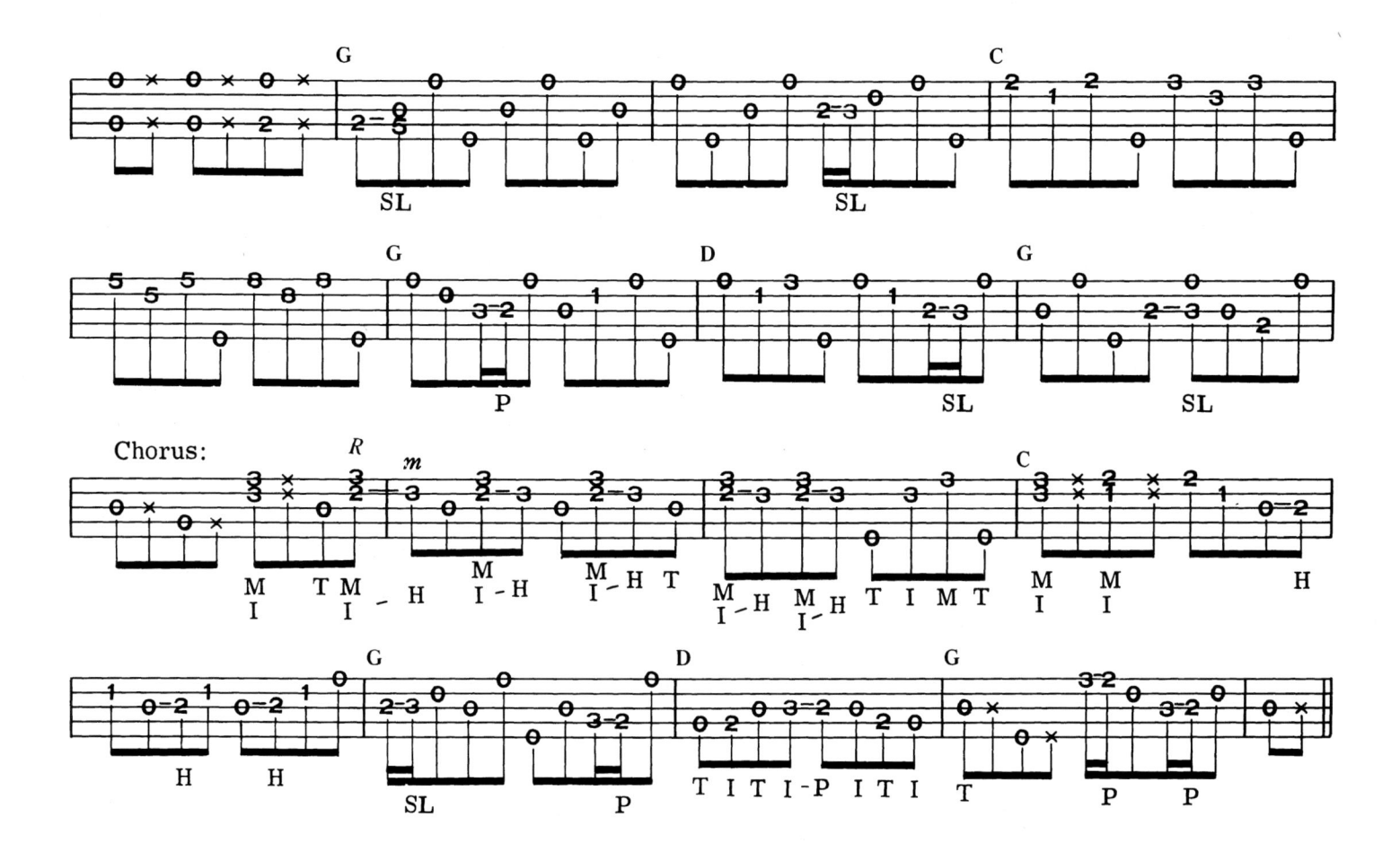

TRAIN 45

This song is usually played in the key of B, with the capo placed on the 4th fret of the banjo.

I. <u>MELODY</u> and <u>CHORDS ONLY</u>:

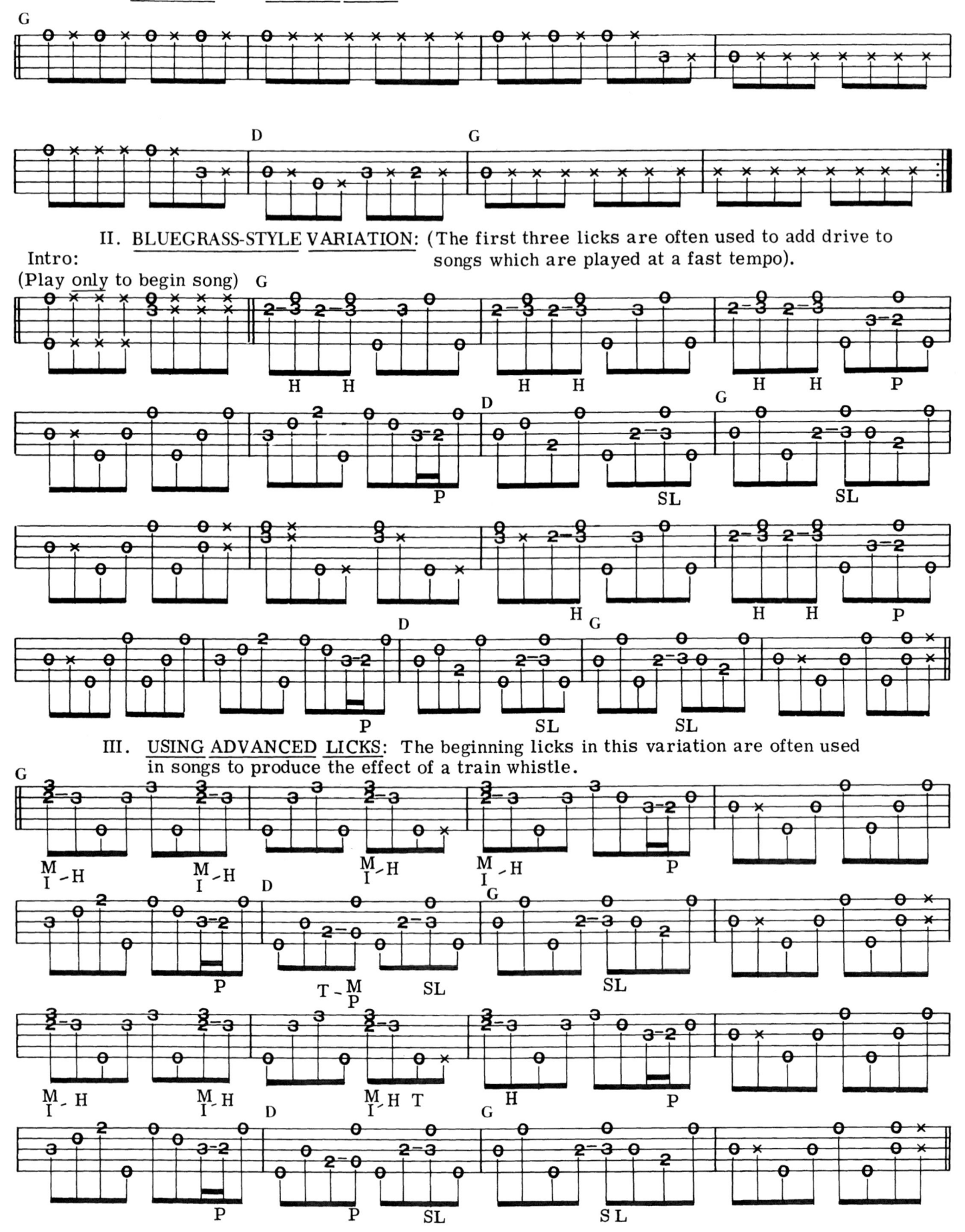

II. <u>BLUEGRASS-STYLE VARIATION</u>: (The first three licks are often used to add drive to songs which are played at a fast tempo).

Intro: (Play only to begin song)

III. <u>USING ADVANCED LICKS</u>: The beginning licks in this variation are often used in songs to produce the effect of a train whistle.

IV. <u>USING</u> <u>ADVANCED BLUEGRASS-STYLE</u> and <u>CHROMATIC-STYLE LICKS</u>:
(Notice that the first two measures of this variation are simply Forward-Reverse Roll Patterns.)

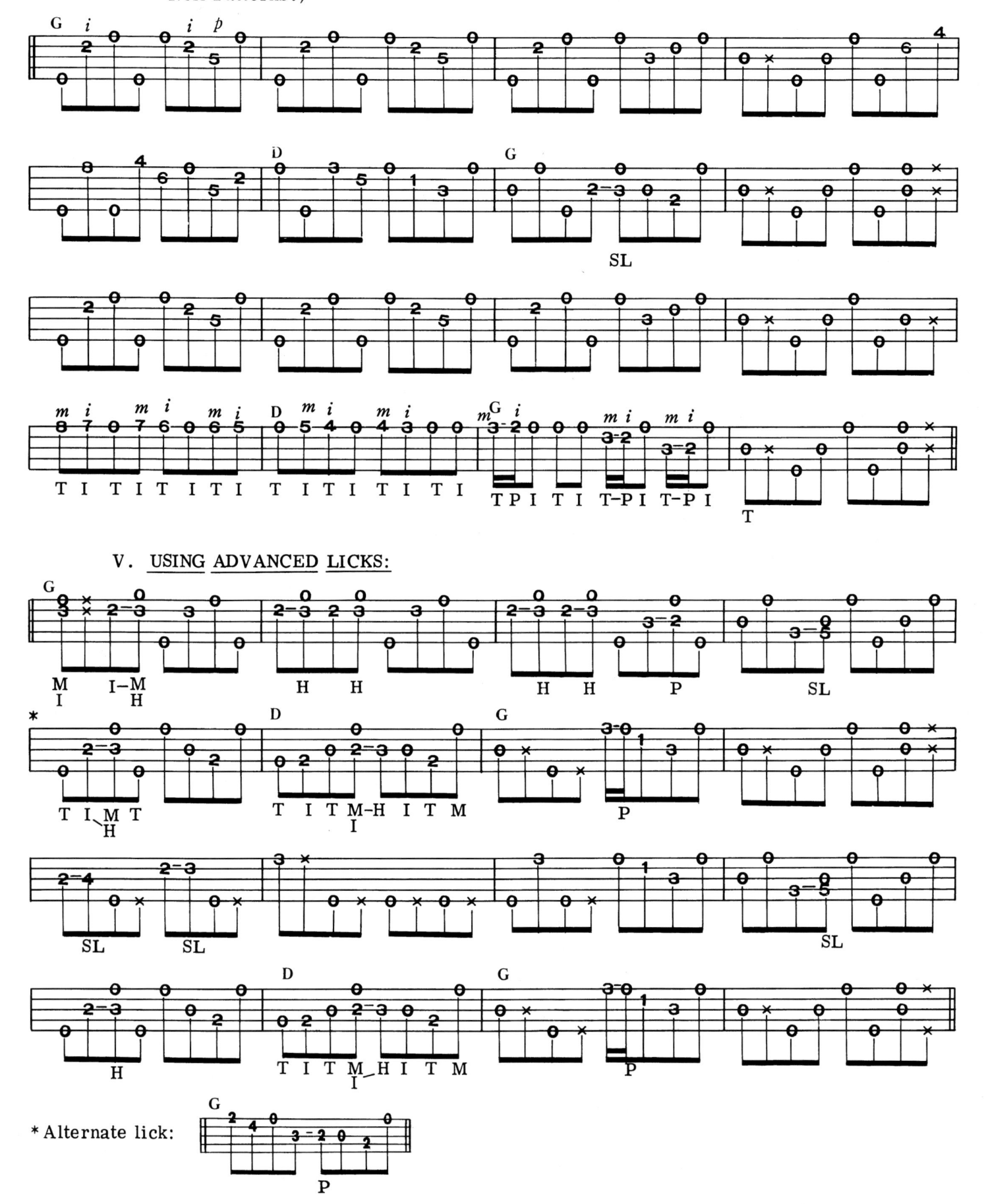

V. <u>USING</u> <u>ADVANCED LICKS</u>:

*Alternate lick:

SALT RIVER

This tune is frequently played in the key of A, with the capo on the 2nd fret.

I. <u>MELODY</u> and <u>CHORDS ONLY</u>:

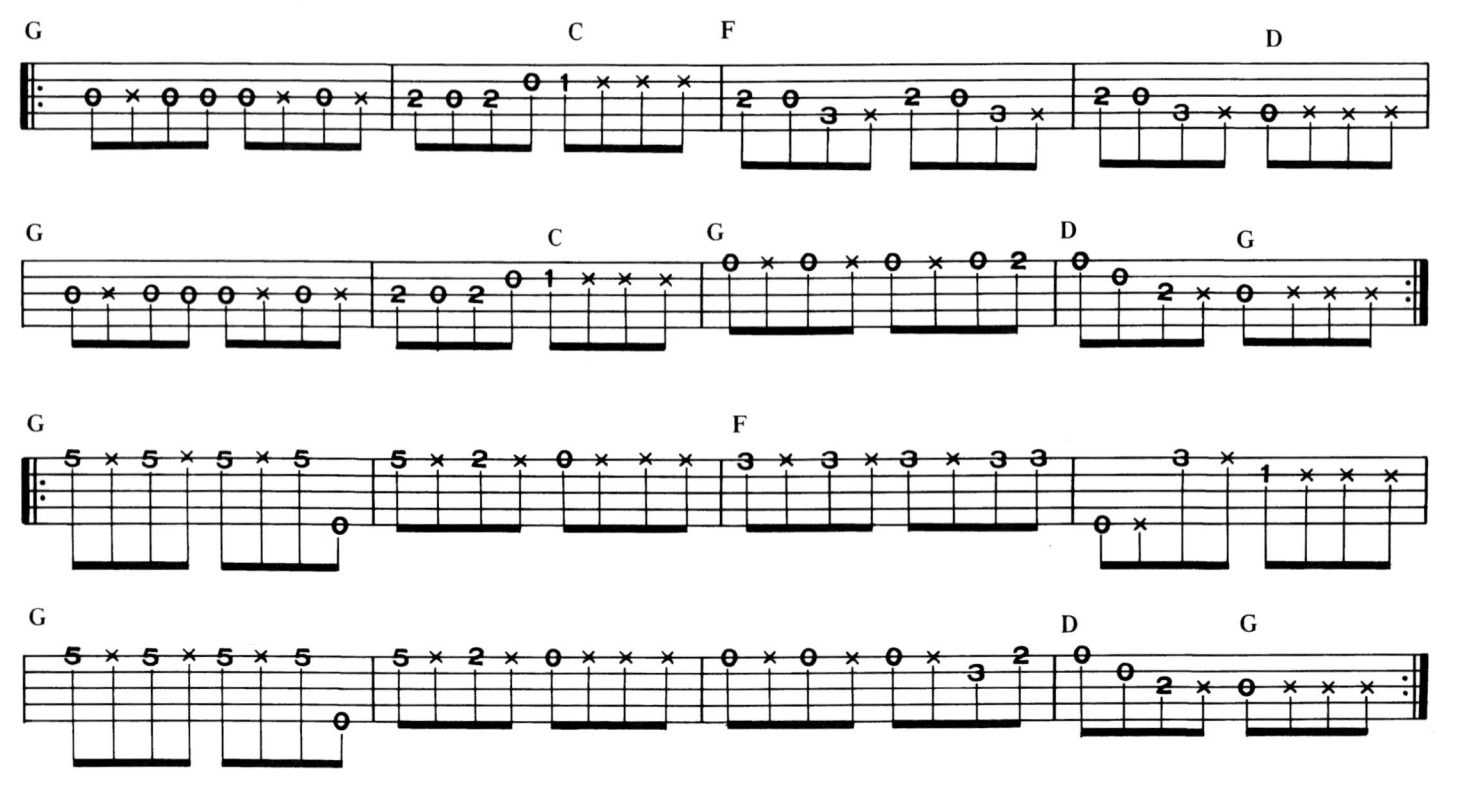

II. <u>BLUEGRASS-STYLE ARRANGEMENT</u>: This arrangement involves:
1.) Picking the <u>same</u> string several times in a row.
(Alternate the right thumb and index finger.)
2.) The use of <u>triplets</u>: Play three notes in the same amount of time two eighth notes are normally played.

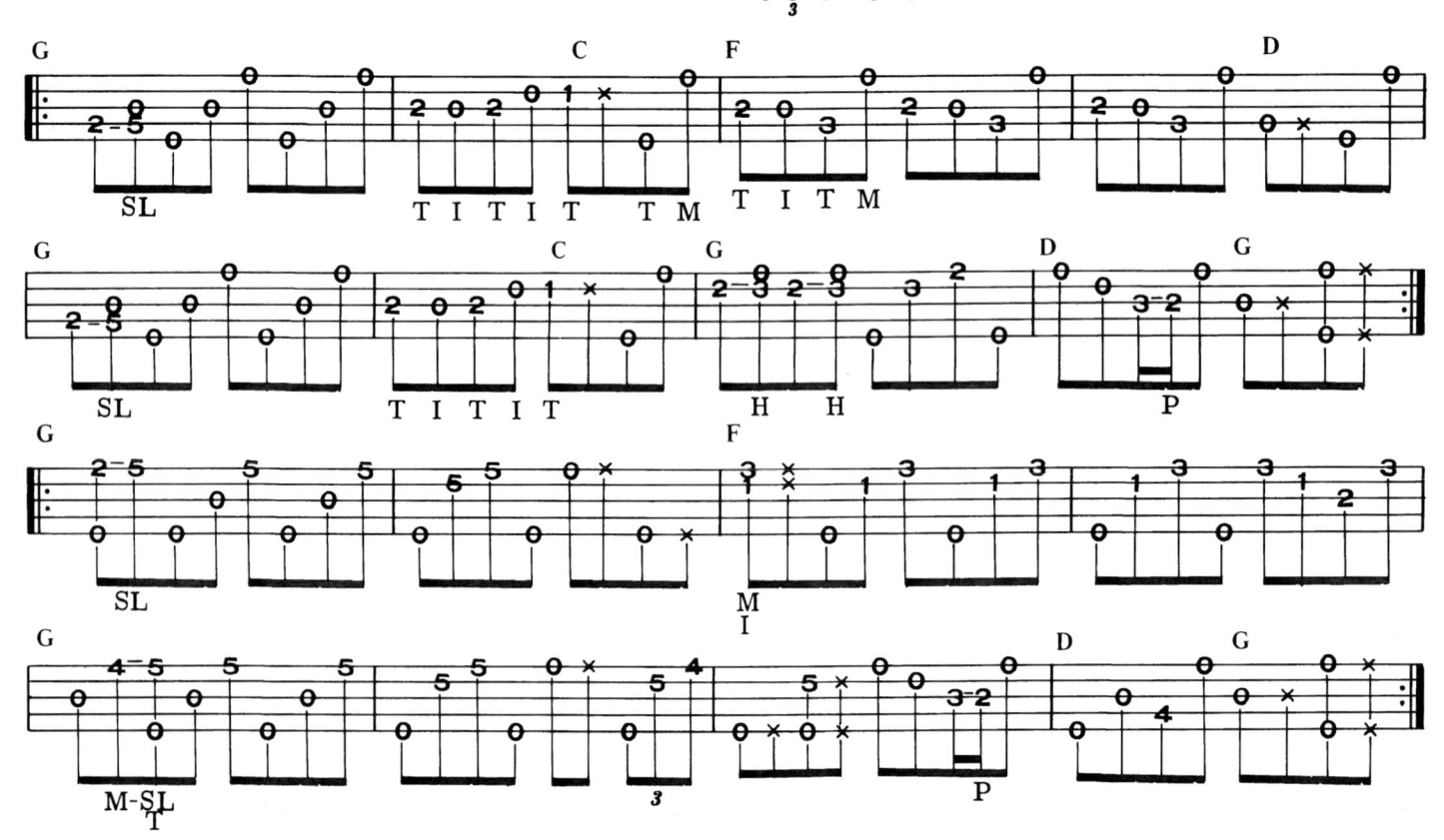

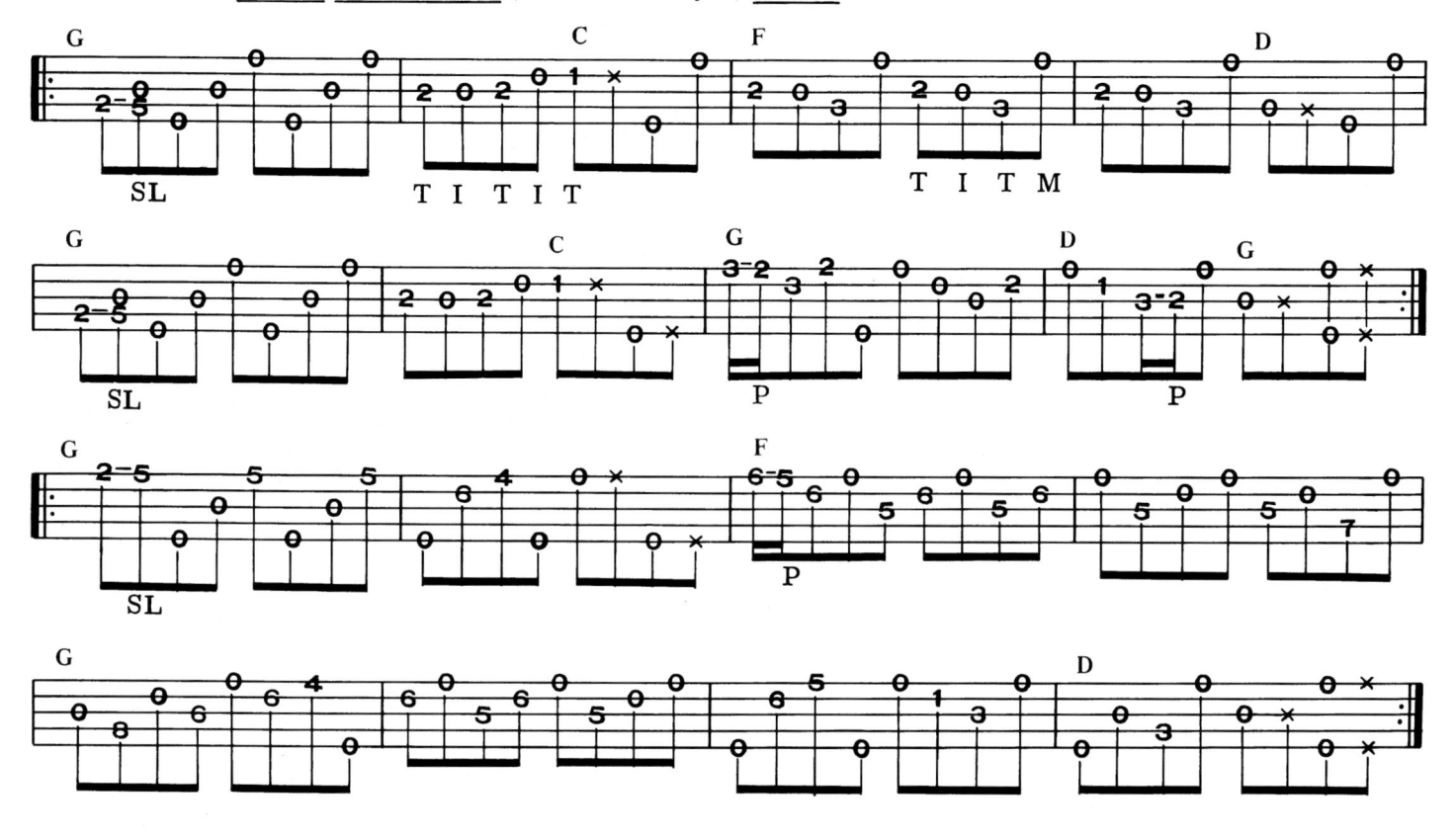

III. **USING ADVANCED** (chromatic-style) **LICKS:**

HAMILTON COUNTY BREAKDOWN

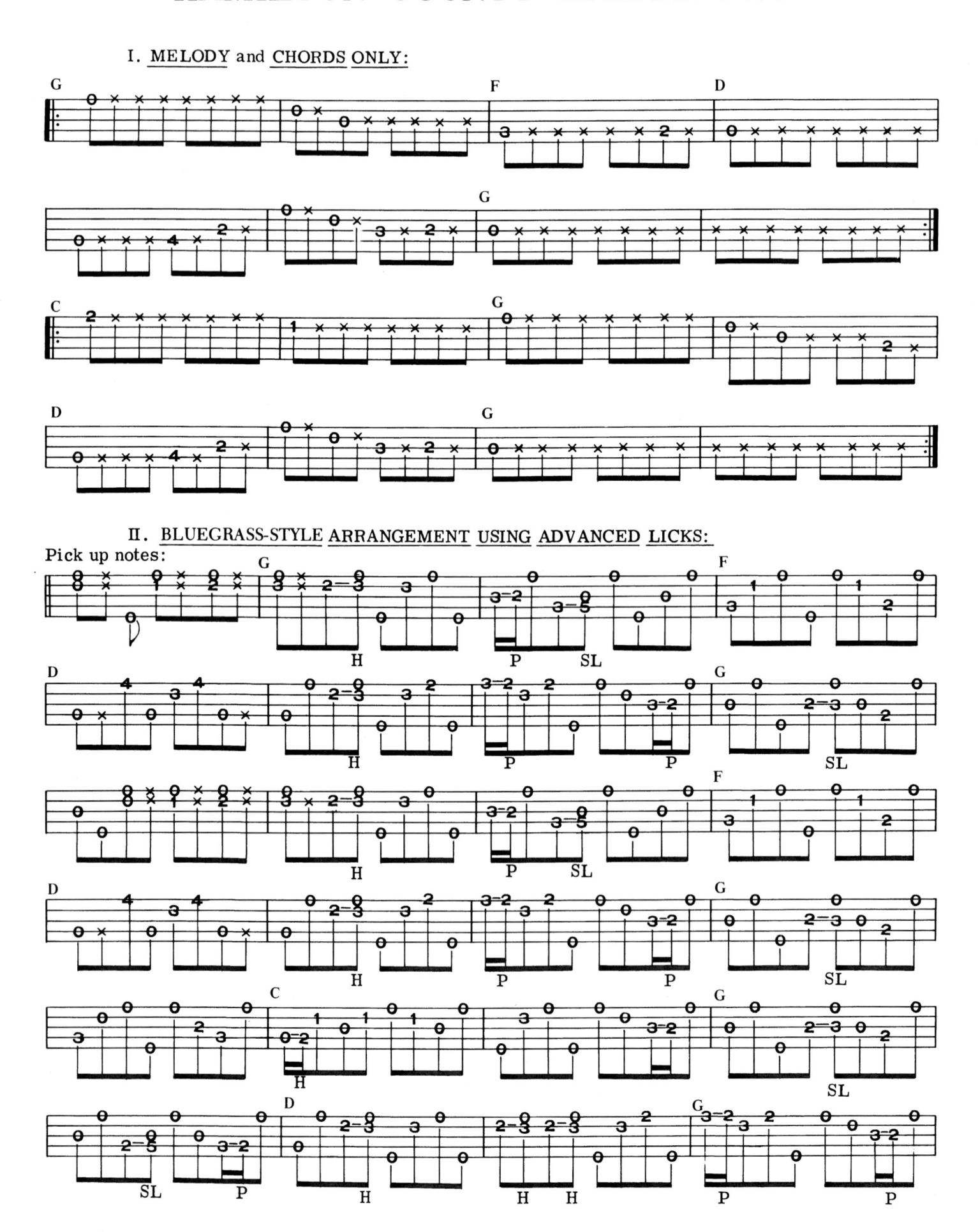

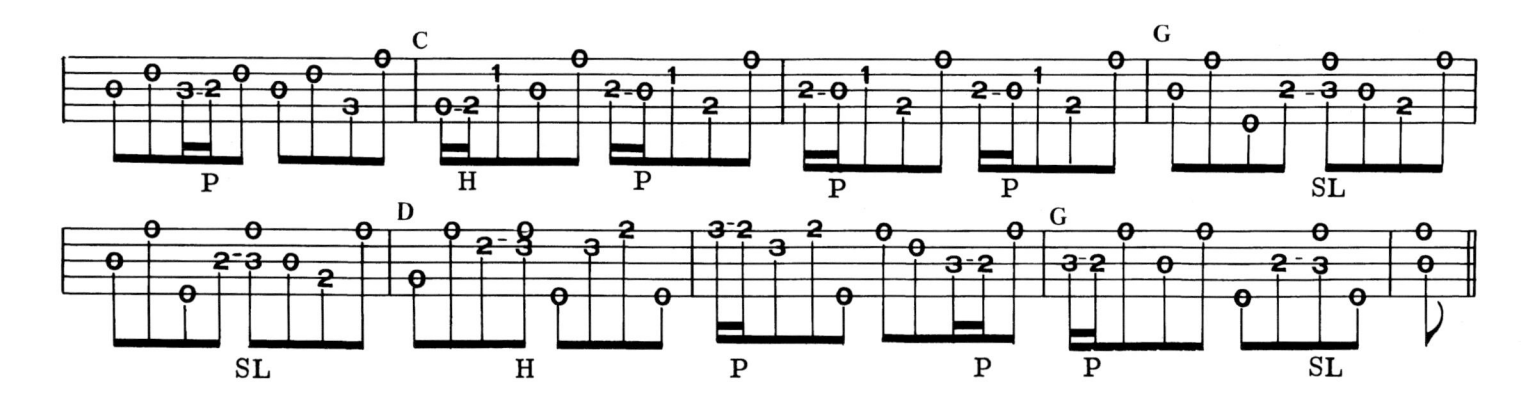

III. <u>USING ADVANCED LICKS:</u> (Bluegrass-style and chromatic style)

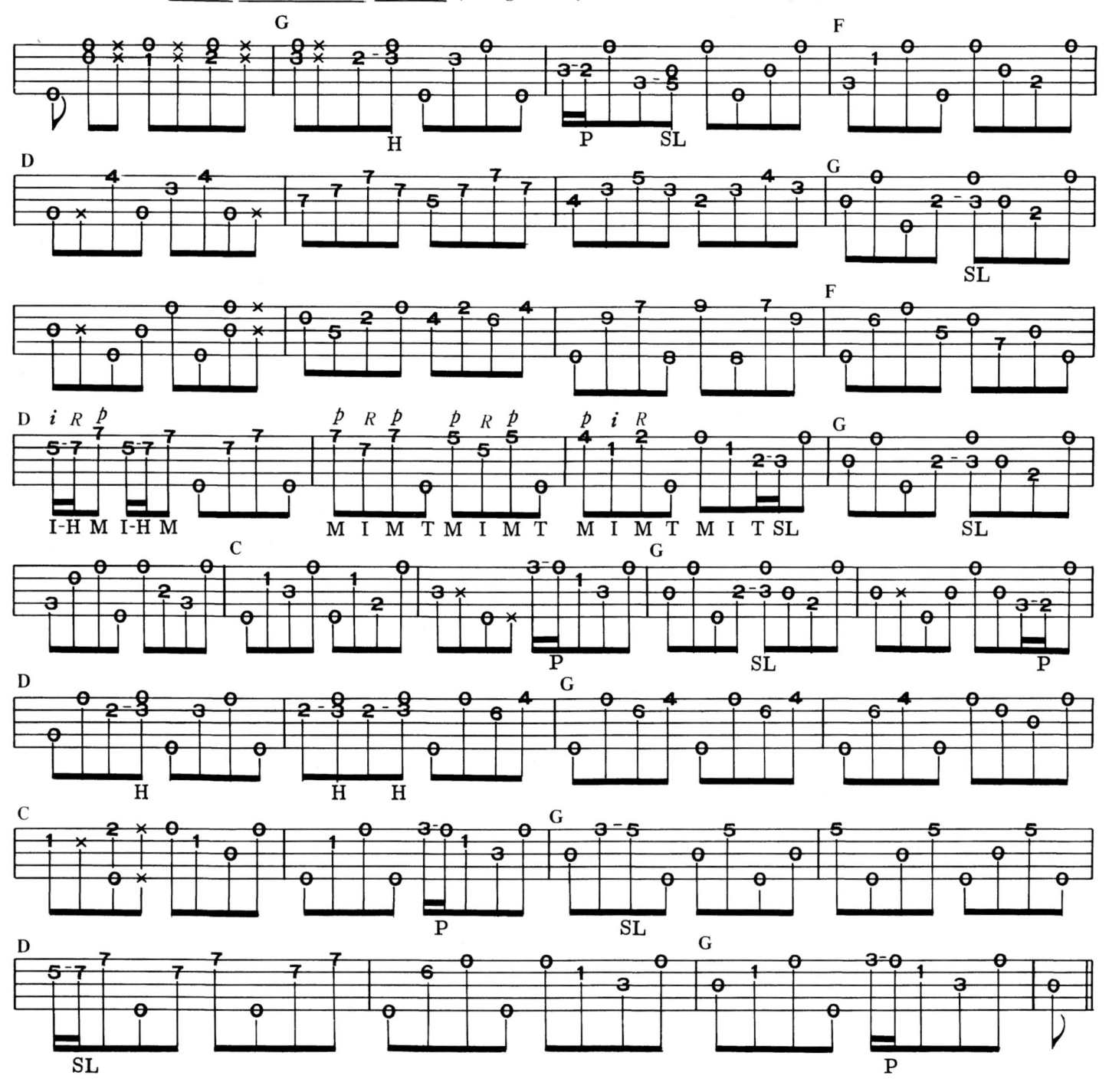

UNDER THE DOUBLE EAGLE
–MELODY ONLY–

(Uses standard G tuning)

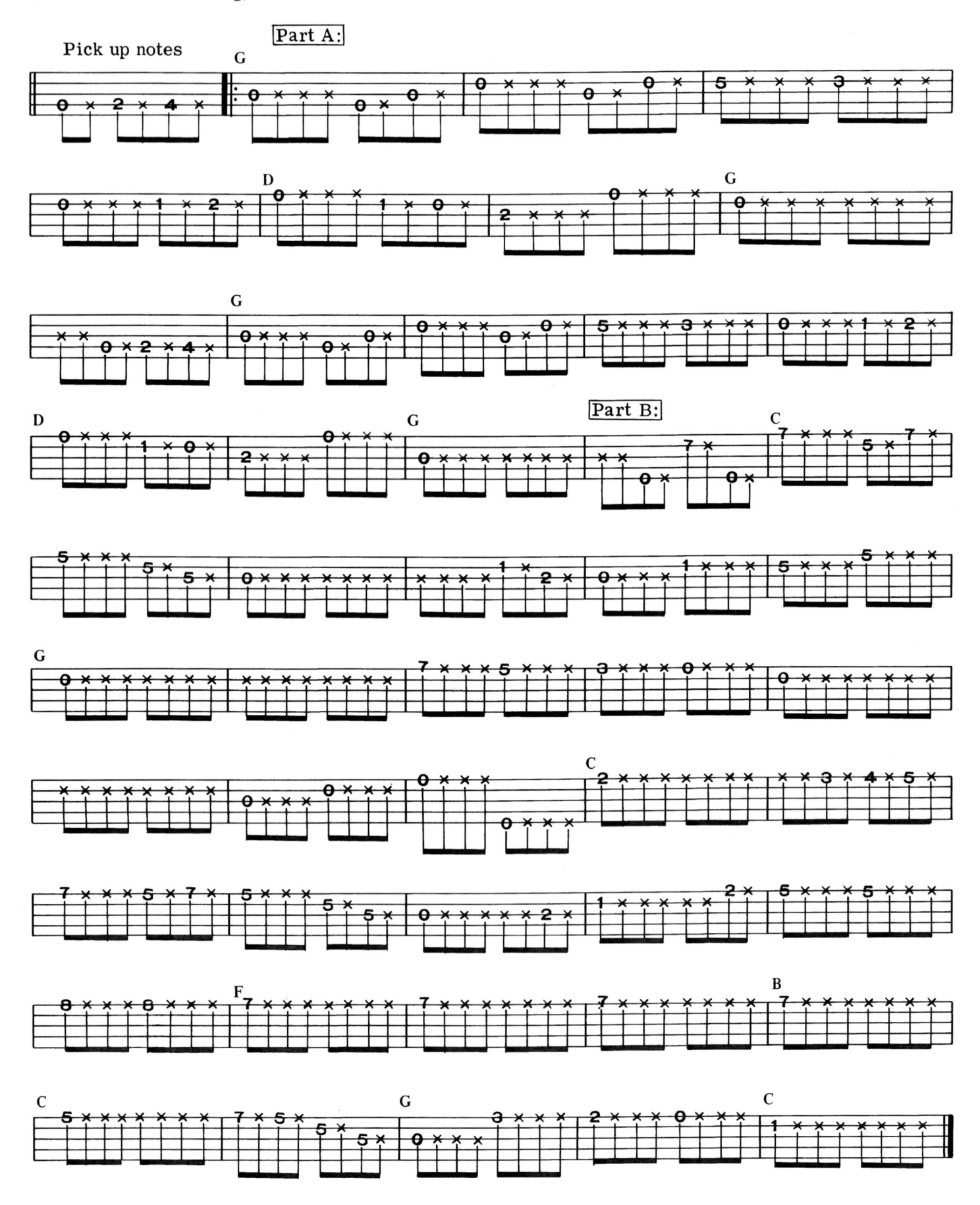

This song is usually played with the capo on the 5th fret of the banjo. (Part A is played in the key of C, and part B is played in the key of F.)

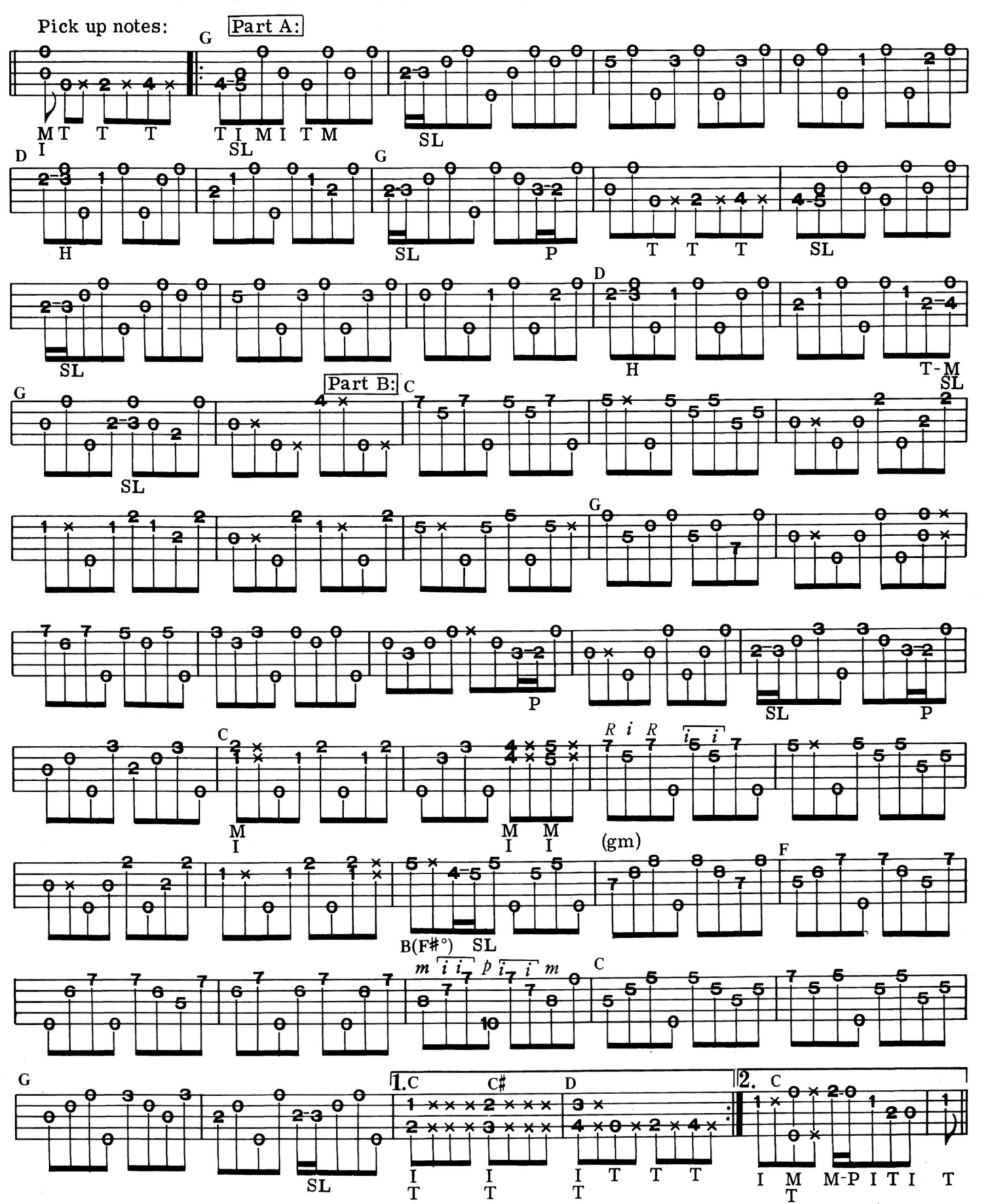

BUILDING ENDINGS

The final step to arranging a song is to provide an effective ending which can be played with the last variation of the song. (Even in a band situation, when another instrument might play the final lead break, or when a vocalist sings the final chorus, the banjo player is often called upon to provide the ending.)

The function of an ending is to provide a firm impression of finality, (usually by emphasizing the I chord). Endings which are played on the banjo, can be divided into two categories: 1.) Tag Endings -- which are added to the basic structure of the song, (also called a Coda); and 2.) Two measure Endings -- which are played for the last chord of the song, in the place of the licks which are normally played for that chord.

The examples on the following pages are commonly used by many banjo players to end songs which are played in the key of G. (Many of these can also easily be transposed for use with other keys.)

NOTE: The "BRUSH" is a technique which is frequently used with an ending, either at the beginning of the warning part to notify the listener that the song is about to end, or for the last chord of the B Part, to emphasize the final chord of the song. In the tablature:

BR ↓ means to brush across all of the strings with the right Thumb, toward the floor, from the 5th string through the 1st string.

BR ↑ means to brush across all of the strings with the right Middle and Index fingers (as a unit), toward the ceiling, from the 1st string through the 5th string. This brush technique is used primarily for the final chord. It is more effective if the right hand is placed near the area of the banjo where the fingerboard joins the drum, or head. (I generally brush the strings over the fingerboard, in the area around the 17th fret). This results in a mellow sound, as opposed to a harsh sound.

TAG ENDINGS

A Tag Ending, or Coda, is added to the end of a song, after the licks for the last chord have been played. This type of ending is usually used to end instrumental songs, (i.e. Train 45, Hamilton County Breakdown), but is rarely used to end vocals. (For vocals, see Two Measure Endings.)

A Tag Ending normally consists of two parts:

Part A: serves as a warning that the song is about to end. This part usually equals two measures of tablature, and begins and ends on the I chord, (i.e. G in key of G).

Part B: strongly emphasizes the feeling of finality, generally through the use of the V chord to the I chord, (D to G). This part is often referred to as the "Shave and a haircut" part, although it doesn't necessarily carry that theme. Part B usually consists of two measures of tablature, although it can also be extended.

FOR PRACTICE: Combine the Part A section of one ending with the Part B section of a different ending. (Many banjo players prefer to have a standard way of playing the warning part, (Part A), and combine it with a different B Part, depending upon the song they are playing.)

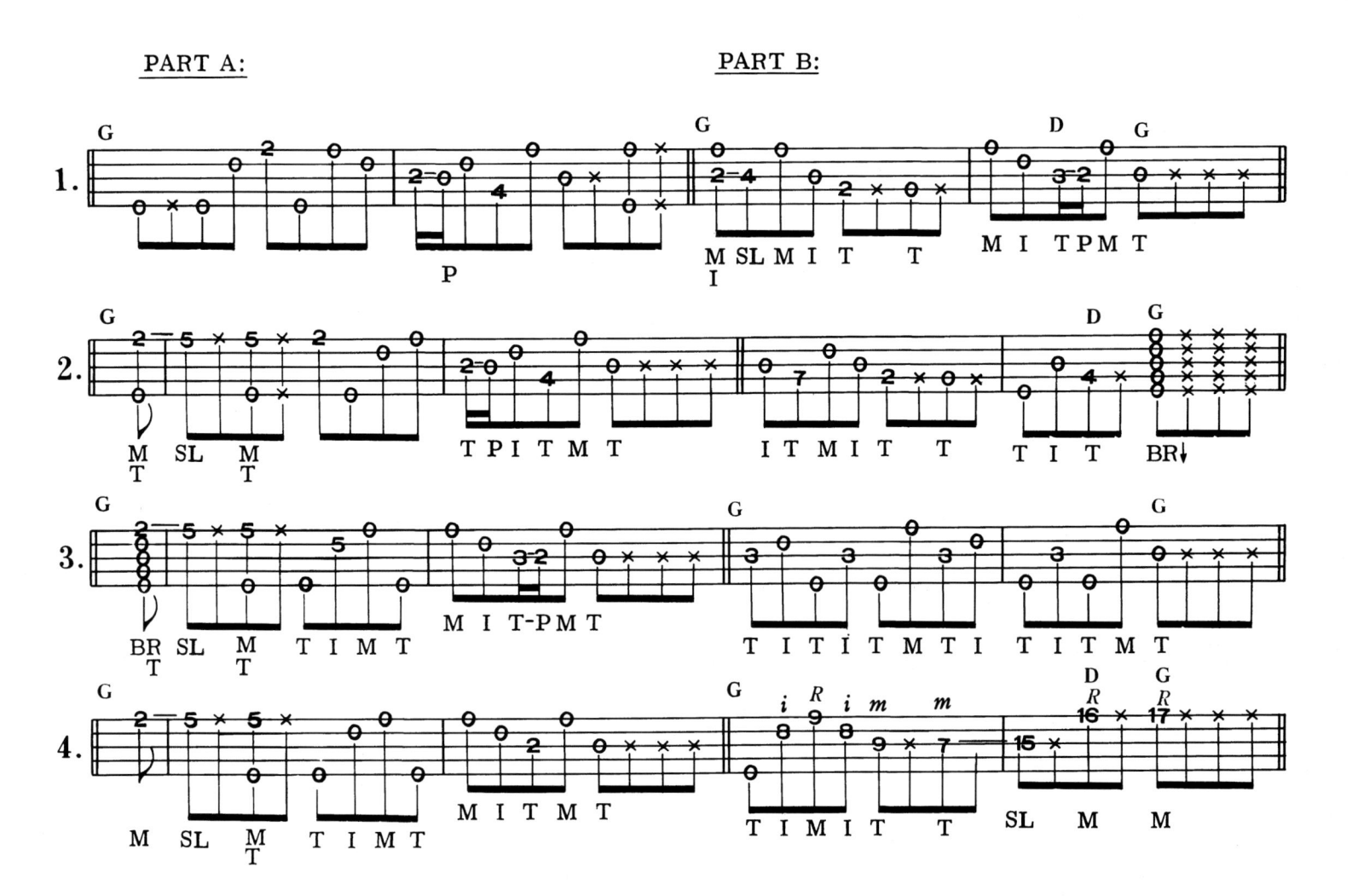

PART A: PART B:

[Banjo tablature examples 1-4 showing Part A and Part B tag endings]

99

Part A: Part B:

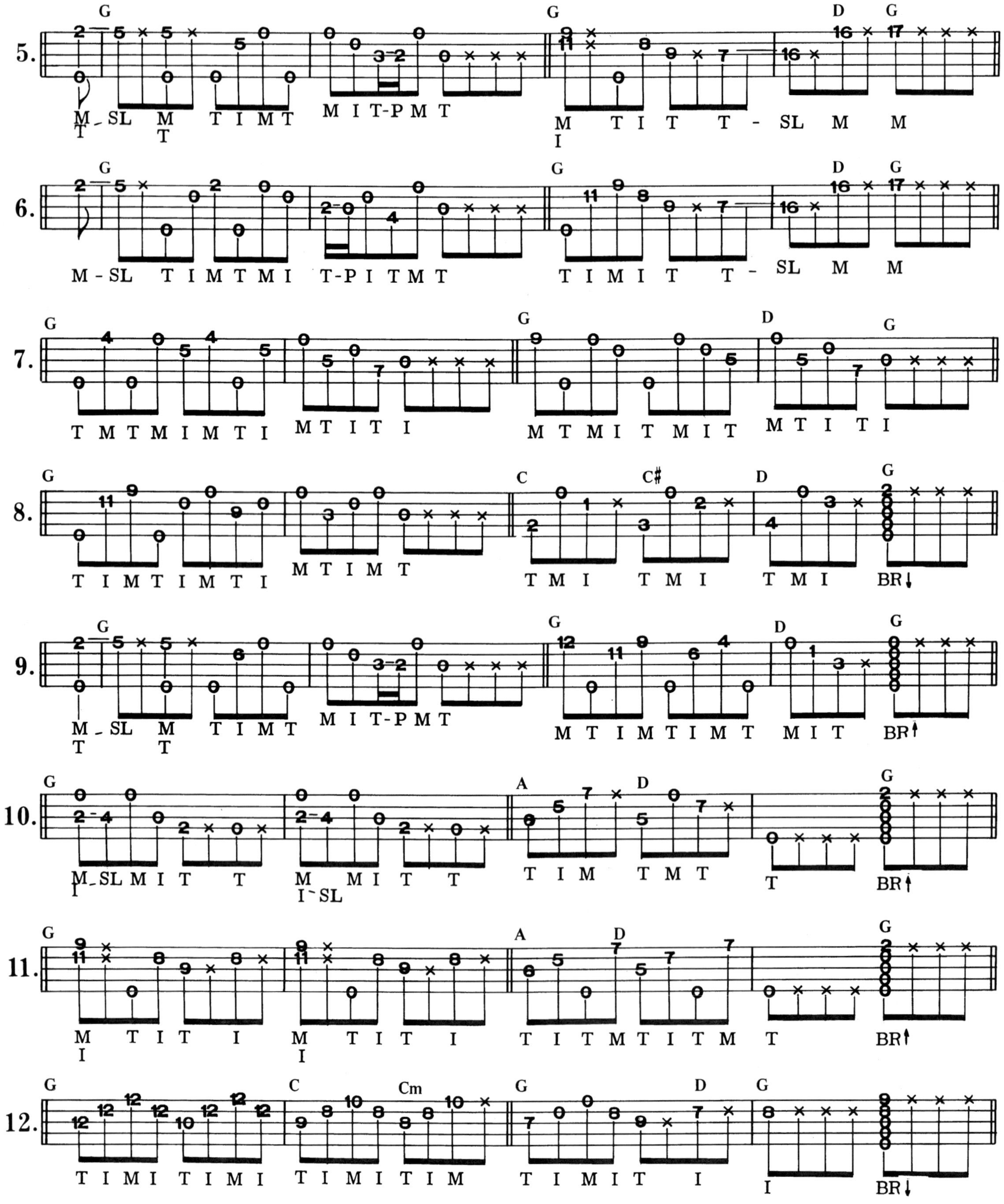

TWO MEASURE ENDINGS

The "Two Measure Ending" is usually <u>substituted</u> <u>for</u> <u>the</u> licks which are normally played for the <u>last chord</u> of the song. (For songs played in the key of G, this type of ending will be played for the final G chord, immediately after the D chord.) This ending almost always consists of two measures of tablature. It is usually played at the close of the final chorus of a vocal, or singing song, and this type of ending can also be used for instrumental songs. (See the last two examples.)

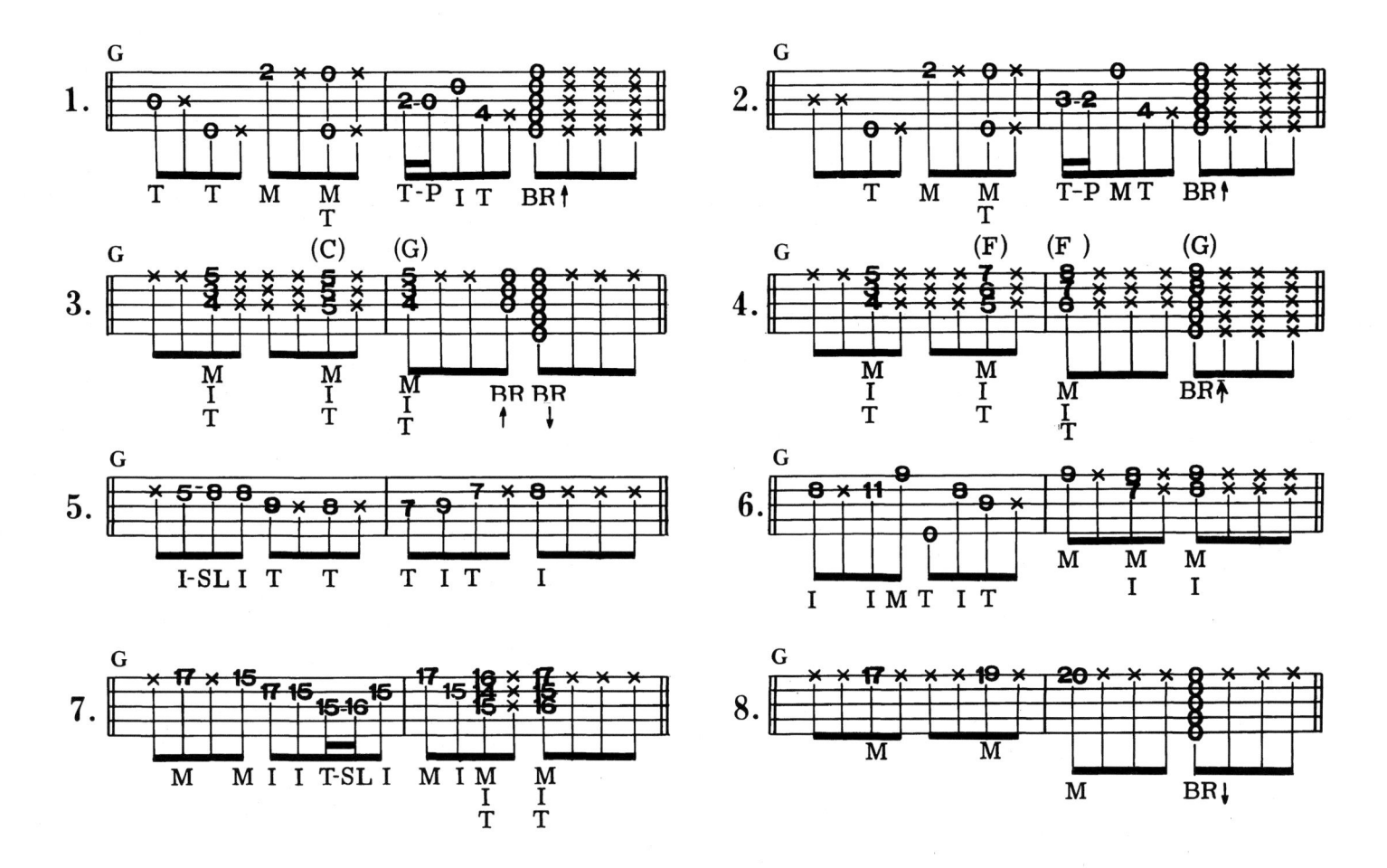

The following examples demonstrate how a two measure ending (#8) sounds when combined with the final D chord of a song. These are effective endings for instrumentals such as "Foggy Mountain Brkdwn"., "Shuckin' The Corn", "Train 45", and "Lonesome Road Blues".

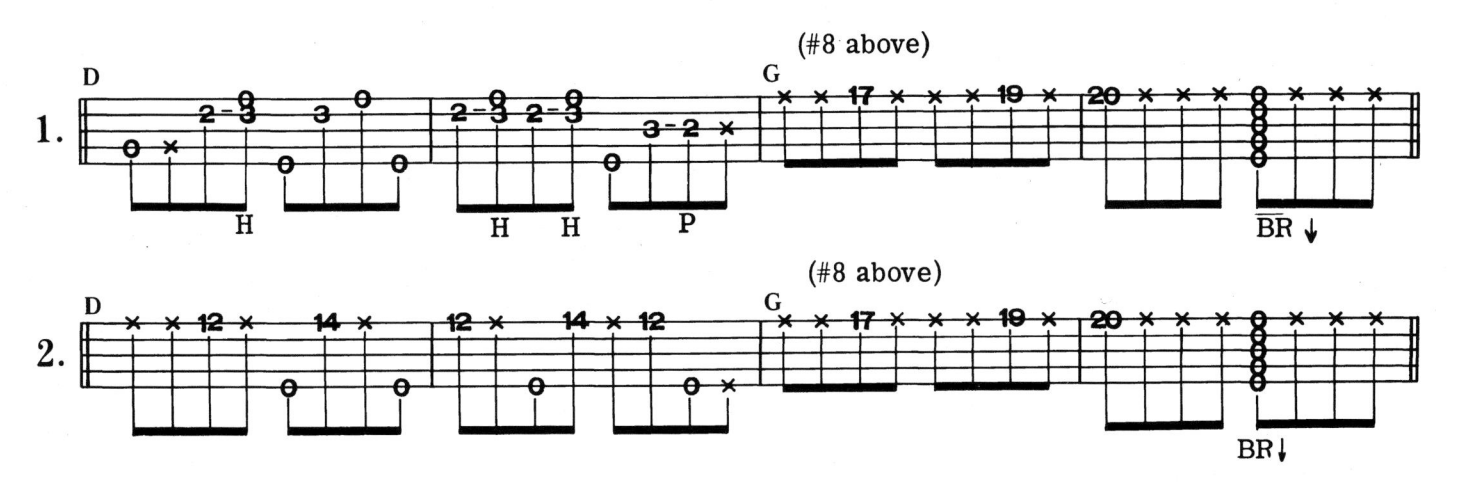

CHORDS

When working out songs on the banjo, it is helpful not only to realize that songs are built with melodies (tunes), but also, that the melodies are supported by <u>chords</u>. When working with the deeper tonal area of the banjo, (i.e. open-5th frets), the left hand may not necessarily hold a chord position for the G chord or for the D chord. This is because the open strings are chord tones which belong to these two chords. (The first and fourth strings are D chord tones, so you are generally required to fret only the two inside strings when playing D licks. All 5 strings are G chord tones when played open.) However, almost every other chord in a song will involve working from full chord positions. Therefore, CHORDS ARE IMPORTANT!

To learn the chord positions for every chord on the banjo, you actually need to learn only three left hand patterns. Any major chord can be played with these three patterns, and the other types of chords, (i.e. minor, augmented, diminished, seventh chords), can be found from each pattern.

THE MAJOR CHORD PATTERNS

The following left hand patterns can be used to play any major chord.

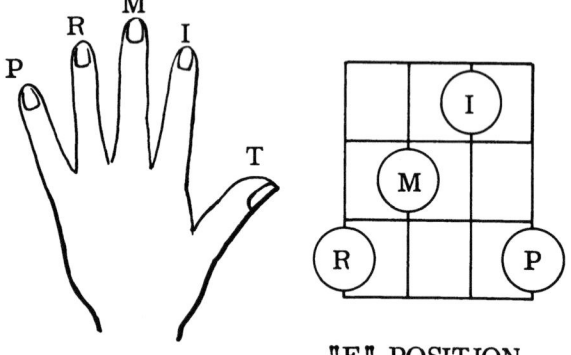

"F" POSITION 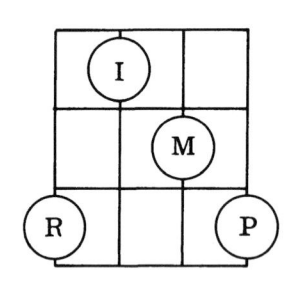   "D" POSITION 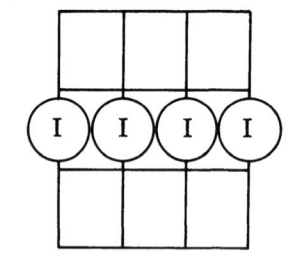   "BARRE" POSITION
                                            (Lay the index finger
                                             across all 4 strings)

The Chord Chart on the following page demonstrates how each chord pattern can be moved up the fingerboard to play any major chord. Notice that the chord names change in alphabetical order as each pattern travels up the neck.

MOVEABLE CHORD POSITION CHART
MAJOR CHORDS

* The number by each individual diagram tells you what fret the chord starts on.
* Use the correct left hand fingering to form each chord position.
  (I=index; M=middle; R=ring; P=pinky)

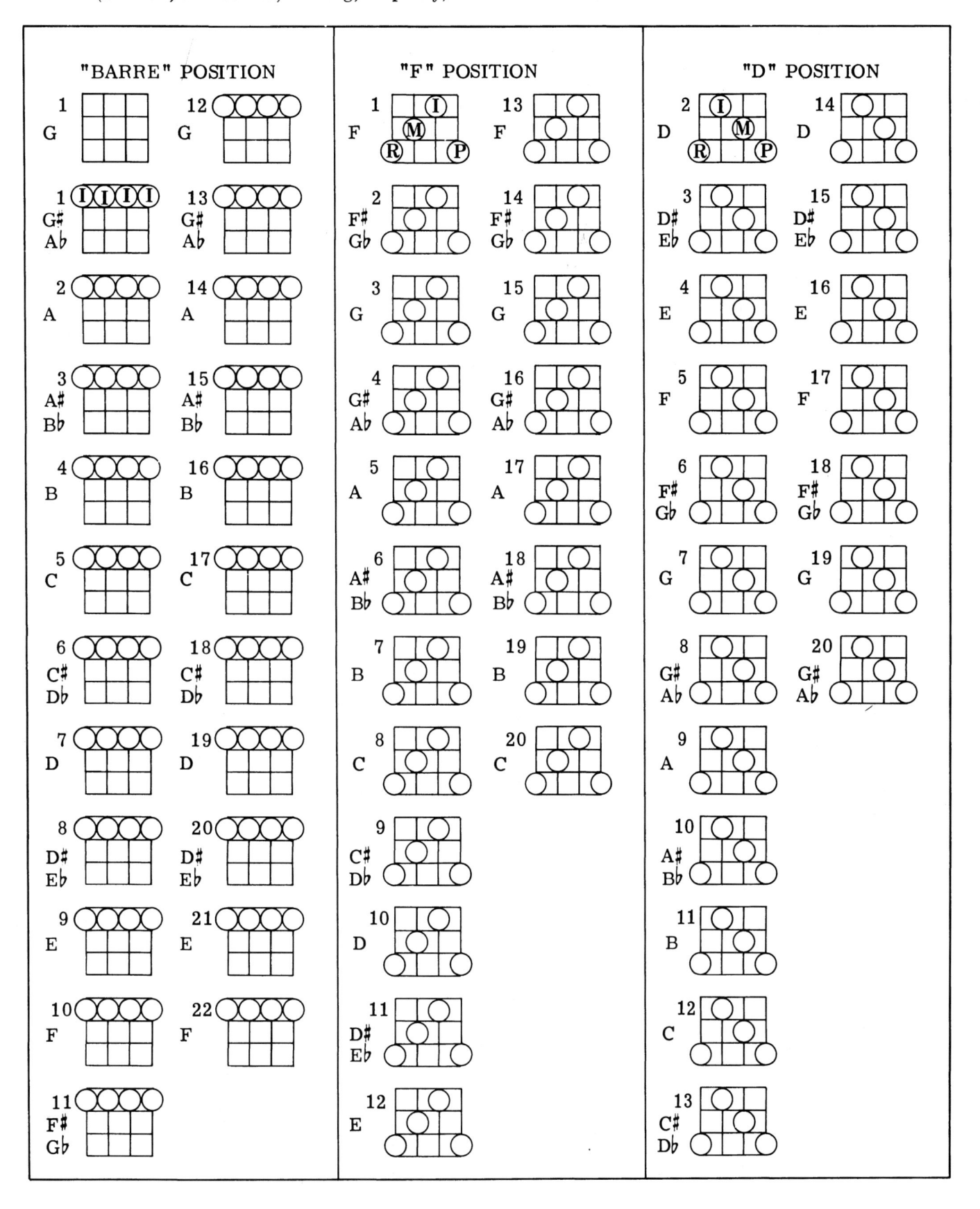

"BARRE" POSITION

Fret	Chord	Fret	Chord
1	G	12	G
1	G#/Ab	13	G#/Ab
2	A	14	A
3	A#/Bb	15	A#/Bb
4	B	16	B
5	C	17	C
6	C#/Db	18	C#/Db
7	D	19	D
8	D#/Eb	20	D#/Eb
9	E	21	E
10	F	22	F
11	F#/Gb		

"F" POSITION

Fingering: I (index on top), M (middle), R (ring), P (pinky)

Fret	Chord	Fret	Chord
1	F	13	F
2	F#/Gb	14	F#/Gb
3	G	15	G
4	G#/Ab	16	G#/Ab
5	A	17	A
6	A#/Bb	18	A#/Bb
7	B	19	B
8	C	20	C
9	C#/Db		
10	D		
11	D#/Eb		
12	E		

"D" POSITION

Fingering: I (index on top), M (middle), R (ring), P (pinky)

Fret	Chord	Fret	Chord
2	D	14	D
3	D#/Eb	15	D#/Eb
4	E	16	E
5	F	17	F
6	F#/Gb	18	F#/Gb
7	G	19	G
8	G#/Ab	20	G#/Ab
9	A		
10	A#/Bb		
11	B		
12	C		
13	C#/Db		

CHORD CHART-G TUNING
MAJOR CHORDS

Major chords are formed from the 1st, 3rd, and 5th tones of the major scale of the chord name. There are three left hand positions for all major chords.

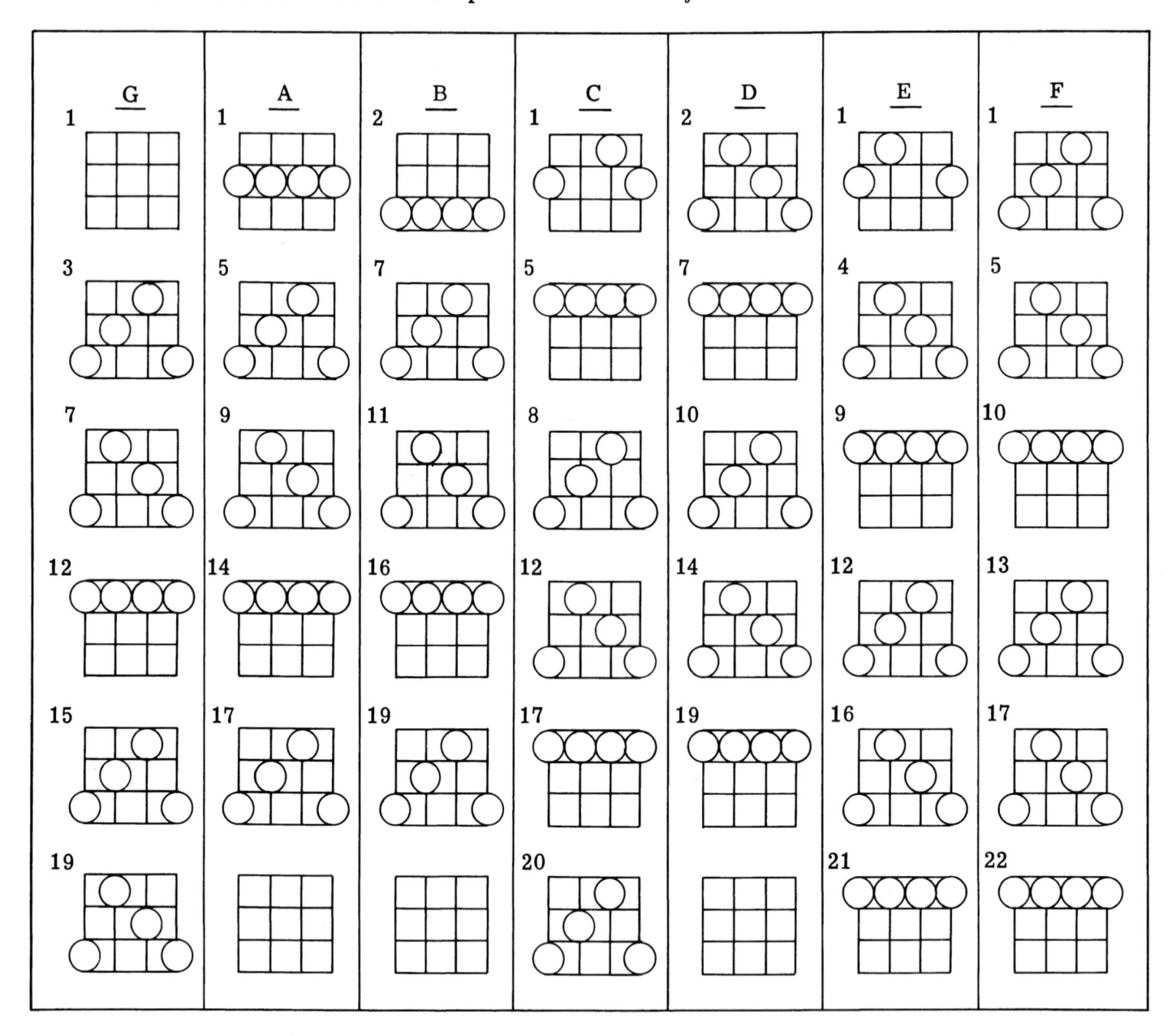

G	A	B	C	D	E	F
1	1	2	1	2	1	1
3	5	7	5	7	4	5
7	9	11	8	10	9	10
12	14	16	12	14	12	13
15	17	19	17	19	16	17
19			20		21	22

* The number beside each diagram indicates the fret number where the chord begins.

Major chords provide the primary chords for songs played in major keys. (Most bluegrass songs fall into this category.) In addition, they can also be substituted for other chords in a song, either to fulfill the function of those chords, or to act as passing chords or to add color.

* NOTE: ♯ means to "sharp" or raise in pitch one fret. If a ♯ follows the letter name of a chord, the chord should be played one fret higher than the regular position.

♭ means to "flat" or lower in pitch one fret. If a ♭ follows the letter name of a chord, the chord should be played one fret lower than the regular position.

MINOR CHORDS

(Symbol=m)

*   The number beside each diagram indicates the fret number where the chord begins.

**   Minor chords are usually indicated with a small letter followed by a small "m".

NOTE: ♯ means to "sharp' or raise in pitch one fret. If a ♯ follows the letter name of a chord, the chord should be played one fret higher than the regular position.

♭ means to "flat" or lower in pitch one fret. If a ♭ follows the letter name of a chord, the chord position should be played one fret number lower than the regular position.

LOCATING CHORDS WITHOUT A CHART

1. Notice on p.103, that the chord names change in alphabetical order as each chord position pattern is moved up the fingerboard. (The musical alphabet = A through G, repeated over and over.) Notice that B is located next to C, and also that E is next to F, but that all other letters are separated by a fret. (The frets in between work like the black keys on a piano.) To locate a specific chord without a chord chart, you can start with one of the chord position patterns, such as the "F" Position F chord, and move it up the fingerboard until you arrive at the desired chord alphabetically. If you know all of the positions for the G, C, and D chords, you can also find the other chords in relation to these chords. For example, the E chord is always located two frets higher (in pitch) than the D chord.

2. ♯ means to "sharp" or raise (in pitch) one fret. Therefore, any chord with this symbol following the letter will be located one fret above the position of the chord letter. i.e. G♯ is located one fret position above the G chord.

3. ♭ means to "flat" or lower (in pitch) one fret. Therefore, any chord with this symbol following the letter will be located one fret lower than the regular position for this chord i.e. B♭ is located one fret lower (in pitch) than B.

4. Minor chords, diminished chords, and augmented chords can be located by first locating the normal major chord position of the desired chord. Each of these chords requires altering a tone of the major chord. (See chart for more explanation.) The following diagrams demonstrate how these chords can be located from the major chord positions.

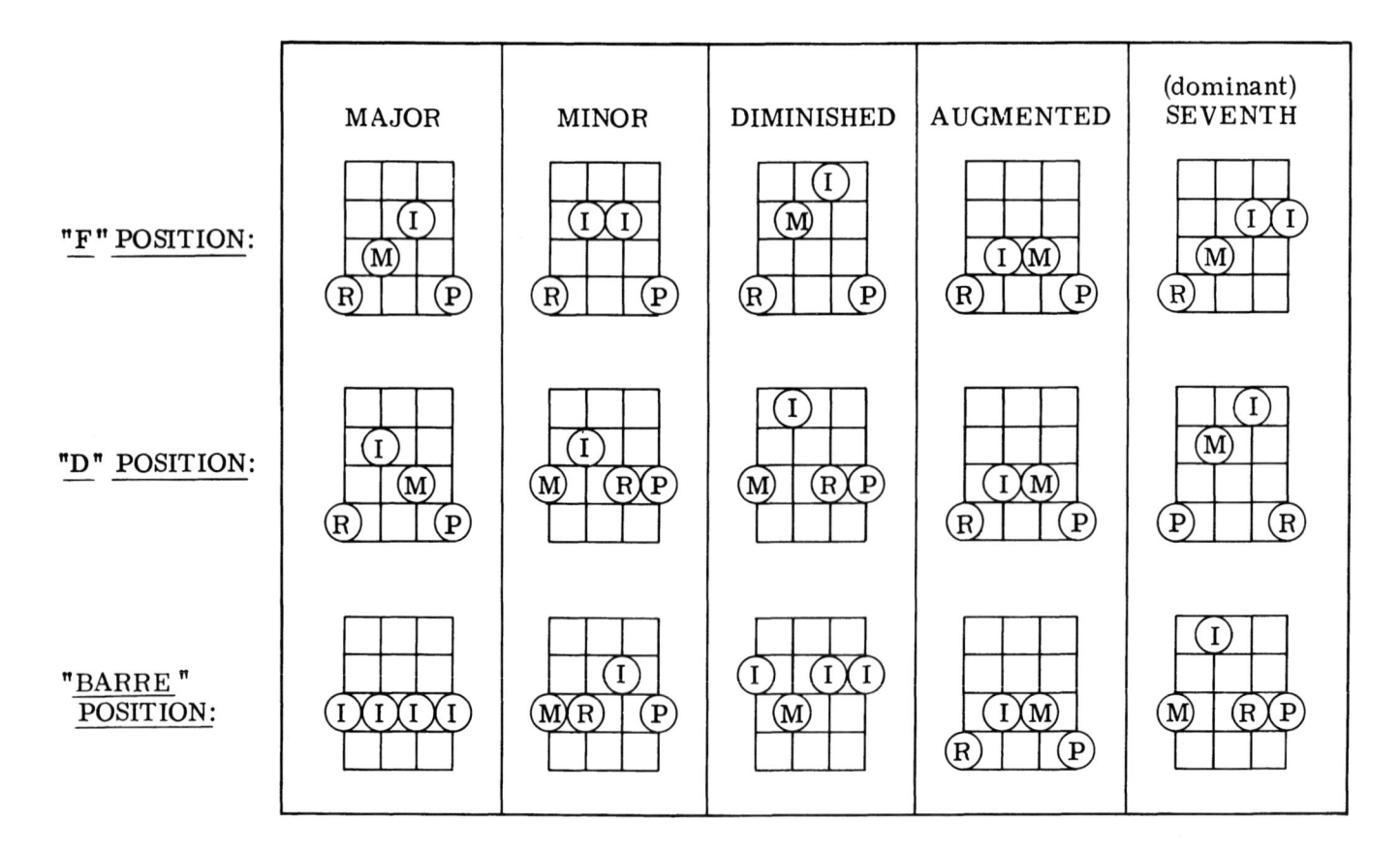

NOTE: Barre the left index finger across the strings, when it is indicated on more than one string in a chord position.

5. A number following a chord symbol, (i.e. G7 = dominant 7th chord) means that an extra tone is added to the chord. (The major chord can also be substituted for chords of this nature.)

MEL BAY

Great Music at Your Fingertips